My

My Son Carlo

Carlo Acutis Through the Eyes of His Mother

ANTONIA SALZANO ACUTIS

with
PAOLO RODARI

Our Sunday Visitor
Huntington, Indiana

Published for
PIEMME
by Mondadori Libri S.p.A.
© 2021 Mondadori Libri S.p.A., Milano

28 27 26 25 24 23   1 2 3 4 5 6 7 8 9

Published in English in 2023 by Our Sunday Visitor Publishing
Division, Our Sunday Visitor, Inc., 200 Noll Plaza, Huntington, IN
46750; 1-800-348-2440; www.osv.com.

ISBN: 978-1-63966-025-4 (Inventory No. T2764)
eISBN: 978-1-63966-026-1
LCCN: 2022944948

Cover design: Tyler Ottinger
Cover art: Courtesy Carlo Acutis Center
Interior design: Amanda Falk

PRINTED IN THE UNITED STATES OF AMERICA

I dedicate this book to my son Carlo. May his dream that the entire universal Church, under the maternal guidance of the Most Blessed Virgin, live the following words with ever more fervor and conviction: "The Eucharist manifests that the Church and the future of the human race are bound together in Christ and in no other reality. He is the one, truly lasting rock. Therefore, Christ's victory is the Christian People who believe, celebrate, and live the Eucharistic mystery" (XI Ordinary General Assembly of the Synod of Bishops, Instrumentum Laboris, 2005).

Contents

1

"I'm Not Getting Out of Here Alive. Prepare Yourself"

September 2006. After a few weeks spent mainly in Santa Margherita Ligure and then in Assisi, where we spent a few months of the year, we had by now reached the end of our vacation. My son Carlo, as was the case every year, went to Saint Francis's tomb before leaving to ask for and place his trust in his protection for the new school year. He was very upset because he was not allowed to enter. They had closed the basilica early, but he prayed anyway from outside. Milan welcomed us with its usual bustling. The streets were already full of people doing a thousand different things. Back and forth. Daily life had not wasted any time in starting up again after the August break.

Carlo loved starting anew. He was fifteen. And as always, the first days of the month passed for him without any particular nostalgia for the summer, which was fading away, but rather with great anticipation. He wanted to see his friends again, his classmates, his teachers. He wanted to get back in the game. Anticipation — this was one of the words that described it best, the attitude of someone who knows that every moment can bring something new, that in every moment something can happen.

When we got home, we found a book in the mail. It had been sent to us by an editor friend and dedicated to young saints. Carlo wanted to read it right away. He held it in his hands and told me, "I'd really like to put together a website about these people."

Websites were his passion. He had created various ones, and one in particular, about Eucharistic miracles, had gained worldwide acclaim. He created them on his computer and then let them run their course. Requests arrived even from afar, from Milan, from around the globe. Creating websites was his way of satisfying his great desire to proclaim the Good News to everyone. He was animated by an irrepressible desire to constantly bring the beauty of the contents of the Christian faith to light, to be proactive in seeking out the good in all of life's circumstances, and to always remain distinctive in accordance with the unique and unrepeatable plan which God has designed for each of us for all of eternity. "Everyone is born unique, but many die as photocopies," was not surprisingly one of his most well-known phrases.

The book received made a particular impression on him. It told stories of heroism, of the lives of young people cut short at a tender age and at the same time given as offerings. The main thing that emerged was these children's faith in a God who loves us infinitely and never abandons us, even while allowing suffering and contradictions, and the way that they knew how to believe in fundamental goodness even in times of difficulty. Life had often given them struggles and pain, but in their hearts they were able to remain cheerful and find the light.

This message fascinated Carlo. He saw himself in it. I remember, in fact, that at that time he had wanted to stay particularly close to a classmate who was sick. Her parents were very worried because, initially, they had not been able to figure out what was causing the illness. They suspected leukemia. Carlo called her often over the summer. He told her to trust in God. In the end, fortunately, it turned out that the illness was simply mononucleosis. "God still wants you here," he joked with her on the phone.

My son was also not feeling particularly well in those weeks. He had minor aches in his bones and a few tiny bruises on his legs. Nothing, however, made us suspect anything serious. He played a lot of sports, and we thought that that was causing his aches and pains. He also tended to play down the pain. So we did not worry much. School started in mid-September. I remember these days as particularly luminous. Milan was still in the height of summer. Autumn did not seem to want to arrive. The evenings were sunny, and we loved to take long walks through Parco Sempione. We started the school year with a sense of lightheartedness. My feelings, in particular, were those of joy and serenity. I could have imagined anything, truly anything, happening to me, happening to us, except for the storm that arrived, unexpected and violent, which tore up our lives and struck us like a sudden summer thunderstorm. A true clap of thunder in a clear sky.

Carlo's last day of school was September 30, a Saturday. He got home from school particularly tired. He had had an hour of physical education, and the teacher had had him run laps around the large soccer field. We thought that it was the laps that had tired him out. That afternoon, at any rate, he found the energy to go outside with me and take Briciola, Stellina, Chiara, and Poldo, our four beloved dogs, to the park for a walk.

The next morning, my husband, mother, and I decided to go out to eat with Carlo. A *trattoria* near Venegono, the town where the Archdiocese of Milan sent its future priests to study, had been suggested to us. When Carlo came down to the kitchen to have breakfast, I noticed that he had a small red spot on the white of his right eye. It looked like he might have caught a cold. I did not worry too much about the spot, either.

Before leaving for Venegono, we went to Mass. At the end of the service, Carlo wanted to recite the Prayer to Our Lady of the Rosary of Pompeii, a prayer that he was particularly attached to. By now, we knew our son well. He had had a close relationship with the Virgin Mary since he was little. He spoke about her frequently. He always prayed to her and invited us to do so with him. We obliged. My husband and I had come back to our faith a few years prior. We discovered it thanks to Carlo. It was he who brought us close to God. In my life, before this happened, I had only gone to Mass three times: the day of my baptism, the day of my first Communion, and the day of my wedding. My husband — even though, in contrast to me, he had more religious parents — also went to Church only every so often. It was not that we were opposed to faith. We were just used to living without it. We were like many around us — we filled our days with lots of activities, but we did not know their fundamental meaning. The Roman philosopher Seneca (Lucius Annaeus Seneca the Younger) neatly describes this way of existing: "The largest portion of our life passes while we are doing ill, a goodly share while we are doing nothing, and the whole while we are doing that which is not to the purpose" (Letter to Lucilius, I, 1, 1).

The arrival of Carlo in our lives, in this sense, was like a prophecy, an invitation to look at things from another angle, to be different, to dive deeply.

After Mass, we got into the car. We arrived in Venegono, where we ate outdoors. Briciola, Stellina, Chiara, and Poldo were also there with us. After lunch, we took a walk in the surrounding woods and collected chestnuts, filling an entire bag. A bit of sunlight filtered through the tree branches, rendering the atmosphere almost like that of a fairy tale. We had let the dogs off the leash, and I remember that they ran lightheartedly back and forth in the underbrush. Every so often, Carlo amused himself by tossing them branches to bring back to him. He smiled; he was happy. This day has remained a beautiful memory for me. Light and peacefulness are the feelings that I remember most. When we got home, around evening, Carlo started to run a fever. It hit 38 degrees Celsius. I gave him a Tylenol and decided that he would not go to school the following day.

• • •

Monday, October 2. I called the pediatrician and asked if she could come see Carlo. She came immediately and only noted that his throat was a bit red. She prescribed him a simple antibiotic and said good-bye. I was not worried yet. In fact, I had heard that half the class had the flu. I thought that Carlo had come down with the same illness.

My son spent the rest of the day relaxing. He recited the Rosary with me, as he often asked me to do. It was natural for him to interrupt his daily activities to pray. His relationship with God was continuous, incessant. Everything he did, he thought of God, turning to him. His prayers helped him, as he said, to gather up energy and start the day's activities with increased strength and serenity. He did his homework and worked on his websites a bit on the computer. His fever did not go away, but he was able to be active and present.

We all came together to keep him company while he had dinner in his bedroom. Out of nowhere, he said, "I offer my suffering for the pope and for the Church, so as not to go to purgatory and to go straight to heaven."

In that moment, we thought he was teasing us. Carlo was always happy and playful. We thought that he was joking and therefore did not pay any particular attention to these words, which it seemed he had spoken to make us smile. Even though his fever had not come down, it had not gotten worse. Since he was little, Carlo had had sore throats on occasion. And it always took him at least a week, if not more, to get fully better. It was also for this reason that we continued not to worry.

• • •

Wednesday, October 4. The website that Carlo had made over the summer to help with the Jesuits' charity work for the needy and underprivileged was to be presented to the entire school. They asked Carlo to do it because he was comfortable with computers and complex software, and because, since he was young, they thought that other students might pay more attention due to his involvement with them. They might follow his example and give their time free of charge to help others. The Jesuits told me that when the volunteer committee consisting of some parents of students at the school met, they were all struck by the vivacity with which my son presented his work, by the passion which drove him, and by his creativity. The mothers were literally fascinated by Carlo's approach, by his leadership qualities, and by his style, which was so kind and at the same time lively and efficient.

Carlo had already invested so much of his energy for those in need. He did it every day, both on planned occasions and when the circumstances arose. For him, these were natural, obvious actions. He loved the example of the saints who dedicated themselves to the needy. He wrote down some quotes by Mother Teresa of Calcutta that he particularly liked: "Many talk about the poor, but few talk to the poor." "Don't search for Jesus in far lands; he is not there. He is close to you; he is in you." "You can find Calcutta anywhere in the world. You only need two eyes to see. I know that you'd like to travel to Calcutta, but it's easier to love people far away. It's not always easy to love the people nearby."

It was decided to present Carlo's website about volunteering without him. In the early afternoon, they called and told him that everyone liked it. The presentation was a success. Carlo was beaming and flattered. Doing things for others and doing them well was a source of joy for him. I went out and bought chocolate cakes for the feast of Saint Francis. I did so every year. Carlo went crazy for them. On that day, he also dug in and ate a lot. He was still a bit tired, but as always he smiled and tried to show us that everything was fine.

• • •

Thursday, October 5. My son woke with glands that were a bit swollen. I called the doctor again. She came to see him and said that he probably had mumps. She recommended that he keep taking the medicine that he was taking, so that is what we did.

The next day, however, there was another surprise. Carlo had blood in his urine. The pediatrician had us bring a urine sample for testing in a clinical laboratory close to our home. The results were reassuring. It really seemed like it was nothing serious.

When my son had a sore throat and ran a temperature, he often suffered from night terrors, a nonpathological sleep disorder which happens fairly frequently in children and teenagers and causes parasomnia and nightmares. For this reason, I preferred to spend the night with him when he was sick. I slept on a mattress on the floor, next to his bed. I remember that on the night of October 3 I dreamed that I was in a church. Saint Francis of Assisi was there.

Higher up, on the ceiling, I saw the face of my son, a very large face. Saint Francis looked at it and told me that Carlo would become very important in the Church. Then I woke up. I spent all morning thinking about that dream. I thought it was a small prophecy about the fact that my son would become a priest. In fact, he had told me about a particular dream of his many times, and I convinced myself that the dream was related to that.

The next night, I slept in his room with him again. Before I fell asleep, I recited the Rosary. While half-asleep, I heard a voice which distinctively told me the following words: "Carlo will die." I thought that this was not a voice that came from a good place. That it was a bad thought and not to pay attention to it. So I gave it no weight.

• • •

Saturday, October 7. Carlo woke up early. He wanted to go to the bathroom, but he realized that he could not move. He could not get out of bed; he did not have the strength. He had been struck by severe fatigue and called me for help. With a lot of effort, together with my husband, we were able to bring him to the bathroom.

We were very alarmed. We decided to call our son's old pediatrician, a famous Milan professor who had retired and who we trusted with anything. He told us to take Carlo to the De Marchi clinic, where he had been department chair for many years, immediately. He was very kind to us. Before we got to the clinic, he told the doctors we were coming. And in particular he told the head of pediatric hematology to investigate immediately and try to figure out what was happening.

It was hard to bring Carlo to the hospital. Rajesh, our housekeeper, had taken a day of vacation. So my husband and I decided to have our son sit on his desk chair, which had wheels. Somehow, we were able to get him to the elevator and into the car. I remember that Milan was cordoned off because of a marathon that was to take place the next day. With much difficulty, we reached the clinic. Two nurses came to the entrance and brought Carlo inside. They immediately comforted us and surrounded us with affection. They were very caring with us and with him.

In the doorway of the clinic, my thoughts raced. I immediately re-membered that I had been here once before, when Carlo's old pediatri-cian vaccinated him against hepatitis B. It was 1996. I remembered it viv-idly because the clinic specialized in the treatment of cancer in children. The professor told me that the mothers who had sick kids also got sup-port from external volunteers who made themselves available to com-fort them. These volunteers took training courses called Bailint groups, which were named after their creator, Michael Bailint, who designed a program aimed mainly at doctors but which had also been extended to external volunteers in this clinic. The program mainly consisted of pro-viding psychological help to the parents of sick children as well as to the children themselves, staying close to them, being present, and trying to support them through the struggle and pain. I remember that the pro-fessor told me that if I wanted, I could join the group. When he told me this, I felt a strong sense of anguish and fear. The thought of those sick children and their mothers deeply upset me. I did not feel ready for such an undertaking. Since I am also a hypochondriac, just thinking about it terrified me. This was also because, due to my character, it would have been natural to put myself in the place of those mothers, and I think I would have suffered too much. When I think about it now, I think that in some way God wanted to prepare me for my son's illness through that offer. I believe, in fact, that from time to time God gives us experiences as a "taste" of what we will later have to experience ourselves. They are rehearsals for events that only he knows about, for which only he knows the plot and how it ends. Life is a great mystery. Sometimes, signs come down from heaven. As St. John Paul II emphasized, we must always re-member that "the future starts today, not tomorrow." Today, I would say that the professor's words were an early warning: This is the pain that you will also have to go through.

That thought was not my only thought that morning. While the two nurses brought Carlo into the clinic, in fact, I turned around instinctively to look at the other side of the street. I noticed the church of the Barnabite order where the relics of St. Alexander Sauli are held. I knew this church well, but that morning I felt a pull toward it. Something was telling me, "Turn around, look there." Immediately, I understood the reason. Saint Alexander had incidentally became Carlo's companion in life for that year.

Each December 31 in Milan it is customary to go "draw for a saint." It is said that the saint which comes up will accompany the person who "drew" him in a special way for the whole year. For this reason, you are invited to learn his story, and to sort of become his friend. Carlo had always drawn the Holy Family, or Jesus, or the Virgin Mary. We teased him for this — we told him that he came "recommended." That year, however, he got Saint Alexander, a Barnabite bishop who lived in the 1500s, the patron saint of young people, whose feast falls on October 11, a day which will always be etched in Carlo's story. I was struck by the fact that this church was right in front of the De Marchi clinic. Instinctively, I entrusted him to Saint Alexander and entered the clinic.

· · ·

I remember the words the doctor told us right after the initial exams as if he had said them today: "There is no doubt that Carlo has been struck by type M3, or promyelocytic, leukemia."

The doctor told us, in a serious voice and without beating around the bush, that it was a silent disease which does not reveal itself until the last minute, suddenly, without any warning signs, and that it was not genetic. It is a disease that leads to very rapid proliferation of tumor cells. In practice, it makes blood blasts go crazy. He told us that Carlo needed to be hospitalized and that they needed to immediately begin serious treatment to try to save his life. They told Carlo the same things. They did not hide anything from him.

When the doctor left us, Carlo was able to stay calm. I remember that he gave us a big smile and said, "God has given me a wake-up call!"

I was very struck by his attitude and by his ability to look at his situation with positivity and serenity, regardless of the circumstances. The memory of that luminous smile he gave us still comes to mind today. It was like when someone walks into a dark room and suddenly turns on the light. Everything is illuminated and takes color. This is what he did. He lit up our darkest hour, the shock of upsetting news. He did not waste words worrying. He did not allow anxiety or anguish to conquer him. He reacted by trusting in God. And in this trust, he decided to smile. In addition to the smile, I was struck by his composure. I think that he was clear that the situation was desperate, but he delivered himself into the arms of Our Lord, who conquered death. Sometimes, I think of those moments, and I ask myself what my son's real feelings at that juncture were, but I am not able to come up with any answer other than, "Christ knows 'what is in man.' He alone knows it," which Pope John Paul II said during the homily for the inauguration of his pontificate.

On the other hand, serenity was one of the distinctive characteristics which always accompanied Carlo. He knew how to infect everyone with happiness and joy. Even in the darkest moments, he was able to infuse people with tranquility and peace and warm hearts. He transmitted serenity, calm, and composure. "Joy that lives in intimate silence is deeply rooted. She is the sister of seriousness; where one goes, so does the other," wrote Romano Guardini.

Carlo was always an optimist. And even when everything seemed to be falling apart, he never stopped hoping and never gave in to resignation. A concept which John Paul II expressed well, in other times and in other circumstances: "Do not abandon yourselves to despair. We are the Easter people and hallelujah is our song."

· · ·

A few minutes passed, and they came to bring Carlo to the intensive care unit. They put a mask on his face that administered oxygen and helped his breathing. It really bothered him. It kept him from moving. He could not cough well. The medical term for this life-saving device, which we later became used to seeing in ICU rooms during the COVID-19 pandemic, is a CPAP machine. Carlo confided in me that this device was true torture for him, but that he offered it up for the conversion of sinners. When I saw all these people hospitalized with CPAP machines during the pandemic, I often thought back to 2006, the year of Carlo's death, and I was met with proof that the deep wounds caused by those terrible days of his passion are still "bleeding."

They only let me stay with him in the intensive care unit until one in the morning. Then Carlo had to stay by himself. Before I left, he wanted us to recite the Rosary together. He could barely talk, but he still wanted to do it. These were terrible moments for me. The words of the Book of Job bounced around inside me, and I had no way of stopping it. "'The LORD gave, and the LORD has taken away; blessed be the name of the LORD.' In all this, Job did not sin or charge God with wrong" (1:21–22).

God was allowing this. A part of me wanted to praise him, to accept, and another part was torn apart by seeing my only son suffering in a hospital bed without being able to do anything to prevent it. It was in these moments that I felt the desire to give my own offering to Jesus arise within me. Regardless of how the story of Carlo's disease ended, I decided to offer up my profound suffering for greater love toward the Sacrament of the Eucharist on the part of the People of God. The Eucharist was Carlo's great love. And so it also became my own. I prayed and made an offering so that those who had not been able to get to know the love of Jesus Christ could experience it at least once in their lives. I especially asked for this blessing for my dear friends, the Jewish people. Since I was a girl, I had the opportunity to spend time with many people of the Jewish faith, many of whom were my playmates in Rome, where I was born. I lived in a building in the city center where a Jewish family lived on the top floor. My parents became friends with them and, consequently, so did I. I knew their entire community.

Many of them were relatives of the chief rabbi. I went to their parties; we often went on vacation together. Paradoxically, I knew Jewish customs better than I knew Catholic ones. I was always struck by the fact that Jewish children were not allowed to eat pork, and they were very diligent in following every rule that their religion imposed. I found their attention to the rules and commandments to be a great testimony of their faith.

In London, where I was a student, I had a young Jewish woman come live with me. She was from Brussels, Belgium. I had met her because I was friends with a young Belgian man who had dated her for a while. They had lived together, but later broke up. The woman found herself without a home and did not know where to go. They did not have a lot of financial resources. I remember that she was very depressed. Moved to pity by the situation, I suggested that she come live with me. A great friendship was born. It was she who taught me to speak French, while I in exchange taught her Italian. Thanks to her, I was able to come into contact with the English Jewish community that lived in the capital. Once again, I learned to appreciate and love them, to care deeply for them.

That was why that night, in the intensive care unit, while my Carlo suffered, I felt that I should offer up this pain for them as well. For me, it was a natural gesture that I believe bore fruit. God often works in mysterious ways. We do not immediately see the result of our actions and our prayers. But answers come from heaven sooner or later, when and however God wants.

• • •

That night was not easy for me. My mother and I stayed in the clinic so that I would be present whenever anything might happen. I convinced my husband to go home and rest. At dawn, I went to Mass at the Barnabite order church to ask for the intercession of God and of the Blessed Virgin Mary. I also prayed to St. Alexander Sauli. Through Carlo, I had learned that the saints are always present, and that, if we pray to them, they help us from heaven. And so I did. Soon after, I went back to the clinic. They let me see Carlo. He was still wearing the mask, still suffering. He confided in me that he had not slept much.

Soon after, his doctor decided to transfer him to the San Gerardo Hospital in Monza, where there was a center that specialized in this type of leukemia. We were not allowed to ride in the ambulance with him. However, the doctor was very kind and accompanied him personally.

My husband, my mother, and I followed by car. In Monza, they immediately performed a special kind of cleaning of the blood which separated red blood cells from white blood cells. The procedure was a success.

They brought him to the pediatric hematology department, on the eleventh floor, where they had reserved room number 11 for us. The department left an impression on me. There was a modern kitchen and lots of comforts. They told me that it was used by many mothers who lived in the hospital with their children, some even for years on end. Mentally, I prepared myself for this possibility. I was aware that the severity of the disease meant that Carlo could stay there for a long time.

Some nurses eased him into his new bed. A woman who organized distance learning came to see us. She reassured us that he could continue his studies and that Carlo would not lose a school year inside the hospital. Carlo asked that the Sacrament of the Anointing of the Sick be administered to him. The nurses called the hospital chaplain, who also brought us Communion. He came back in the following days.

My son had a great faith in this sacrament, and it was not the first time that he received it. He wrote the following about it on his computer:

> The anointing of the sick (no longer, as was previously the case, extreme unction): The moment of death, whether a person is aware of what is happening or not, is full of worries for most people because we are never purified or prepared enough. This is why there is a Sacrament specifically for this important moment. And there are special prayers. But it is also necessary for the faithful to participate in order to prepare themselves well in advance. That is, existence should be a continuous preparation for death. We should not allow them to fall into the terrifying temptations of dejection and terror, but nor should we allow them to be superficial and negligent. We need to find a middle ground, first and foremost a great balance powered by trust and directed towards the gates of hope. This second theological virtue should be a guiding light and strength. The Scripture admonishes us to 'recognize the hope that is in us.' When existence is attacked by disease or when the definitive sentence of death is pronounced, we must gladly adapt ourselves to Divine Will. Moreover, it is a very good exercise to unite ourselves intimately to the Passion and to the Death of the Lord. Paul said that Christ

did through him what was lacking in his Passion. This means that the mystic body always climbs Calvary and is subjected here and there to vexations and persecution and struggles. Like creation, the Passion continues. That is, until the end of the world, of this world. This joining is echoed through the entire people of God, to their benefit. In this way, a continuous circuit of pains and offerings and martyrs is established. This circuit joins that of the Masses, five of which are celebrated every minute-second. "Jesus, my Communion." "Jesus, I join myself to the Masses of the world." These are two very worthwhile short prayers. Very worthwhile! Why not take advantage of them?

I remember the nurses and doctors were all astonished by how Carlo faced those moments. He never complained. His arms and legs were swollen and full of fluid. Nevertheless, when they brought him back to his room from the radiology department, where they had performed a CAT scan, he tried everything to move from the stretcher to his bed on his own. He did not want the nurses to be inconvenienced in any way. This was typical of Carlo — even in the most critical of situations he thought of others instead of himself. I remember how he struggled to get into his bed on his own — struggled, but with a smile. He often repeated, "Not I, but God." And also, "Not love for oneself but rather the glory of God." "Sadness is looking inward toward oneself, happiness is looking toward God." How those words must have resounded within him at that time!

The doctors ordered the mask back on his head. They asked him how he felt, and he answered with a smile, "I am well; there are people who are suffering much more than me."

They looked at each other incredulously. They knew the pain that this type of leukemia produced. However, that is how he answered. Other patients had been through that pain. The pain is piercing. It does not let up. Carlo seemed to possess a strength that did not come from him. I remember that only his strong, close relationship with the Lord could have made him face this situation in such a manner. It was not momentary heroism. It was the fruit of a relationship nurtured day by day, hour by hour. Without knowing, Carlo had built himself the ability to experience that moment in that way. He built it with years lived under the light of God, under his continuously requested protection, under his continuously desired light. Afterward, many who saw him in those hours in the hospital told me that they had the impression that they were standing before a special young man, who due to his almost inhuman strength was able to not show his suffering, to not disturb, to smile through the storm.

Christian philosopher Blaise Pascal was eighteen years old when he wrote this beautiful prayer during the course of an illness that nearly paralyzed him in his bed, which describes the way in which Carlo faced his "Calvary" well:

> Grant then, Lord, that such as I am I may conform myself to thy will; and that being sick as I am, I may glorify thee in my sufferings. Without them I could not arrive at glory; and thou, too, my Savior, hast only wished to attain it through them. It was by the tokens of thy sufferings that thou wert recognized by thy disciples; and it is by sufferings also that thou wilt recognize thy disciples. Acknowledge me then for thy disciple in the evils which I endure both in my body and my mind, for the offences that I have committed. … Enter into my heart and soul, to bear in them my sufferings. (Prayer, to Ask of God the Proper Use of Sickness)

Evening arrived, and night fell. From the windows of the Monza hospital, I looked west, toward Milan. And I started to ask myself if I would ever go back there with my Carlo. My mother and I were allowed to sleep with him. Around one in the morning, I drifted off for a few minutes. Carlo, on the other hand, was not able to sleep due to his pain. However, I heard him ask the nurse on shift not to make too much noise so that I could rest. But I woke up soon after.

Despite my many fears and doubts, I still hoped that he could pull through. I latched on to anything and everything in the hope that he could get better. Even though the words that he had wanted to tell me when we first arrived in Monza kept popping into my mind. I remember it clearly. They had just gotten him down from the ambulance. He looked at me and told me, "I'm not getting out of here alive. Prepare yourself." He said these words to me because he did not want me to arrive at the moment of his death unprepared. He also explained that he would send me many signs from heaven, and so I should not worry. He knew how much I cared about him, and how apprehensive I was. I think that his greatest worry was that he would leave me here, on Earth without him. He wanted to warn me somehow, so that his death would not arrive as too much of a shock.

• • •

A few moments before he fell into a coma, he told me that he had a bit of a headache. I was not particularly alarmed because even though he looked to me as though he was in pain, he remained relatively calm.

A few seconds later, however, he closed his eyes with a smile.

He never opened them again.

It looked like he was only dozing, but he had fallen into a coma due to a cerebral hemorrhage which, over the course of a few hours, led to his death.

The doctors considered him to be clinically dead when his brain stopped all vital activity. It was 5:45 p.m. on October 11, 2006. October 11 was the same day on which his saint of the year, Alexandro Sauli, died.

I felt like I was living in a dream. In some ways, it all seemed inconceivable. Carlo had left us so quickly! Was it possible that it had happened? There was little to say. Carlo was no longer here. This was the reality. The Lord took him away at just fifteen, at the height of his youth, at the peak of his energy, full of joy and splendor.

We wanted to donate his organs. We were not allowed, however, because they told us that they had been compromised from the leukemia.

The doctors decided not to detach the respirator until his heart stopped beating on its own. For this reason, they sent us home, telling us that they would call us as soon as his heart ceased to beat.

We were told that Carlo's heart stopped beating at 6:45 a.m. on October 12, the eve of the final Marian apparition in Fátima. We believe that this was no coincidence. We had lost our only son, which caused immense pain, but the hope that he had not disappeared from our lives forever and even that he would be even closer to us than before and that he waited for us in a better life, gave us strength.

I remember that my husband and I were convinced that the Lord would perform a miracle and heal him until the very end. But that is not what happened. After they called us, we went directly to the room of my mother, who lived with us, and told her that Carlo's heart had stopped beating.

I remember that my mother told me that she already knew, because she had heard Carlo's voice tell her: "Grandma, I am in heaven with the angels. I am very happy. Don't cry, because I will always be there beside you."

• • •

The morning of October 12 the Monza hospital gave us permission to bring our son's body home. A Milan city ordinance, in fact, allowed for this. It was the funeral home which went to the hospital, prepared Carlo, and brought him to our home.

His room was transformed into a funeral home. His body was laid on his bed. I looked at it, and it did not seem real. Carlo was not here anymore.

The news of his death made its way around the entire neighborhood, through his school, to his acquaintances and friends, and even through the social networks of the time, such as Messenger. All of his classmates, from preschool to high school, were informed. The hullabaloo involved a great many people. Everyone was incredulous and disconcerted.

Our house was soon bustling with people. So many wanted to come to say good-bye. What remains most etched in my memory from those days was the fact that rather than being consoled, it was I who was consoling others. I am grateful for this. Because being forced, as is often the case, to comfort someone who is crying, to tell them to keep faith because our Carlo was alive in another life, was what most helped me to not succumb and to allow my deep pain to lessen a bit. Mysteriously and truly, my consoling

of others in some way even allowed for the pain to be exorcised and transformed into an offering. As the Holy Scripture recalls, our God "comforts
us in all our affliction, so that we may be able to comfort those who are in
any affliction, with the comfort with which we ourselves are comforted by
God" (2 Cor 1:4). I listened to myself talk, and I marveled at myself. I had
lost my only son, but I was still able to transmit hope and peace to everyone
who wanted to visit him before the funeral.

• • •

Among the many people who came to visit us was a friend of Carlo's wearing a yellow sweatshirt. The color reminded me of an episode from my
childhood, when I had not yet passed the boundary which marks adulthood. For a few minutes I went back to those years, and without wishing
to I remembered that when I was a teenager I had confronted death once
in my life, even though I had removed it to some extent from my memory.

It was the summer of 1979. I had gone, as was the case every year, to
visit my grandma, who was at a resort in Anzio, a seaside town near Rome.
I saw many of my Roman friends there, as they were also on vacation in
the same place. One of my friends had introduced me to a friend of hers
who was older than me. Her name was Claudia. She was very beautiful,
kindhearted, pure, and sincere. I remember that when it rained, she always
wore yellow rain boots together with a raincoat of the same color, like that
of Carlo's friend's sweatshirt. She had just turned fourteen. Despite the difference in age, we became fast friends.

The summer holidays were almost over, and before I went back to
Rome, Claudia insisted on taking me to see a market where you could find
many interesting things. We agreed to meet early the following morning,
near the front of her house, a small cottage near the sea. The following day,
I went to the meeting place with another friend of mine. Several minutes
passed, but Claudia did not arrive. We tried to ring the doorbell. At a certain point, we saw a sullen man come out of the house. He was walking
quickly and just avoided knocking us over. I will never forget that figure,
so dark and brooding. He was a bald man, middle-aged, and almost scary.
When he saw us waiting in front of the house, a bit chilled by the biting

morning wind, he stopped and looked at us gravely. "Claudia is dead," he said. And he immediately ran off without giving us any further explanation. I never figured out who he was. Maybe he was the doctor who was there to pronounce the death, but I still do not know his identity.

We thought he was playing a prank on us. We did not have the slightest inkling that he might have been telling the truth. We kept waiting. The minutes went on by, and it was getting late. We thought that Claudia forgot about us or that she had not woken up yet. We decided to ring the doorbell again. Someone opened the door without asking who we were. We leapt up the stairs to the second floor, where Claudia lived. When we came into her house, Claudia's older sisters and her mother were there to greet us. They were all sobbing.

The girl's father was not there. He was in Rome for work. Claudia died of a cerebral hemorrhage in her sleep. Her mother told us that she had complained of a bit of a headache the day before. That night, that headache led to her death. I listened, paralyzed by the pain. Every word that I tried to say died in my mouth. [I think of] Edvard Munch's *The Scream*, an image evocative of all of the world's tragedies. Each time that I see that painting, I think of Claudia and of the loss that I felt that day.

If we think about it, there is a word for sons or daughters who lose their parents (orphans) and husbands or wives who lose their spouses (widower), but there is no word to describe a parent who loses a son or daughter, because it is the most unnatural and terrible thing that can happen in a person's life.

I will say it again: I felt immense despair mixed with loss! How much anguish and shock! Suddenly, all joy had vanished and what remained was space for a deep pain that broke my heart, filling it with an immense sadness. I thought of Claudia's father, who did not yet know, and I was saddened by the idea that her mother would still have to tell him.

At a certain point, mysteriously, something changed in me. I tried to gather my strength, and to the extent which I could, I started to console her mother and sisters, telling them such nice things. While I was speaking, I was myself surprised by my words. Where had they come from? How was I able to say them? I said that Claudia was certainly in heaven, together with the angels and the Blessed Virgin Mary. I was surprised by these words, which popped out of my mouth without any input on my part. I do not know if in that moment I believed what I was saying, or if I only pretended to, but at any rate it worked, and somehow I was able to bring them a little bit of comfort.

Without meaning to, the girl in the yellow sweatshirt had unleashed a series of memories which, although painful, helped me to reflect and convince me that the Lord had once again prepared me to confront the premature death of my son. It is life's most tragic situations that bring out the best in us and teach us who we really are. I was struck by myself, by the strength that I was able to find within me, by the fact that, like years before, I was able to console others following Carlo's death.

This time, however, unlike years before, the words which I spoke to bring comfort to the people who came to say good-bye to my son were the result of a walk of faith I had begun years ago, a walk of faith I had started most of all due to Carlo, a path which had opened my mind to new perspectives, always illuminated by the Word of God. The yellow color of the girl's jacket had brought Claudia back into my mind. It was inevitable that I would juxtapose her and Carlo. The two had both been struck by death at an age which marks the border between childhood and adolescence. Both had budding traits that had just started to bloom, like an early morning landscape covered by a thin layer of frost that casts a veil over its colors but at the same time lets you see everything it could be.

All those people who came to the house to say good-bye to Carlo reminded me of the friends who came to say good-bye to Claudia for the last time, and who in the following days continued to meet to exorcise that premature death, to try to calm the anxiety of eternity which torments everyone who is forced to confront death sooner or later. Somehow, their presence brought Claudia back to life, just as the poet Ugo Foscolo describes in his *Dei Sepolcri*, who replaces every prospect of faith and hope in celestial life and in a provident creator God with a "correspondence of such deep affection."

My encounter with Claudia represented my first true encounter with "sister death," to use the same words as Saint Francis. That unexpected death had shaken and marked so many people, myself included. At the time, I was able to bring comfort without, however, having made my life a true life of faith. In the days following Carlo's passing, I found myself, much to my regret, in the same role, but the more I spoke about it, the more I felt the truth of what I was saying within me. I felt Carlo close; I felt that while I comforted the others I was not lying. Carlo was truly there, although in a mysterious manner, next to me. Carlo was alive, but in another dimension. Hope was no longer an empty word — Christian hope is faith in things which we hope for and which we cannot see. It was a certainty, something to latch onto because it was real, because it was the truth.

• • •

Before Carlo was born, I did not have faith. I was born and lived for years in the center of Rome. My parents sent me to study in a school run by nuns. I learned some notions of catechism, some prayers, but nothing more.

I grew up, like so many teenagers, without a real spiritual life, without developing a relationship with God, which I can say today is something that I believe is decisive for each person because it is a question of personal realization. In this sense, I very much agree with what theologian Carlo Molari, author of *Il cammino spirituale del cristiano*, writes. He believes that without interior life, spiritual life, there can be no realization. Because it is only when we leave space for the spiritual dimension that we can acquire our true identity, "or as Jesus said, our name which is written in heaven."

Molari explains:

> Now, we are becoming. And how do we become? Through the experiences that we live, the thoughts that we develop, the desires that we feed, the relationships that we experience. Interior exercise teaches us to experience our relationships and live through our experiences, to confront situations, to experience sickness, to experience joy, to carry our burdens in a way that allows us to develop our spiritual dimension and grow as children of God.

And,

This is the reason for spiritual work, which does not involve only ourselves but also the whole world, the communities of which we are a part, the cities in which we live, our generation, everyone we meet, the people with whom we have relationships, to spread the dynamics necessary for the life of humanity all around, so that it is not destroyed but can arrive at new forms of brotherhood.

Only when Carlo came into my life did things change. Since he was little, he was constantly attached to Jesus. This relationship of his changed me. Due to his presence in my house, and his faith, I also had to learn to start asking myself questions, coming back to myself to go deeper and deeper and capture the things that had to change in me.

While Carlo lay dead on his bed, I found the strength to bring a bit of this new life, a bit of this "eternity" that surrounds us without ever abandoning us, to those who came into our home. I found a light inside me, a light which was not mine, and I discovered that saying certain things no longer took effort.

Many people who came to our home were far from any practice of faith — that is, nonbelievers, for whom death was no more than a leap into nothingness. I saw their anguish, I saw their despair. I understood it, and I understood them, because these feelings had also been mine.

Before Carlo was born, I was also like them. I was a prisoner of the relative, which is a limitation, a dead end, a boundary, an attachment, slavery. I lived in the most complete ignorance, just like the slaves described in Plato's myth of the cave. Since they were children, they had lived chained inside a cave, unable to move, and believed that the shadows of things from outside which bounced against the wall in front of them were the only reality. One day, one of the prisoners was able to free himself from the chains and discovered the truth. That is a bit like what happened to me.

Carlo showed me how to spend my days in the light of eternity. He taught me always to look toward heaven, toward the absolute, and not bent down toward the temporary, the relative. Day by day, he helped me glimpse a way to leave the relative and become a pilgrim of the absolute, which is a synonym for the supernatural and also for grace. And grace is nothing other than the recognition of this absolute. As St. Thomas Aquinas wrote:

And that [people] are "turned" to God can only spring from God's having "turned" them. Now to prepare oneself for grace is, as it were, to be turned to God; just as, whoever has his eyes turned away from the light of the sun, prepares himself to receive the sun's light, by turning his eyes towards the sun. Hence it is clear that man cannot prepare himself to receive the light of grace except by the gratuitous help of God moving him inwardly.

Grace is the absolute found again. Grace and the absolute are connected by Calvary, by Jesus' death on the cross, a supreme act of God's love and mercy toward men. From this arose the sacraments, through which we receive grace.

Carlo taught me all of those things. He taught me to direct my everyday life toward the seeking of the absolute, of grace. To do this, one must constantly tap into the sacraments, go look for them, attend them. Living while looking toward the absolute helps us to see that every instant of our life is full of an unimaginable light. And in this way, everything is transformed, everything becomes new, the light inhabits our lives, even in unremarkable or dark times. Everything turns in the direction of eternity.

Thanks to Carlo, I did not arrive at his death unprepared. Even through the immense pain, I interiorized and made certain that death is not a part of God's, because death is a negative reality, while God is the God of life and of good things, my own. However, it is a fact, it exists, but we can get through it together with him. As Carlo wrote, "Man can pass from this existence, limited by time and space, to Eternity without any upheaval." And Carlo continued in one of his more intense writings:

And then came sin, and with it death. Death, which before had not existed, began to exist and became the most terrible reality in the life of each person. Every rational being realizes that death is "the problem." Man struggles to keep finding new answers to what there is or is not after death. In effect, death is for each one of us the truest reality, the most authentic, the most genuine, before which there are no doubts whatsoever. In this way, everyday life becomes a fight and defense against death, which although it is impossible to avoid, we try to banish and make as less cruel as possible. Day by day, we fight with death, if not against death. Death is, for most people, a leap into nonexistence, the abyss of the after, of the never, of the forever, of risk, of danger, of uncertainty, of the sunset, of the end, of the accounting, of the appraisal. All of this leads to darkness. It casts shadows. The peoples are humanity. They are the billions that carry out their lives on this planet. They are the existences that come and go. They are the lives that turn on or off. A swarm of beings that look, that hear, that touch, that smell, that imagine, that dream, that desire, that understand, that want, that choose. This interminable mass, this incredible collection, this multitude that elbows for position, that fights, that wants or does not want, that takes and leaves, that loves and hates, that serves and commands, that helps and abandons … all these "people" are, finally, illuminated. Illuminated, that is to say freed, saved, redeemed. By whom? By Christ. And Jesus, who could choose any way he wanted to redeem humanity, because He is infinite, also chose to die. And so that which for us is the most dramatic moment, the most authentic doubt, the most painful torment, became through Jesus an element of Redemption and of liberation. Jesus chose death, the most terrible, murderous, diabolical death. On that piece of crossed wood, beaten in the most hideous way. In choosing death, Jesus gave us Life back. He is the grain of wheat that in dying bore much fruit. With Jesus, death became life, strength, hope, and trust. Thanks to Jesus, everything was turned over, and death became "life." This is not an absurdity, it is just a change brought about by his death, because the grain of wheat fell, he died, and he bore much fruit. Death is universal, just like sin is universal. The moment of death is unknown. The separated soul acts on behalf of the person and exercises its intellectual faculties. From a spiritual point of view, we need to feel and know that we are not permanent parts of this world.

When people asked Carlo about the future, because they all seemed to refer to him for all kinds of matters, he answered:

We have a stable city down here, but we are looking for that of the future. We have been elevated to the supernatural state, redeemed and saved, and we are destined for Eternity with God, "co-eternity." We need to consider death not as the end of everything. It is not the end. It is not ruin. It is not the fatal conclusion. It is the transition to co-eternity. If we consider ourselves to be passing through this world, if we act as though we are temporary, if we aspire to what is Up Above, if we set our lives up based on the Beyond, if we base our existence on the Afterlife, then everything comes into order, everything becomes balanced, everything is oriented, everything is fed by hope. If we think of tomorrow as the next future to prepare for, then one of the most important virtues of spirituality comes into play: that of hope. Hope, not as poetic rhetoric, not as a change of mood, and also not as an evasion that allows for noncommitment, but as what it is: the second theological virtue which is infused like a seed during Baptism.

Essentially, Carlo invited us to pay attention to an entire series of contrived and conventional concepts which often confuse us. He said:

We often talk about here, there, up, down. This way of thinking and speaking relativizes everything. Since we are immersed in the here, we relate everything to the time and space which enslaves us, which conditions us. If we free ourselves from these chains, if we become accustomed to that which is Up Above, if we gain confidence with the Beyond, if we consider life to be a trampoline towards Eternity, then death becomes a transition. It becomes a door. It becomes an in-between. It loses its drama. It loses its fatality. It loses its definitiveness. Exorcise death. Spiritualize death. Sanctify death. That is the secret. Then we will not think about, and we will not speak about, and we will not measure it in absolute terms, in terms of no return, of total destruction, but we will see death in the light, in the warmth and in the victory of the Risen Christ.

The day of the funeral was a beautiful day, still quite hot, almost muggy. The sun shone in the sky, and surrounding us was nothing but light. It was October, but it seemed like August. The funeral home came to prepare my son and to place him in the coffin. I did not want to remain there with them. I chose to leave the room and wait outside.

Time seemed to stand still. Then the door of the room opened and I saw the coffin with Carlo inside.

It is very difficult to express what I felt. I felt like I was living in a dream. I thought that only a few days prior everything had been so different! In that room, Carlo joked, played, laughed, lived his teenage life. And now look at him, lying lifeless in a wooden box.

Carlo's laughter still echoed in my mind together with his ever-joyful voice. Fate had changed the course of my life and the lives of my family in a few hours, over just two weeks. I could be certain of only one thing: What was true yesterday was no longer true today.

I had spent my life waiting for something to happen, for a better future that should have arrived. I had never much appreciated the present. I have always been a real dreamer.

The present felt constraining, because it forced me to take note of and confront the contradictions and disappointments which sooner or later turn everyone's life upside down. I had learned to take refuge in the future, in the dream of a future which let my imagination run wild because it is unknown to all of us. I was not much interested in the past, since by now it was gone. I lived my life projected into a time when everything became possible through my imagination.

Until Carlo's death, essentially, I had never been able to perceive the beauty of the present moment. I had always allowed the minutes and then the days and years to pass, consoling myself with the thought that surely things would be better tomorrow. When I saw the coffin leave the room with my son inside, I thought of his words: "Mom, even if all our dreams were to fall apart, we could never allow cynicism to take over and harden our hearts. From each disappointment, a new dream is born."

That is how Carlo was. This was his constant optimism. It was the feeling that he had always shared with us.

From Carlo's death, I learned that even when everything seems to be telling us the opposite, we can never stop dreaming with passion and stop being optimists. Tomorrow is never in our hands, but it is also not in the hands of a fickle fate which determines the outcome of our existence. It is the thought that it is in God's hands which gives us hope that death has been definitively defeated, because it is nothing more than the gateway to eternity.

If we have this awareness, we learn to experience the reality that surrounds us with passion, and we can expand our horizons and take flight toward dimensions that would otherwise be unreachable. Reality, when illuminated by faith, allows us to tear down the veils that go beyond our small little world, made of guises and contradictions, and open ourselves to the infinite.

Carlo's unexpected death forced me to change perspective, and especially to reevaluate and appreciate the present moment, along with the little things that normally distract us and to which we are normally almost addicted.

The loss of Carlo helped me better understand old people who live in memories. This reminds me of a passage from the first book in Marcel Proust's celebrated series *In Search of Lost Time*. The passage is from *Swann's Way*, and the author describes how the taste of a piece of cake, a *madeleine*, made the beautiful memory of his Aunt Léonie and feelings of a forgotten time bloom within him:

> And soon, mechanically, weary after a dull day with the prospect of a depressing morrow, I raised to my lips a spoonful of the tea in which I had soaked a morsel of the cake. No sooner had the warm liquid, and the crumbs with it, touched my palate, a shudder ran through my whole body, and I stopped, intent upon the extraordinary changes that were taking place. An exquisite pleasure had invaded my senses, but individual, detached, with no suggestion of its origin. And at once the vicissitudes of life had become indifferent to me, its disasters innocuous, its brevity illusory. … I had ceased now to feel mediocre, accidental, mortal.

Memories cancel out the distance between the present and the past and become one single time. And this is what has constantly been of great comfort to me when I think of Carlo. If the past had not existed, there would be no present, which, at each instant, becomes the past. If today, right now, we can write about the past — and with ease — it means that we have lived it, we have built it, we have taken advantage of it. But even though in that moment I had been experiencing profound darkness, I felt that no difficulty, no fear, would have been great enough to stamp out that optimism which had always characterized me and pushed me to keep going. To cite Carlo once again: "Our existence on planet Earth has meaning. It has meaning, if we think of it as a direct yet personal walk towards the Savior. So our problem, my problem, your problem is this: to rush towards this meeting, to realize this meeting, to make this meeting concrete."

As the poet Alexander Pope writes, "Hope springs eternal in the human breast," and we must never allow it to die within us! Think of the eyes of a child — always full of hope. We are not the sum of our weaknesses and failures; on the contrary, we are the sum of the love that the Father has for us and our real capacity to become the image of his Son.

While I had Carlo before me, lying in the still open coffin, thoughts continued to bounce around my mind, untamed. Various parts of his life, events that I experienced with him, flashed before my eyes.

For a few moments I thought in particular of a trip that we took together in France. Carlo was about twelve years old. My mother and my husband were with us.

We went to visit the town of Chartres. We were driving, lost in the wheat fields of the immense French countryside, when a magnificent cathedral emerged out of nowhere. It looked as though it was suspended between earth and sky, solitary, solemn.

Carlo was moved in the face of such beauty. He wanted us to take his picture in front of the western facade, where the main entrance was. It recalled the mystical door about which Scripture speaks and which leads to eternal life. On the facade was a beautiful relief of Jesus, glorified and surrounded by images of the Last Judgment.

After we took the picture, we entered. We were immediately attracted by the beauty of the windows that framed the naves, from which rays of light filtered in, reflecting in a symphony of a thousand colors and creating a surreal atmosphere.

My attention was captured by the enormous labyrinth depicted on the floor of the central nave. Built in the twelfth century, it measures almost 13 meters in circumference, and the entire route measures 261 meters. This ancient labyrinth has always been recognized as depicting the walk toward New Jerusalem, because it represents the soul's pilgrimage toward eternal life. It is subdivided into four main zones and eleven concentric rings through which you have to pass before arriving at the destination, represented by a flower consisting of six petals. The central part is missing, because it is left to be completed by those who are able to arrive. Carlo started to walk through it. He quickly arrived at the center. That path seemed almost to foreshadow what was to become of his life.

Everything happened in an instant. When, after proceeding with the visit, we arrived in front of the relic, a veil which belonged to the Virgin Mary, I had a terrible thought. I was acutely aware that Carlo would soon die.

I was grasped by fear.

Carlo was my only child. I had always tried to have him avoid even the smallest dangers, considered innocuous by most people. I probably got this extreme caution from my father, who often reminded me on the phone to be careful when crossing the street even when I was an adult and living in London.

In Chartres, everything happened in an instant. A feeling of ending, of premature death, which I relayed to my mother, who has the natural tendency to minimize everything and reassure me. However, this premonition came true.

The sight of my son lying on his bed with his rosary, which had accompanied him through all these years, brought that trip to France and the premonition that I had had, that Carlo would soon die, back to my mind for an instant. Once again, it was as if God had wanted to warn me. Somehow, in Chartres, he wanted to come forward and reveal to me what would happen to my son. I do not know why. The only explanation that I can give myself is that sometimes heaven wants to prepare us for what is to come.

They carried the coffin away. I did not want to follow right away. I stayed there for a bit, in Carlo's room, alone. It had gone quiet. Everyone had left. Around me, there was only emptiness. I let a great silence descend into my heart. It was not a silence of desperation, of anger, of retreating into myself, but rather a silence that tried to let God console me and help me to be, despite everything, a living testament.

Fate had separated me momentarily from my son. My life had changed. A thousand thoughts filled my head. Suddenly, we had been divided. I had been relegated to the present life and Carlo to the afterlife. I remember that I had a strange dream a few months before my son died. Carlo was there, dressed in red, on the other side of a gate, while I was stuck outside.

I could talk to him, but we were separated. I was on one side and he on the other. For me, this dream was also a premonition that our lives would be separated. In the moment I did not pay attention to it, but I later understood that this piece also fit into the puzzle of my life.

However, suddenly a certainty arose in my heart. Despite this apparent human defeat, Carlo had been called for a great mission by heaven, a mission that would be revealed slowly and in which I, somehow, would take part. The words of Saint Paul in the First Letter to the Corinthians came to mind, when he reiterates that "Jews demand signs and Greeks seek wisdom, but we preach Christ crucified: a stumbling block to Jews and folly to Gentiles, but to those who are called, both Jews and Greeks, Christ the power of God and the wisdom of God. For the foolishness of God is wiser than men, and the weakness of God is stronger than men" (1:22–25). As previously mentioned, Carlo said, "Starting from birth, our earthly destiny is marked: We are all called to climb up Golgotha and pick up our cross."

Before leaving the room, another thought came to me. It was a memory of Good Friday of that year. We took part in our church's Stations of the Cross. At one point, the priest stopped with the cross right next to our pew. This also seemed to be an omen. God called us to share in the cross together with him.

• • •

Carlo's casket went down toward the hearse that was to take him to the church for the funeral. Before my eyes were Jesus' Stations of the Cross, an incomprehensible mystery which reveals God's immense love for us to us, and as Carlo had said:

> Even though it cannot be fully understood, it must be welcomed
> with gratitude and love. Once we have welcomed it, this mystery
> will change and transform our hearts and our lives and will help
> us understand true love according to God and to not be deceived
> by all the surrogates for love that the world presents us with and
> which are of no benefit to man. The Word of God is made flesh
> and has come down from Heaven to restore the Mercy we lost
> through original sin and which we continue to lose each time we
> sin today. Jesus could have easily performed his redemptive act
> in a less painful manner. He certainly did not lack for the means,
> systems, and methods to reach salvation without having to resort
> to suffering. But that is not what he chose. He chose Calvary. He
> chose the Cross, he chose humiliation, he chose the Passion.

We, too, as his disciples, must accept suffering in our lives with faith and
trust, trusting in what Saint Paul tells us in his Letter to the Romans, which
is that "we know that in everything God works for good with those who
love him" (8:28).

I thought of Carlo, who said that due to his extraordinary sensitivity,
Jesus fundamentally always suffered, since his birth, even from the moment in which he took on human form. This detail is not emphasized
enough. For Carlo, it was not so much the manger as the passage from
divinity to humanity that marked his great humiliation and suffering. It
was a passage that was surely not painless — it involved going from the
infinite to the finite. We who cannot possibly have a similar experience
cannot evaluate the humiliation suffered by the Word. We also emphasize
poverty and deprivation too much. But how much poverty and deprivation is found in the passage from the infinite to the finite! Then the exile
in Egypt, a difficult journey, a painful trip. He grew up, therefore, in pain,
in deprivation, in tightness. Then there was his public life, which lasted
around a thousand days. He did not allow himself any privileges. He underwent humiliations and challenges. Just think of the silent fight with the
scribes and the Pharisees and the Sadducees and the Herodians and the

priests, including the Sanhedrin. They followed him, they tailed him, they spied on him. They were always trying to catch him making a mistake. The Gospels tell us that every day was a battle. And then we arrive at the famous week. Days of unspeakable suffering. The flight of the disciples. The arrest, with clubs. The public trial.

The insults, the mockery, the contempt. The Stations of the Cross. The strikes of the hammer on his hands and feet. But why did he choose death, and death on the cross, when he could redeem us without suffering? The only answer I can find for myself is that Jesus accepted such a violent death for love alone. And in God's mysterious plans, I was also called to embrace this cross with Christ.

During his Calvary in the hospital, Carlo assured me that he would send me lots of signs and help from heaven. This thought brought me a lot of comfort, because I knew that my son was particularly inspired by and close to the Lord, and, if he stated something, he would always keep his promises. I looked out the window in his room and watched the movements.

After my son's coffin was slowly eased into the hearse, it began to move toward the parish church of Santa Maria Segreta, not far from our home. I stayed and watched until the car turned the corner and left my field of vision.

As soon as the car disappeared, I felt a great wave of sadness and pain wash over me. The fact that I could no longer see the car with Carlo inside served to emphasize the chasm, the break that had been created between myself, still on earth, and my son, who had gone to heaven forever.

However, a voice called to me and distracted me from my thoughts. It told me to hurry. I had to come back to reality.

I got ready, and with my mother and my aunt, I walked toward the church to meet my husband, who was already on his way. When I got there, I found it already crowded. It continued to fill, to the point where some people were forced to wait outside. I saw many people sobbing, many grieving faces, many emotions that leaked from the faces that looked at me embarrassed because they did not know how to comfort me.

The funeral was proof of how much Carlo was admired and loved. There were all of his friends, and also everyone that Carlo had helped. The beggars, the homeless, the various foreigners that he had helped over the course of his life were there because they had lost a true friend. I remember that it was the first time I saw some of them there. Carlo had truly created a great network of friendship, a silent network which was not fully visible when he was alive but was displayed in all its greatness and beauty in that moment.

Many had the impression that they were not at a funeral but rather a party. It seemed like the celebration of the passage to another life, a true life. True, everyone was crying, but at the same time everyone felt the presence of so much light. It was as if the life in which Carlo had landed wanted in some way to make its presence known. And, in some ways, it was really there with us.

When the priest gave the final benediction, saying, "Mass has ended, go in peace," by sheer coincidence the church bells began to ring. In fact, the Mass had ended precisely at noon. The numerous priests that had celebrated Mass with us told us that they thought that this was a sign that Carlo's death was the beginning of his life alongside God. And, in fact, it appeared that way to many. The bells rang, and it was as if Carlo wanted to share the heavenly party that had begun with his arrival.

The parish curate read from a text he had written and compared Carlo to the prophet Jeremiah.

My son performed his first miracles on the day of the funeral. A woman who had breast cancer and had not yet started chemotherapy invoked Carlo and was healed. Another woman from Rome, forty-four years old, who had come from the capital just to say good-bye to Carlo for the last time, prayed to him because she was not able to have children. She asked Carlo for this grace, and a few days after the funeral, she learned that she was pregnant. Nine months later, a beautiful baby girl was born.

People began spontaneously to pray to my son, to ask for his intercession. It was as though they already felt that he was consecrated. In fact, Carlo's leap into the glory of the altars started the day of the funeral, through the testimony of his friends and acquaintances. Unexpectedly, his reputation for saintliness spread very quickly and around the globe.

It was a movement by the people, spontaneous. The faithful, his friends, and the people that my son had encountered during his life started to pray to him, believing him capable of intercession. Various miracles occurred and continued to occur, because people believe that Carlo can intercede. It is the Church which, through the devotion of those who pray to him, recognizes sainthood. It is their faith which moves the heart of Jesus to grant grace and miracles through his intercession and due to his merits. My son told me that he would help me a lot from heaven, and that has been the case since the day of his funeral, since we brought him to the cemetery to bury after leaving Santa Maria Segreta.

I remember that I had a strange dream during those days. I was in church with my husband. We walked down the long aisle that leads to the altar. The church was full of people. Everyone was looking at us as though we were the protagonists of something special. That is how I felt immediately after Carlo's death: the protagonist of an important story, not because of merit but because of divine will. Carlo said his "yes" to Jesus, and his generosity sparked the beginning of a story of mercy which continues today, even though he lives in another dimension. After the funeral, Carlo's body was transported to the cemetery in Ternengo, in the province of Biella, where one of the family's tombs is located. There, he would wait until the tomb that we had purchased in Assisi was prepared and completed. My son had often said that Assisi was the place where he felt happiest. That was where he wanted to be buried. So that is what we did. His tomb immediately became a destination for pilgrims, especially groups of young people accompanied by their teachers, a constant stream of people that never stopped flowing. The people who address Carlo and who he continually helps number in the thousands.

• • •

Not long after his death, the parish priest of Santa Maria Segreta, Msgr. Gianfranco Poma, came to visit me along with a sacristan named Neel, a man from Sri Lanka. Neel had gone back to his home country for a period of time to take care of his sick mother. Upon his return, he told me that he had run into Carlo, who had grown up quite a bit. He had become very tall, and for a moment, Neel didn't recognize him. It was Carlo who reminded him who he was. He confided in me that he was struck by how Carlo conducted himself, which was in a very different manner from the others of his age, and he kept repeating to me that he was not like the others. He was friends with everyone and respectful of everyone. He remembered, for example, that he never shouted. He was always kind to everyone. He always greeted him with a big sunny smile. Neel brought me a beautiful poem that he had written and dedicated to Carlo in which he compared him to the brightest star in the sky. He wrote that no one else was like him, and lots of other beautiful things.

I was intrigued by his poem and thought Carlo must have been a close friend of his. I was very struck when I came to know that Neel had never spoken directly to him, and that those beautiful verses had poured out from his heart just because of how my son greeted him when they ran into each other. A simple "hello" spoken by Carlo was like a golden arrow that struck people's hearts. And that is what happened to Neel.

This was also something that I learned from Carlo. Every minute can be different if we live it with the right intensity. Even a simple greeting accompanied by a smile, which can appear insignificant, can be very important and have a profound impact on those we address. In a certain sense, this is also what Mother Teresa of Calcutta believed. She always said: "We shall never know all the good that a simple smile can do. There is no better moment than this one to be happy." She believed that we should fully experience this moment, not others in the future. She did not regret the past and did not live thinking only of the future. No, she lived in the present, and so did Carlo. He knew how to dispense these special greetings and these smiles to everyone he encountered.

Neel also told me about how he sometimes ran into Carlo on the street with our housekeeper, Rajesh, and saw that their relationship was like that of two old friends. He was deeply convinced that he was a truly special young man. Carlo was always calm, never gloomy or angry or sad. Neel had been very struck by his mild-temperedness, and he said that most kids Carlo's age had mood swings written all over their faces. He also stood out for his behavior in church and looked composed and immersed in prayer before the tabernacle. He was surely deeply moved by the fact that Carlo participated in Mass every day, because in today's world young people are almost never seen in church. Here are some lines from the beautiful poem that he wrote in his memory which I find particularly meaningful:

> There are many stars that sparkle in the night sky. Some have a brighter light, and there is one that stands out for its brilliance, and it makes me think of you, Carlo. Not everyone who looks at the sky sees the difference between one star and another. You, Carlo, are unmistakable. Until now, I have never found someone like you.

I met with the parish priest of the church that we went to multiple times soon after Carlo's death. He told me that he had discovered that Carlo belonged to an important family only through the newspapers, when he saw our son's obituary. With him, like with everyone, Carlo always came off as a simple person. He wore classic clothes, and he rode around on a broken bicycle. He never talked about himself. The priest told us that he was always very struck by his discretion. He wrote the following words about him:

> The months pass, and in the meantime, it is becoming clearer and clearer to me that young Carlo Acutis's "passage" towards the gateway of the Easter of our Lord is a sign of Grace, an uncommon sign, exceptionally accessible and very familiar. I have my reasons for noting its importance and beauty, especially in terms of the "normal evangelical everyday-ness" of how he lived his life, which I saw on many occasions when I came into contact with him. But today, I am more and more struck by his echo, which comes to me spontaneously through many people of all ages who feel the need to talk about him. All these memories have something in common, something striking: the perception that Carlo had an absolutely normal way of living but with an absolutely special kind of harmony. There was no ostentation, no inclination to appear "special," no volunteering aimed at creating an image of supremacy for himself — on the contrary, he always seemed comfortable letting his integrity, passion for life in its various expressions, and simplicity of ways and of language (in the sense that it was naturally free of duplicity and uncalculated), shine through. He was a talented young man, as everyone recognized, with a clear and concrete

intelligence and sense of responsibility, a refined sense of humor and clear values that he would never compromise. A frank and affectionate young man, not prideful and a stranger to possessive maneuvers, with a passion for deliberate and disinterested action, where he knew how to invest his energy, capability, and amiability; punctually patient when it came to the effort of realizing group projects, habitually removed from the revenge of resentment and obstinacy.

As mentioned, Carlo had promised to send me various signs once he had reached heaven, and that is what he did. Soon after his death, one morning, I woke with a start. A voice inside me spoke clearly to me and kept repeating, "Testament."

I was convinced that it was Carlo talking to me. He wanted me to find a testament of his or something similar. In life, he was always full of surprises, and I thought, "He is the same in death."

Excited, I ran to his room. I hoped to find a letter, a message that had escaped me until that moment. However, I searched in vain.

On impulse, I decided to open his computer and started to look at some of his notes. At a certain point, I was drawn toward a video from two months prior which was clearly visible on the desktop. I had never opened it. I opened it in that moment. Carlo had filmed himself. I think he used an old camera. It lasted a few seconds. It said, "I've put on seventy kilograms and am destined to die."

He smiled as he repeated these words, and looked up toward heaven happily, displaying a certain serenity. I was very struck when I watched the video. And it brought me a bit of comfort. It was as if he had wanted to tell me, "I felt that God was calling me." Since he was a child, in fact, he was convinced that he would die of a broken vein in his brain, which is what in fact occurred, since the cause of his death was a cerebral hemorrhage. And every so often, when Rajesh worried that his hair was going gray, he said jokingly, "I will always be young."

On multiple occasions in the past, he had said things which seemed not to make sense which later came true. And somehow, this had also come true: Carlo died young. He had never known maturity or adulthood.

• • •

On the first Sunday of October, a few days before Carlo died, we had recited the Prayer to Our Lady of the Rosary of Pompeii together. We asked the
Virgin Mary to help us become holy, to help us not go through purgatory
and to bring us straight to heaven after death. Our requests had been for-
mulated directly by Carlo.

Not long after his death I received confirmation that the Virgin
Mary had listened. I had gone with my husband on pilgrimage to Monte Sant'Angelo in the Gargano in Apulia. We arrived at this holy place by
car. It was built on an enormous limestone cave, on a promontory at over
eight hundred meters above sea level. In this sanctuary, where it is said
that the Archangel Michael appeared four times, plenary indulgences and
the remission of sins are granted daily. It is the only holy place which was
consecrated directly by the Archangel Michael.

To get there, you have to go down an Angevin staircase with nearly
a hundred steps. Carlo loved this place, and we had gone on pilgrimages
there together on multiple occasions. Each time he went down that staircase, he became very excited. The long descent into the cave seemed to him
to symbolize somehow a mystical descent "within ourselves" which each of
us should complete in order to get to know ourselves better and be able to
improve.

I attemded the last Mass of the afternoon with my husband.

It ended at around 4:30 p.m. The church had just emptied.

In fact, there was no one remaining. I decided at that point to stay a bit
longer, and I sat down to pray in front of the altar with the statue of Saint
Michael.

I began to think of Carlo, asking myself whether he was already in
heaven with Jesus, and suddenly I heard an interior locution. A voice told
me these simple words: "Carlo is in heaven and this is enough for you."

This answer brought me much comfort. Later, I received further confirmation from priests devoted to Carlo who lived abroad and who had
dreamed of my son. They told me that he had also told them that he had
gone straight to heaven after death, without passing through purgatory.

2

"I Thirst"

The summer of 2006 was the last one that Carlo experienced on this earth. Of those months, the ones I remember most clearly are the days that we spent together in Santa Maria Ligure, at his paternal grandparents' house. I remember many things, but I want to start from what still comes back to me as most important. We were coming back from afternoon Mass and walking along the beautiful road that winds along the coast. With his characteristic simplicity and bluntness, Carlo asked me what I would think if he were to become a priest. In the moment, I did not know how to answer. I listened kindly.

I was not unfamiliar with his love for Jesus and the Church. For this reason, his revelation did not strike me as unnatural. Additionally, I later discovered he had also told my mother, his grandmother, about this intimate desire. Evidently, he had been thinking about embracing religious life for a long time. As Czech Cardinal Tomáš Špidlík wrote, vocation is "becoming aware that God is asking us for something that he already has in mind, and that he is counting on us."

I did not say much. I tried to make him understand that above all I cared about his happiness. If his desire to embrace religious life was something serious and sincere, then I would be very happy for him.

If he had made it to priestly ordination, he probably would have decided to become a diocesan priest. He admired them greatly. He appreciated their unassuming everyday work, far from the limelight, work dedicated to the life of the faithful entrusted to them — everyday Christianity, in essence. For Carlo, it is in everyday life that Jesus reveals himself and walks among his people. He did not look for him in great things but rather in the minute ordinary vicissitudes of life.

Multiple times, I asked myself what kind of priest he would become if he had embraced consecrated life. The most convincing answer came to me from a great priest, the Curé of Ars. "It is the priest who continues the work of redemption on earth," St. John Vianney said. "When you see the priest, think of Our Lord, Jesus Christ. ... All good works together are not of equal value with the sacrifice of the Mass, because they are the works of men, and the holy Mass is the work of God. The priesthood is the love of the heart of Jesus." I am certain that this description is also the one that Carlo felt in his heart.

For me, Carlo's simple question revealed an important desire. He asked it with extreme naturalness, without fear of my judgment and with his typical characteristic candor. Of course, if he were still alive today, it is not a given that he would have necessarily embraced that path. No one can say. Sometimes, I like to think that he would. I was much aware that God had dug deeply into his heart to find himself. For him, Jesus was "his everything." For this reason, it was somehow natural that he should choose to dedicate his life to him.

Surely, the shining example of some priestly figures contributed to the sparking of the desire in him. He had many important friendships, including those formed out of sight of his family. However, I repeat, more than anyone else, that I believe it was God who burrowed into his heart.

In Santa Margherita, we were often able to take boat trips. In fact, my father-in-law had a small motorboat with a cabin where we could spend the whole day out at sea. I remember various trips we took toward Cinque Terre. We stayed at sea for long hours, immersed in pristine nature, in clean water full of fish.

On one of the last days of a vacation, we went as far as Porto Venere, not far from La Spezia. We were sailing along breezily when suddenly a group of dolphins came up to the boat and started to swim alongside us. Carlo's grandfather said that he had never seen such a thing in his life. Sometimes one or two dolphins would come up to the boat, but never dozens and dozens. A whole pod had come up to us. Fish leapt around the boat. They followed us everywhere we went. I had the sensation that they wanted to act as a shield for us and share their joy with us. I remember Carlo's face. He was in ecstasy, radiant. I learned only later that in the previous days he had prayed to Jesus multiple times asking that he be allowed to see dolphins in real life before we went back to our everyday lives. They were his favorite animals. (The first time he had seen them was at Gardaland, where we went every year for a day of fun on his birthday. Among the various shows was one with dolphins.)

The dolphins stayed with us outside Porto Venere for quite some time. When I think back, I am convinced that their presence that day was a special grace, one of God's delicacies, for Carlo. Ever since he was little, he had been the recipient of particular attention from God. His dialogue with him was constant, and Carlo told us that somehow the Lord always answered his prayers.

This was his secret: that he had a constant, intimate relationship with Jesus. He wanted everyone he encountered to have this kind of relationship, like he did. He did not consider it something just for him. He was convinced that this relationship was accessible to all. He asked everyone to go to God for every need. "He listens and answers," he used to say. "You have to believe, however, and have faith that this dialogue is possible and real."

Carlo did a lot of research into what dolphins represent in Christian iconography. They are the symbol of salvation brought by Christ. In ancient times, in fact, dolphins were already thought of as animals that were friends of man and protectors of sailors at sea. They have always been seen as mediators, bearers of peace and harmony, and as a point of reference for man.

In the *Inferno* from the *Divine Comedy*, Dante himself tells of how dolphins protected sailors from an imminent storm. Italian historian Franco Cardini reminds us that from the time of the catacombs "Christian iconography used the dolphin in two fundamental ways: to represent the soul of the Christian, which reaches the gate of salvation through the sea of existence, and to represent Christ himself. In this context, the anchor could take on the role of the cross, and the trident an analogous one."

Tertullian calls the faithful "little fish," and says that they should take inspiration from the "Great Fish" — that is, Christ. Paulinus of Nola, writing to a bishop named Delphinus, plays on the name of his correspondent and compares it to the "True Dolphin," which is Christ. Cardini continues: "The cetacean also makes an appearance in hagiographic legends: when Saint Callistratus was thrown into the sea by Diocletian, two dolphins brought him to shore; the body of Lucian of Antioch was carried by another dolphin; and Saint Martinian escaped the temptations of lust riding a dolphin. And people riding dolphins are found, for example, in the mosaic on the floor of the Otranto cathedral. Their loyalty in friendship and the story of Saint Martinian explain how the dolphin — which for the Greeks is Aphrodite's partner, which helps explain her marine origin — was taken as a symbol of faithfulness and especially marital faithfulness."

I do not know whether Carlo knew all of this. He certainly loved dolphins and felt a certain connection with them, and he knew the meaning that they had in the life of the faithful very well. Carlo loved all nature. He saw clearly how it was a gift from God. And his favorite part of nature was the dolphin, the creature which made him feel closest to God and closest to Jesus Christ.

• • •

I remember many events from that last summer that we spent in Liguria, and especially one evening in which Carlo and I stayed home alone. My in-laws had been invited to the house of some friends. We had dinner together and sat on the balcony that looked over the beautiful port of Santa Margherita, on the northern part of the horseshoe-shaped inlet where the town was built. It was a beautiful summer evening, a bit breezy. The air was warm and light, which kept the heat, which often became very muggy, from bothering us too much. Despite the murmur of voices of people walking down the street, it was fairly quiet. Far away, along the coast, were the lights of houses. They decorated the landscape, creating an atmosphere like a fairy tale. The moon and stars in the sky were reflected in the calm sea, and it reminded me of Vincent Van Gogh's marvelous painting *Starry Night Over the Rhône*, found at the Musée d'Orsay in Paris.

I started to work on the computer, and Carlo also began working on his summer homework. At a certain point, a friend called him. He moved away a bit so as not to disturb me, but without trying to I heard the entire conversation. I was never a nosy mother. I never eavesdropped on his conversations.

On the contrary, I always tried to stay away. But that evening, I could not avoid hearing. I was struck by what Carlo said. I remember that he talked to this girl in a way that was both very paternal and at the same time stern. That is how Carlo was: nice, but also decisive, even authoritative, I could say. As far as I could understand, his friend had met a boy in a night club and had intimate relations with him that same night.

Carlo was very attached to chastity. He was not a prude — quite the contrary — but he recognized the special dignity in each person that was to be respected and not consumed. He thought that you needed to take time before giving the whole of yourself to your partner. Multiple times he chided his friends if he thought they were rushing things and even indulging in pre-matrimonial experiences.

Chastity was not an end in and of itself. It was not due to mere asceticism that he suggested it. It was rather due to the awareness that if experienced as a gift from God, each relationship can lead to one hundred times the happiness. If it is abused, however, it does not bear the fruit that it could. To tell the truth, sometimes it felt like listening to a priest, and it made me smile to listen to him tell others that the body is the "temple of the Holy Spirit."

He often spoke of the Holy Trinity and said the Father has a throne in heaven, and also the Son, who sits to his right, but the Holy Spirit has our hearts for a throne, which become a temple of God. For this reason, he continued, we must respect the sacredness of our soul and our body and not trivialize love by reducing it to a simple "economy of pleasure" aimed only at satisfying self-serving desires and not at true goodness. When I listened to him speak, I felt like I was rereading from the famous novel *The Little Prince*, written by Antoine de Saint-Exupéry, where the main character explains the difference between wanting and coveting his little rose:

> "I love you," said the little prince. "I care for you, too," replied the rose. "But that's not the same thing," he replied. "Caring for something means taking possession of something, of someone, it means looking for the things that fulfill our personal expectations for affection in others. … Caring for something means making something that does not belong to us ours. … Loving means wanting the best for someone. … Loving means allowing someone to be happy even when his path is different from ours. It is a disinterested feeling which is born from the desire to give oneself, to offer oneself up completely from the bottom of one's heart. When we love, we offer ourselves up completely without asking for anything in return."

Carlo loved *The Little Prince*. It was perhaps the book in which he saw himself reflected the most, even though he read broadly and extensively. I could say that he grew up alongside *The Little Prince*. He first read it when he was little. He read it and reread it, over and over.

When Carlo spoke of love, of the love between a boy and a girl, he always referred to the teachings of saints who were able to love without coveting. Carlo knew how to maintain a separation that was not disinterest but rather an entrusting of others to God. For him, each man was sacred, each man was a child of God, as was each girl. For this reason, he loved one and all without trying to take possession, without subjecting them. It was as if he related to others while allowing space between himself and others for a third person, God himself. He let Jesus come into his relationships, to live inside them, and he left him the last word. He entrusted them to Jesus, sure that in this way they would not want for anything. Since he considered Jesus to be truly present, he did not dare to dirty others, to allow himself to be won over by selfishness, but rather to love with the same love reflected in the Gospels, the love of Jesus.

Carlo cared a lot about chastity and the Sacrament of Matrimony. He was convinced that married couples, through the gift of the Holy Spirit which they receive at the point of marriage, are made participants in Jesus Christ's capacity to love — a capacity which, if embraced with open arms and made one's own, allows for the full and complete realization of all of the goals of conjugal and family life, allowing them to cooperate in the plan of love that God has for everyone. He said that marriage is rooted directly in the heart of God, our creator, and it is an effective sign of Christ's alliance with the Church. "Husbands, love your wives, as Christ loved the Church" (Eph 5:25), Saint Paul wrote, giving your lives for them. If one of his friends criticized the Sacrament of Matrimony or trivialized it, he always repeated with deep conviction that we must follow Jesus's teachings and wait for marriage before having sexual intercourse.

On multiple occasions, I remember hearing him yelling at friends of his who bragged about visiting pornographic websites, or who read things that he defined as "damaging to the soul," or talked openly about practicing "autoeroticism." He told them that in doing so, they were becoming like the marionettes in *Pinocchio*, the ones that Mangiafuoco used for his shows and then threw directly into the fire. It was his metaphorical way of illustrating what happens to souls who are not able to resist temptation and allow themselves to be led astray and overcome by their vices. I want to re-emphasize that for him staying away from pornographic websites or inappropriate literature was not prudishness. It was rather the only way not to be poisoned, not to open the door to attitudes that can leave a bitter taste in your mouth and not make you happy. Happiness, he said, is loving others like God loves them, and not unloading your own selfish desires on them.

• • •

Carlo often demonstrated his convictions in this regard. He did so without fear and even with those who he did not know. I remember that a year prior, in the summer of 2005, in Assisi, we sometimes went to the town pool for a few hours. It was outdoors and surrounded by the beautiful green slopes of Monte Subasio.

It was during one of these afternoons that I noticed Carlo become very angry. I saw him get up suddenly and go to the lifeguard because on the opposite side of the pool two teenagers, about sixteen years of age, were kissing in front of some children, who watched them, a bit amused and a bit embarrassed. The lifeguard went directly to the teenagers and asked them to stop. That is how Carlo was. He did not tolerate vulgarity, especially when it scandalized innocent souls.

Carlo was always ready to explain the reasoning behind the Church's thinking, even when it came to delicate subjects, including when it came to the dignity of life and of the embryo. He spent that summer working on a research project that his religion teacher had assigned. It was about different religions' perspectives on in vitro fertilization. He was very disturbed to learn that these techniques often produced extra embryos, which were then frozen or used for medical experiments. During this period, he told me that he had had a nightmare. In his dream, he had seen dozens of frozen people. It made a strong impression on him. He said that it would be a holy act if women volunteered to "adopt" one of these frozen embryos in order to give them the opportunity to come into the world.

Carlo was not interested in judging people. He said that only God could do so. He avoided Catholics who attacked those who, according to them, were stained by "criminal acts" with force and near cruelty instead of trying to find solutions that worked for the good of everyone. And for him, what was good was simply to try to find a way to bring birth to those lives. His intent was not to be an opposing force, as though he needed to build walls to keep out those who thought differently. On the contrary, he felt it right to look toward the light and to look for answers to darkness, to that which was wrong, in the light.

• • •

He often thought of his friends. He brought them everywhere in his heart. He always prayed for them, even offering small sacrifices. Friendship was truly important to him. For Carlo, caring for his friends, wanting the best for them, meant wanting the best for their souls. In a certain sense, he also took instruction from *The Little Prince*, a book that had a truly decisive influence on his life, in this regard. He often cited a quote from the fox, who says, "It is the time you have wasted for your rose that makes your rose so important." It is the time that we dedicate to our friends, he repeated, that makes them special and unique. However, this time should always have love for God at the center. Only then will it truly be quality time.

Even from far away, even from Santa Margherita Ligure, Carlo was always there for his friends, via telephone or the internet. He tried to make each one feel unique, special, one of a kind. Many of them spoke about the way he had of seeing them after his death — a way of seeing that always turned into action. They were not just words for him. Words and thoughts were always followed by facts. In Saint-Exupéry's book, the fox explains to the little prince how both the boy and the rose need each other. He said that if the little prince had spent his time taming her, he would have become unique for her.

For Carlo, in this way, each person had something unique to give the other: sharing, becoming special for each other, and contributing to the realization of everyone. Dedicating time to others allows for the creation of unique bonds which can hold up against the storms of time. It is no accident that Jorge Luis Borges, another author who Carlo often read, wrote, "I cannot give you solutions to all life's problems, nor do I have answers to your doubts or fears, but I can listen to you and share it with you." For Carlo, friendship was this sharing.

He always said that each person brings the reflected image of God along with him. And for this reason, each person is unique and one of a kind. Unsurprisingly, he often said, "No fingerprint is just like any other." To put it once again in the words of *The Little Prince*, "It is only with the heart that one can see rightly; what is essential is invisible to the eye." We are responsible for what we "tame." That is, the effort that we put into our relationships with others makes it essential that we each take on our responsibilities, that we get involved and do not run away, otherwise we will be like *The Little Prince*'s geographer, who refuses to explore his own world, the one closest to him, and instead takes refuge in research on worlds far away, missing out on the most fundamental part of life and on the people that surround him.

I remember that last summer as days and months in which Carlo, even from afar, was able to dedicate time and energy to his friends. In fact, he worried little about himself. Each day was dedicated to others, to his world, which was in the end small but in his heart special and unique.

• • •

In Santa Margherita, we slept in the same room. It looked out over the main road below. It was always very hot. At night, we kept the windows open, hoping for a bit of cool. One night, at about 2:30 a.m., we woke suddenly to the sounds of kids yelling. They blasphemed against the Lord, laughing coarsely. Their voices sounded like those of devils incarnate. I truly do not know how better to define them. Carlo believed in the existence of the devil. He knew that evil is almost always the act of man. But he also knew that the devil is a real creature who pushes man toward evil. It was as if he recognized his presence. He could see his actions in the voices of those kids. He often repeated the words that popes had dedicated to evil and to its personification, the devil. He said that we must never talk to him and that it is very dangerous to do so. We must confide only in the Lord. And when we feel the presence of the devil, we must not fear, because the Lord is stronger than everything and everyone.

Carlo was always harsh with those who insulted the saints, the Virgin Mary, and God through blasphemy. For that reason, we decided to recite a Rosary for those kids who, Carlo maintained, surely did not know what they said. "They do it without reflecting," he said, convinced. "They do it because their heart is conditioned by those who wish them evil, and they do not realize the gravity of their words. They are not fully aware."

He believed that they were victims of people older than them, from whom they had unfortunately learned these ugly habits. Interceding for them was not something new to Carlo. Many times, I had seen him pray for others, dedicating hours to prayer to ask the Lord that people like this understand the gravity of their gestures and words.

Carlo said that blasphemy was a very grave sin that greatly offended God. In addition to praying for them, he often intervened directly. He never did so brusquely, but rather gently. What an impression it made on me to see such a young man approach kids that he did not know and tell them that they should not continue to blaspheme, and that they should stop because they did not realize the damage that they did.

On a similar note, during one of our trips to the Assisi town pool, which was a hangout for local kids over the summer, we heard many of them blaspheme. On this occasion, he was threatened by one of these young men who he had courageously confronted, asking him to stop swearing against God. He did not become demoralized, but rather responded. He told them what the saints said about blasphemers. He had taken note of what Padre Pio had said: "It is the most secure way to hell. It is the devil in your mouth," he told them.

He also knew the writings of Saint Augustine, who railed against those who offend God: "Blasphemy is even worse than the killing of Jesus Christ because Christ's crucifiers did not know what they did and did not know that Jesus was really God, while blasphemers usually know what they say and know who God is." And the words of St. Thomas Aquinas: "Blasphemy is the greatest of all sins." And, finally, St. Bernardino of Siena: "It is the greatest sin there is … greater than pride, than murder, than wrath, than lust, than gluttony. … The tongue of the blasphemer is a sword which pierces the Name of God."

The kids listened to him. A bit stunned, they did not react. They stopped threatening him and went away. I do not know what they were thinking. But I am sure that once they got home Carlo's words started to work in their hearts. With the kids on the street in Santa Margherita, on the other hand, Carlo decided not to do anything. He closed the window and asked me to pray for them with him. And that is what we did.

• • •

In Rapallo, there is a beautiful sanctuary dedicated to the Virgin Mary. It is located on the top of the Montallegro hill. Many pilgrims visit there every year to pray. It is considered to be a miraculous place. It is said that in 1597 Mary appeared to the farmer Giovanni Chichizola, asking him to build the sanctuary in her eternal memory. She presented herself to him as "the Mother of God." As a sign of her appearance, she left an icon depicting her assumption into heaven and a spring of water considered to be miraculous.

I went to the Sanctuary of Our Lady of Montallegro every year with Carlo. That summer was no exception, although I would never have imagined that it would be our last pilgrimage together. Carlo asked Mary for the special grace of going directly to heaven without passing through purgatory. We had brought some empty plastic bottles with us. We filled them with water from the miraculous spring and took them with us to Santa Margherita.

Carlo was very attached to these places of grace where Mary had made springs of holy water flow. He said that it was important to take advantage of these gifts from heaven, because all these free gifts are useful for progressing along your spiritual journey and in growing and being helped to overcome flaws and weaknesses.

That day, a group of disabled people had also made a pilgrimage there, including some in wheelchairs. Carlo offered to give them a hand, as they were struggling to make it up to the sanctuary. That is how my son was — even in the supermarket, for example, if he saw that someone did not have enough money to pay, he offered to pay for them. He paid attention to everyone, even on the metro or on buses, to cite another example; he always gave up his seat to older people. That day, he spent a fair amount of time with people with disabilities. It was natural for him.

I have to say that he had a soft spot for people with disabilities. He considered them to be a gift from God. He always said that they had a special place in God's heart. Often, their disabilities made them fully dependent on others, and therefore capable of recognizing God's presence in a simple and direct manner. Carlo admired their ability to accept reality and to humbly accept the condition in which they were brought into the world. For him, they were a testimony to look toward, and one based on which to remake oneself. It is true that he often offered to help, to spend time with them, to keep them company. But at the same time it was they who taught him the proper proportions in life, the true meaning of things, the true measure.

Carlo had read *Nati due volte*, the book in which Giuseppe Pontiggia describes the relationship between a father and his disabled son. He was struck by the father's journey. Through his son, he came to understand over the years that what was important was not so-called normality, but rather to be yourself in any situation. Carlo read the final paragraph of the book over and over again. He cited it as an example and model. In it, the father talks about his son. He says: "I tried closing my eyes and opening them again. Who is that boy who is walking, swaying, along the wall? I see him for the first time. He is disabled. I think of what my life would be without him. No, I cannot. I can imagine many lives, but I cannot relinquish ours."

• • •

Carlo had a great fondness for the sick, especially those that suffered the most, and also for the elderly. I saw him help elderly ladies bring their groceries so many times. He would just offer. He would tell me, "You go home, I'll be right there." And he disappeared, together with those elderly ladies who would not stop thanking him. The whole neighborhood knew him, and many thought of him as an angel. But he did not do anything extraordinary — just ordinary things with a lot of heart.

In a certain sense, he was a boy from another time. I do not know what else to call it. That summer in Santa Margherita, Carlo's little cousin Giovanna stayed with us. She was eight years younger. Carlo adored her. He played with her and always tried to make her happy. He was an only child, so he saw her a bit like the little sister that he so wanted. I remember that before leaving the seaside and returning home, he wanted to buy her a gift with his savings. He was a bit sad that after we left his cousin would be alone with the nanny. His paternal grandparents were also about to leave, and her parents were away for work. He tried to convince my husband to bring his cousin home with us. However, we could not do so because we were not able to get in touch with her mother who was in a faraway country at the time. He was very sad. It was the last time he saw her.

In the following years, during the Mass that we would attend to celebrate on the anniversary of Carlo's death, Giovanna cried inconsolably through the entire service. Carlo had also conquered her heart. There is no doubt that she felt how deep the love he had for her was.

• • •

One evening, we went out to dinner in Portofino. When we left the restaurant, I saw Carlo step a bit to the side. It was as if he was not there. He seemed a bit sad and melancholy. I did not say anything to him. He had those moments every so often. Over time, I had learned to give him space, to leave him alone. I noticed that he also seemed particularly quiet during the trip home. We went into the house, said goodnight to the grandparents, and went to our room to sleep. I looked for him for perhaps a bit too long, and he felt that he had to say something to me. He was very sensitive. He did not want me to worry, so he took the initiative and told me what he was feeling.

He said that when he left the restaurant, he heard a voice inside him speak to him. He said that he had realized that it was the voice of Jesus. He had told him two simple words: "I thirst." Yes, the same words that Jesus said on the cross soon before he died.

He explained his interpretation to me. God wanted him to understand how he felt before all that luxury, before the glitz and opulence of Portofino. There was no negative judgment, just mostly Jesus' thirst for the salvation of all people and particularly of those who were there.

I was touched by his words. I understood once more how to relate to material possessions, and I understood more deeply that it is not wealth that brings happiness and that our only true preoccupation should be that of the salvation of our souls and those of the people we encounter. Of what use is it to gain the whole world if we lose ourselves? Carlo himself had confided in me many times that "a step of faith is a step toward being and a step away from having."

Carlo continued to talk to me. He told me that, "If God owns our hearts, then what we own is infinite." And he explained that it is as if those who trust only in material possessions and not in the Lord live life upside down, like a driver who instead of going straight toward his destination keeps driving on the wrong side of the road, in the opposite direction from his destination, constantly risking crashing into someone.

One of the following mornings, Carlo's grandparents invited us onto the boat of some friends of theirs. Some were nobles. If I remember correctly, one was a count. Before boarding, one of them asked the two sailors who looked after the boat and helped his grandfather dock and push away to help "the Count" aboard. They emphasized the word "Count," as if they wanted to highlight his "status." I remember that Carlo turned red. He was so embarrassed by the way that those people spoke.

He felt light-years removed from that sort of snobby attitude, and he was very embarrassed. That is how my son was. He was very simple. He did not like titles or the trappings that some liked to attach to their first and last names, as if you always needed to underline the difference between you and your neighbor or distinguish yourself from the person in front of you. Carlo did not like those who felt important, who made others feel inferior, and who emphasized differences in wealth or status through actions or words. He believed titles and money to be nothing more than waste paper destined to become pulp.

He often said that one did not choose to be born rich or noble, and that there was no merit in being so. "Noble of heart, on the other hand, that you do choose to become, through your own free will, and those who are able to do so will have much merit in heaven." His heart was always with the weak and close to the meek. He repeated that people of means should not make others feel inferior, not embarrass them, but rather thank God for what they have received "freely" and help those that Providence places along their path and who are less fortunate. For Carlo, sharing was a categorical imperative. He said that giving makes us all brothers — allowing others to enjoy what we have and at the same time enjoying the riches of others. Everyone has something to give, even if it is often hidden. And these gifts are for everyone. He said that the Communion of Saints is not something that belongs only in heaven, but rather is something that should be sought out here on earth and can begin in this world. Earthly paradise is precisely this kind of sharing.

Carlo could not abide social injustice. He never tired of saying: "All men are creatures of God. God loves everyone, and no one is excluded."

• • •

On the same subject, I would like to tell a story which did not take place during that last summer, but is connected to the topic. A nobleman belonging to a chivalric order came to visit us in Milan. He had an apartment in the city and wanted to come over for lunch. He was dressed in knight's garments. His chest was covered by so many medals that you could not see the fabric underneath. Carlo was highly amused by this person. As was always the case, he did not look at him in a judging or accusatory manner. He was simply amused by his mannerisms and by the slightly old-fashioned way in which he moved and spoke. When he left, Carlo presented himself to us with paper medals, that he drew himself, taped to his chest to make us laugh. He did not do so to denigrate him, but rather to take the drama out of the situation and bring his slightly dated mannerisms back into perspective. For Carlo, the most important medals should be hung in silence in your heart — medals of love, of sharing, of charity. In his opinion, trappings to hang in plain view on your own chest did not have much purpose.

One winter, we had been invited by Carlo's paternal grandparents who had a house in Switzerland to spend a weekend skiing in the mountains. The house was near Gstaad, a renowned ski resort. We stayed in a small hotel not far away. His grandparents really wanted Carlo to learn to ski well. They had hired a well-prepared, good teacher for two weeks. She took us skiing from dawn to dusk, just us and her. At the end of the vacation, Carlo had learned to ski so well that he entered a little competition and even won a medal for second place. One morning, one of her previous students, a middle-aged, very famous baroness who spoke English with the accent typical of high nobility, joined us to ski. Carlo was highly amused by her English, which was so exaggerated, and in the following years, every time he wanted to joke about someone who was acting a bit too snobby, he started to imitate the accent.

I can remember many episodes like this. One day, Carlo was invited to lunch at his friend's house. The family was very well-known. Our housekeeper, who was fascinated and excited by the fact that Carlo had visited this home, peppered him with questions. Carlo pretended not to hear, but the housekeeper kept going. After the umpteenth question, Carlo kindly replied that their house was like all the other houses — it had a room, a kitchen, and a bathroom. He said it with his typical Roman accent, which he occasionally borrowed from me, and made me laugh. He used it when he wanted to defuse a slightly awkward situation or throw water on the fire and make his Milanese friends laugh.

He was not a gossip. He did not like to give satisfaction to those who wanted to know too much about others. He preferred to be reserved and discrete, especially when it came to those who were not present. He did not like to listen to rumors or slander. On this point, he would not budge. He maintained that evil starts with a thought but strikes when the thought becomes words. He knew that words could be like bullets, that they could harm, and he discouraged everyone from firing them.

Carlo loved our housekeeper, Rajesh, but he wished he was a bit less "materialistic." Starting at a young age, he wrote letters to Jesus, asking him to change Rajesh's heart. I remember that he was shocked to learn that Rajesh spent all his wages on clothes to wear and gifts to send to his relatives in the Mauritius Islands. He was very struck to see him come home one day with an enormous bag full of shoes, looking like Santa Claus. He had found a stand at the market that sold everything for one euro and had bought three hundred pairs of sandals to send to his sister as a gift. For Carlo, this was over the top. Imagine Carlo's shock — that of a boy who, if I wanted to buy him two pairs of shoes, got angry because he said that one was enough. He would tell me, "With the money we save, we can help those who don't even have money to eat."

Carlo would go for months with a single pair of shoes. He dressed more simply than his friends. He did not follow trends in the slightest. He did not like them. He preferred simplicity, parsimony, moderation. He was elegant with his smile, and not because of the clothes he was wearing.

I remember one day — Carlo was in high school — when the beautiful bike that we had given him for his birthday was stolen. He did not care a bit. When we told him that we would buy him a new one, he told me that he did not want it and that he would prefer to use the old bike we had in the garage. I got it repaired, and he started to go around town with it, smiling and happy with his "new" bicycle, which had been fixed up but was still a bit rickety. I can still see him on the streets of Milan, riding around on his bicycle, stopping to say hi to the doorman that he met along the way, and going to visit the homeless and needy in the area. He brought his smile along. He brought them his love — a love which bubbled up so naturally out of his heart. There was nothing fake about him.

He never compared himself to others. He was modest, simple, and did not like to show off. He did not like those who criticized others and always tried to stay out of such conversations. When there was friction, he backed up or tried to change the subject. Once he told me, "Why diminish the light of others to make yours shine brighter?" He knew that the light of others was a gift for everyone.

I know. I should be talking about Carlo's last summer, but the memories are coming over me like a river in spring, and I am letting them flow along. I will string together lots of little and big memories in the order that they come to me. I like to think that it is Carlo who is guiding my pen. I always feel him close to me, and I am convinced that he really is. It is he who is talking through me in this book. It is his voice which I recall through my own.

One day, we went out shopping. I saw some sunscreen in a display that cost around fifty euro. I was a bit undecided as to whether to buy it. I needed it. It was also brand name, and therefore felt I could trust it. Carlo was a bit scandalized by the price, because he could not understand how a simple lotion could cost so much. We had addressed the subject of superfluous purchases many times. He knew that, unlike my husband, I was a bit spendthrift. And every so often, he called me on it.

That day, he took the opportunity to "catechize" me. He told me about the story of Blessed Alexandrina of Balazar. He had read some books about her in order to prepare one of the pages on his website about Eucharistic miracles. This mystic, the biographers recount, lived for fourteen years on only the Eucharist. Carlo loved her. He also said that he had received a little sign from her.

A friend of ours who worked at Radio Vaticana and who was involved in the services for the beatification of Alexandrina had given Carlo a relic of hers out of the blue. Carlo loved relics from the saints, but he guarded that of Alexandrina jealously. He said that it was one of the most precious things he had. He told me how Jesus had addressed Alexandrina, complaining about those who spent too much to take care of their bodies and became prisoners of their own vanity. He told me that God had also hinted to him once that he was not fond of the vain, those who were too attached to their image. In particular, Carlo did not understand why people were so worried about the beauty of their bodies, torturing and exhausting themselves in order to improve them, but did not pay any attention to the beauty of their souls. In his eyes, this incongruence was too great.

He was convinced that living for others was a personal commitment which each person should make individually. For example, he used to say, "Renouncing superfluous things to help one's neighbor is an endeavor that involves each of us individually. It is a commitment which helps us to become the light that the world so needs." He believed it was too easy to talk about vague topics, like the fight against the arms race, which is absolutely a just cause, but it does not affect us personally because it involves governments. Forgoing some clothes or an item of jewelry in order to help someone, on the other hand, does involve us directly.

• • •

The days passed, and the end of our vacation in Liguria drew nearer. I was unaware that this would be the last summer spent with my son.

We decided to go back to our house in Assisi, where Carlo loved to spend time more than in any other city. For him, Assisi meant finding the simplicity in life again. It was a city immersed in nature, in silence, and in the Franciscan spirituality which he so loved. Saint Francis was a guiding light for him. Francis had chosen to spend time with the neediest; he had no fear of kissing lepers, the marginalized people of his times. He lived absorbed in Jesus, and he looked for him in silence and in prayer, in meditation and in dedication to others.

Assisi was the place where Carlo's soul flew off to unexplored summits and where his heart found the proper space for plans of love and commitments of dedication to the needy. For Carlo, the needy were not just those with the fewest possessions, but also those who lacked a spiritual life.

Carlo loved to withdraw into places that Saint Francis loved and to look for silence there. I remember him walking in the fields surrounding Assisi, through the olive groves where the birds made their nests. For him, quiet was not an escape from the world but rather a place to live with God and listen to his voice. He knew that when we dive into the ocean of our spirituality, heaven can descend to earth and communicate its treasures. If, on the other hand, we are continually immersed in thousands of noises, if we live surrounded by chaos, this voice is unable to reach us — or at least, it is hard to hear it.

Before leaving Liguria, we went to stock up on focaccia. Carlo loved it. The smell of focaccia we bought in a bakery along the shore still comes back to me from time to time. Sometimes, I feel like I can almost taste it. However, I have not been able to go back to Santa Margherita since that summer.

He spent most of that summer working on his virtual exhibits and volunteering for the Jesuit website mentioned earlier. He worked mostly in the evenings. Sometimes, he stayed up until three in the morning. It was a task that he confronted with great determination and always with joy. A catechism for children who were preparing for their first Communion that we were creating with Libreria Editrice Vaticana for the Diocese of Rome was to be published at the end of the summer. My family had owned a publishing house focused on historical and scientific texts for a long time, but I had wanted to create a line of books based on the high-quality Catholic texts that I believed were not given enough space in the Catholic publishing world. Carlo also helped me a lot with this catechism. He even tried his hands at illustrating. Some of the pictures in that book, in fact, were created by him with the aid of graphic design programs.

Despite the fact that he worked late into the night, he was an early bird by nature. We attended morning Mass in the Chiesa di San Francesco or Santa Chiara. Sometimes, we decided to go to a second Mass at the Basilica of Saint Mary of the Angels in the evenings, where the Blessed Sacrament was put out every afternoon for adoration. He adored that basilica, especially the Porziuncola Chapel preserved there, where one night in 1216 Jesus and the Virgin Mary, surrounded by a multitude of angels, appeared, immersed in a bright light directed to Saint Francis above the altar.

Carlo spent a lot of time in worship of Jesus, truly present in the tabernacle. He stayed there in silence, as though he were immersed in an intimate and personal dialogue with the Lord. He said that he liked to spend time in that place, which was special because "he looks at me," he explained:

And I look at him. That gaze is enriching. I let God observe me, to dig deep inside me, to form my soul, to mold it. He is truly present, not an invention. He's there. And if everyone could realize that, how they would run to it! If everyone believed in this truth, how their lives would change for the better!

A text from Franciscan sources tells of a conversation between Saint Francis and God: "I pray thee that all those who repented and confessed their sins and who come to visit this church be granted full and generous pardon, with a complete forgiveness of all sins." God granted this special grace, which the pope at the time, Honorius III, approved. When the pope asked him for how many years he wanted this indulgence, Saint Francis answered, "Holy Father, I do not ask for years, but for souls." And on August 2, 1216, together with the bishops of Umbria, beaming with happiness, he told the crowd at the Porziuncola, "My brothers, I want to send you all to heaven!" Carlo told this story often. And he said that praying there meant opening the doors which lead to our salvation.

Around lunchtime, as I said, we often went to the town pool, where Carlo had made friends with the lifeguards. Every so often, he helped them clean the pool. He was also happy to stand in for anyone who was on shift at the café so that they could eat and take a break. He had asked me for permission to work at the café himself the following year. He wanted first and foremost to better understand the value of money earned through your own effort and not to have to always rely on parents, and to have more means to help the needy. With his savings, in fact, he had sponsored some children. Through certain specialized organizations, he wanted to increase the number of child sponsorships.

• • •

Carlo devoted himself especially to ecumenism. Even though he was young, he was attracted to this topic and to the search for unity among Christians.

When we went to Rome — a place to which I am always happy to return — we would go see some friends from the Dominican and Jesuit orders. They were the first to talk to Carlo about ecumenism and about the attempt to promote dialogue not only among various religions but, most of all, between different Christian denominations.

For my son, this effort was very important. He always attentive to what Pope Benedict XVI, who made this dialogue a priority during his pontificate, had to say on the matter. To the extent that he could, he had also followed the efforts made by John Paul II, but it was first and foremost the words of Pope Benedict soon after his election that made an impression on him.

In August 2005, he followed Pope Benedict's journey to Germany closely. He was very touched by the speech that the pope improvised on August 19 before representatives from the Protestant and Orthodox churches. He explained that he did not believe in ecumenism centered entirely upon institutions. He believed that the real question resolved around how the Church should bear witness to the Word of God in the world — a problem that Christianity had already confronted in the second century, and which had been resolved with decisions that he believed should still hold for today's Church.

In another passage, Benedict XVI repudiated "what could be called ecumenism of the return — that is, to deny and to reject one's own faith history." Because "true catholicity" is multifaceted: "Unity in multiplicity, and multiplicity in unity."

Carlo was fascinated by Pope Benedict. He always said that the Virgin Mary cared deeply about unity among Christians, and we need to pray and make sacrifices toward this end. Each year in January, on the occasion of the prayer for Christian unity, Carlo would say a novena. He was attentive to the needs of the Church, and he also liked to follow ecclesiastical events, such as the pope's visit to Germany.

He had had the opportunity to meet various Orthodox priests. He deeply appreciated their liturgies and songs. He also loved icons and guarded his reproduction of the Virgin of Vladimir, which some relatives of ours had given him, with great devotion and hung it in his bedroom. He said that you could have a dialogue with icons. For him, they were not mere paintings. They do not depict realistic figures, but rather allow those who look at them and venerate them access to a wholly spiritual world through a window. The word *icon* itself recalls the idea of "appearing," or "being similar" to an ideal image, to something that goes beyond the dimension of the real. Icons are never art for art's sake. Their aesthetic qualities are greater when they are expressions of profound truths of faith and instruments which bring us in and allow us to enter a relationship with God, Jesus, the blessed Virgin, and the saints.

It is no coincidence that theologian and Doctor of the Church St. John Damascene maintained that each icon is "filled with divine energy and grace," and is entitative participation in the Body of Christ and of the Virgin, who transmit their holiness to the material where they are painted. In other words, in the history of Christianity, icons have been much more than simple paintings. In displaying a person or an event, they recall the person or persons they depict. They are a kind of theophany, of divine manifestation, and therefore constitute a presence and create a concrete, tangible bond between the Christian and divinity itself. Some icons are still objects of extraordinary devotion today. Carlo was familiar with these concepts and understood the holiness that icons represent for all of Christianity. He also considered them to be important in ecumenical dialogue.

• • •

In Rome, as well as in other parts of Italy, Carlo had come into contact with various religious communities that worked to create dialogue among Christians. He was fascinated by them. He followed their efforts and prayed for them. In Umbria, for example, in Umbertide, there is a men's community of the Monastic Family of Bethlehem, which, although inspired by the Order of Carthusians founded by Saint Bruno, has embraced Eastern liturgy. We went there with Carlo many times for small retreats and to participate in the liturgy. The monastery is surrounded by natural beauty, which invites us to meditate and pray.

Carlo's interest in the Christian East came most of all from a deep conviction that one of the most important challenges for Christianity in the third millennium would be to reestablish the much hoped-for unity among Christians. Carlo said that the Church was founded by Christ and is one and unique, but many Christian denominations promote themselves to people as the true heritage of Jesus Christ. Everyone claims to be a disciple of God, but they see things differently and walk different paths, as if Christ himself were divided. For Carlo, this division was openly opposed to God's will, and it is a scandal in the world because it harms the cause of preaching the Gospel to all creatures.

As previously mentioned, Carlo loved *The Little Prince*. When it came to ecumenical dialogue, he often repeated that it made him think of the passage from the book in which the boy aviator — who is, in fact, the author himself — shows the adults his drawing of a boa constrictor eating an elephant, but no one can understand it because they all see a simple hat. He said that to return to unity we needed to return to the Eucharist. For Carlo, Jesus' words in the Gospel of John — "That they may all be one; even as you, Father, are in me, and I in you, that they also may be in us, so that the world may believe that you have sent me" (17:21) — should be correctly interpreted as a message of union and unity in the bonds of communion.

He would add that the devil was highly interested in division among Christians, and for this reason he influences people to desert the Eucharist. Carlo believed that the true reason for separation among Christians was most of all the slow but relentless general cooling of the fervor toward the Eucharist over the course of centuries. He said:

> The Holy Spirit, as promised, was communicated. The people of the New Covenant, the Church, was called. This people were united in faith and hope and charity. That is, the theological virtues which form the fabric of the union. Faith guides us to a single God. Hope makes us await a single God. Charity makes us love a single God. The theological virtues create unity together. When we believe less, when we hope less, when we love less, unity becomes weak and disappears. The thermometer and barometer of unity are the theological virtues. For this reason, we need to measure and weigh the consistency of these virtues in every Christian.

I know these are difficult conversations, and those of adults. But these were really Carlo's thoughts, and I cannot not repeat them. Carlo believed that the apostle Paul was clearly speaking about unity among Christians, especially when he speaks of one body, one Spirit, one hope, one God, one faith, and one baptism (see Eph 4:4–6).

Evidently, the apostle is thinking only of unity, and he is thinking of it because he correctly feels this is of absolute importance for the Church. In 1054 and 1517, two great betrayals of the apostle occurred. These were the most tremendous breaks: the one between Eastern and Western Christianity, and the one within the West, respectively. They nearly destroyed his apostolic work. Carlo believed that the Mystical Body "is the reality which constitutes the essence of the Church itself." He said:

> The head is Christ, the limbs are the faithful. The head and the limbs are the Mystic Body. This incredible reality which grace powers through one, and [each of] the sacraments [has] unity within it and produces unity. This unity, which cannot be found in any other organization, past or present, is made concrete and experienced through one faith, one hope, and one charity. The theological virtues are actualized through the sacraments.

Carlo knew that from an organizational point of view, union is operated by hierarchy. Union, he said, not unity. Unity comes from faith and the sacraments. Union is maintained through legitimately created and justly administered hierarchy.

Carlo said, "To enter into the third millennium with the seamless garment of Jesus Christ torn into three parts is a crime which cries revenge against the presence of God." He also explained that while we remember the two dates of 1054 and 1517, and we recognize that too much time has passed without arriving at unification, we must hope that the first century, at least, of the third millennium will be marked by renewed union. Jesus spoke of "one flock and one shepherd." He did not say "two" or "three" or "many," but "one alone." And so, he continued, while we hope for this goal, we must not stop at words, as we have too often done in the past, but rather move to deeds.

And the deeds are: We must recognize one another as sinners and as jointly responsible, study the essential causes of our disagreements, look toward the truth — which is not a single truth — with humility and simplicity, return to evangelical poverty, and make the desire for reevangelization reemerge from within. We cannot and must not point to goats from other pens when our own wander around without order or rules.

"To have more grace, we must be assiduous in the sacrament of the Eucharist," Carlo would say. "There are not seven sacraments, but rather six and one. Six give us grace, or renew it. One, the Eucharist, is the source of grace. So 'in' and 'with' and 'due to' this sacrament, the closer we come toward it, the more grace is poured into us. All the prayers, novenas, pilgrimages, and weeks for Christian unity are just 'hot air' without the Eucharist."

Carlo believed:

> Each person should adapt themselves to communion. In other words, you have to make a daily effort to improve yourself. How? By removing one flaw after another and achieving one virtue after another. That's the secret. If many centuries have passed since the schism with the East and the Protestant revolt, it is because we spent too much time studying theology and history and not enough trying to become holy. God's plan of goodness is that grace will circulate to such an extent that Christians from the three denominations feel pushed toward unity. Everyday Christian life must be basically characterized by this accumulation, by this stocking up, by this capitalization of grace. All the rest is profit or, at most, contribution, and nothing more.

Carlo clearly understood that the heritage of the Eastern Church is of incalculable value. It involves stunning rites crafted with careful attention to detail, so that the variety found within the Church does not only not harm its unity, but rather manifests it, reinforces it, and makes it more beautiful. I realize that these are unusual conversations for a teenager. But they were his conversations. Carlo as a teenager was at the same time very simple and very profound.

3

Little Signs

We are the fruit of our decisions and actions. Carlo knew this well. And it is also due to this awareness that he realized and completed the objectives he set for himself in such a brief period of time. He was generous, altruistic, a boy who was always attentive to others. He acted as the better part of his heart suggested he act, and he became the person that so many know and venerate today.

In other words, Carlo listened to the part of himself which had always pushed him in a precise direction. We can all choose what we consider to be "good" for us, what to be and what not to be. Carlo had simply chosen the supreme good: loving Jesus and placing him at the center of his life, and through Christ loving everyone that he encountered along his path.

There is something in my family's DNA that unites all our generations, or at least those from my grandfather to Carlo. It is something I feel continues to connect us even though many of us have gone on to another life. They are small signs, but to me they say a lot. Despite missteps and mistakes which are a part of everyone's life, it becomes clearer to me every day that it is that thread which Carlo chose to make his own — the thread of generosity, of altruism; the thread that, I am certain, was characteristic of the life of my grandmother, my father's mother.

Born in New York, my father's mother moved to Salerno when she was about eighteen years old. She was known as a very generous and religious woman. When she died, many people spontaneously began to pray to her, to ask her for the grace of intercession, especially the fishermen from the port of Salerno. Many testified that they prayed to her and received graces from her. I knew her spiritual director, Father Teodori. He had been a missionary in China for thirty years and was a member of the Xaverian Brothers. It was he who told me about how special my grandmother was and how she had lost a daughter, Renata, at just fifteen months of age. Like me, therefore, she had experienced that great pain.

There have been several saints in my family. My mother's side includes St. Caterina Volpicelli. My father's side includes St. Giulia Salzano and various prelates, including one who is buried in the church of San Domenico in Naples.

And then there was my mother's father, Grandpa Renato. He moved to America. In fact, he was forced to flee Italy during World War II. He took refuge in Venezuela, where he had some friends. He had been a republican partisan. He fought and risked his life to save many Jews from deportation to concentration camps. He was a great skier. During the Nazi regime, he helped many Jews cross the Italian border and take refuge in Switzerland. He was not particularly religious. However, he had studied at the Collegio Nazareno in Rome, where he received a Christian education.

He also helped others while in Venezuela. He became friends with a missionary, and they rented a little airplane to fly over parts of the Amazon rain forest where indigenous people who had not yet heard the Good News of Jesus Christ lived. From the airplane, they threw them supplies, interesting objects and also their photographs. In this way, the indigenous people got to know their faces and later it became easier to make friends. Once, my grandfather was able to save a boy who was about to be killed during a sacrificial rite for the Amazon gods. I am convinced that his great courage, together with a strong missionary spirit, is something he passed down to Carlo.

Once again, there are many threads which connect one generation to another. It is each person's task to take up the best of these threads. Carlo believed strongly in this type of transmission. He used to say that we had to ask our loved ones who are no longer with us for help. It is we who need them, not merely the converse. It is a relationship — the relationship between us and our loved ones — which does not end but continues. From heaven, they can help us, and from heaven they can send us a bit of their light.

Parents do not get to witness the beatification of their son every day. The path toward holiness, however, is a path for everyone. Each of us can travel along it. The more we open ourselves to the grace of God, the more he clears the way of "goodness" we must travel. I do not want Carlo to be remembered as a superhero. Carlo was a boy, and then a teenager like many others who, however, always wanted and knew how to confide in God's love. A path — his path — which, I repeat, can be traveled by everyone.

If I think on what has happened to me, I can clearly understand how everything happens for a reason. I can say that starting with Carlo's childhood, the hand of Providence was at work, discretely drafting a great plan for my son. I did not discover this plan immediately; only after his death did I understand the deeper meaning.

Many things in my life have been important signs. We all receive signs sent from heaven. We need to be prepared to recognize them. My husband, Andrea, for example, was born on the same day that my parents met in Rome. I received the Sacrament of Confirmation in 1980, while I was studying in Cortina d'Ampezzo with the Ursuline Sisters. It was May 3, the same day when Carlo was born. I think this coincidence of the day I received this sacrament, which made me a "soldier for Christ," as we were once taught, clearly shows that Carlo would be my life's most important "mission." Thanks to him, in fact, I began a walk of conversion, which I know I must continue to travel. I know that I will probably end up in purgatory.

I met my Andrea for the first time in Forte dei Marmi in the summer of 1986. We got together that same year. Andrea graduated from the University of Geneva with a degree in political economy. Two years after graduation, he began his military service with the Alpine Corps of the Italian Army in Aosta. He stood out for his seriousness and competence and made an impression on his superiors. He was later allowed to enroll in the branch of the carabinieri at the Caserma Cesare Battisti in Rome, where I lived. After he finished his military service, he moved to London to work for an English bank.

I also went to London, with the excuse of improving my English. I enrolled in a master's program in economics and publishing management. I moved with a friend to a beautiful house in the Knightsbridge area, near where Andrea lived. We spent a lot of time together. Soon, before we married, he signed a lease on a new house where we would go live together after the wedding. The apartment was small, but unique and original. It was located on the ground floor and was one of a series of townhouses that formed an oval around a marvelous common garden. Our bedroom had enormous windows which looked out over the garden and provided me with beautiful views every day. There were many kinds of flowers that bloomed in every season, and the garden was never bare.

Our house was a few minutes from the department store Harrod's, one of the most famous "secular temples" of the city. I remember that I bought Carlo his first stuffed animal in that store, a little lamb with white fur. Heaven inspired that choice. It was also — I am certain — a sign. I myself cannot explain why I decided to pick that particular stuffed animal, since I really liked zebras, giraffes, and dogs. It was a kind of premonition. For Carlo's baptism, I also chose a cake popular in the food department at Harrod's. It was in the shape of a lamb and covered with a white glaze and buttercream with liquor and cream on the inside. I would say it was a memorable cake, given the reception it received. It is still a mystery to me why I was pulled to a dessert in the shape of a lamb.

When Carlo was little, he was very attached to his stuffed animals, and he treated them with particular care. I believe that that lamb foreshadowed somehow his destiny, since before his death, like Our Lord, who offered up his life for us, Carlo offered up his suffering for the salvation of souls.

A few months before my son died, I had a very strange dream. There was a little lamb which was bleeding out and left to die, while a voice in Arabic said words meaning "sacrifice" or "victim." I do not speak Arabic, but when I looked online, I was able to find the exact words that I had heard in the dream, and I understood their meaning. They seemed to ring true to me. I felt they were prophetic, especially in view of Carlo's agony in his last few days of life, when he had many hemorrhages. That dream, somehow, foretold the cruel death of my son, with a lot of suffering and physical pain. I am deeply convinced that Carlo, in imitation of Jesus, was God's chosen victim for the salvation of many. I think that, for Jesus, he was especially associated with the Passion. The fruits of mercy and the graces which have flown from heaven to so many people following Carlo's death bring me further confirmation every day.

Carlo was inspired to offer up his suffering for the Church. His life was truly a *tout court* oblation. His gesture of offering has borne and continues to bear fruit, which is his much-deserved reward after so much suffering and Christian acceptance.

Following Carlo's example, I also offered up this pain which heaven forced me to accept with no ifs, ands, or buts for the Church, for the conversion of sinners, and for the triumph of the Eucharist during those days of illness. I made this offering while thinking of the beautiful words that Carlo found in the XI Ordinary General Assembly of the Synod of Bishops *Instrumentum Laboris* mentioned in the dedication of this book: "The Eucharist manifests that the Church and the future of the human race are bound together in Christ and in no other reality. He is the one, truly lasting rock. Therefore, Christ's victory is the Christian People who believe, celebrate, and live the Eucharistic mystery."

• • •

Andrea and I were married January 27, 1990, in Rome at the Basilica di

Sant'Apollinare, near Piazza Navona, an area which is very dear to me because it reminded me of my childhood. Right after the ceremony, we organized a lunch with a few people in an old restaurant nearby, with our closest relatives and friends. The day after, we went right back to London. We could not take a traditional honeymoon because Andrea had few vacation days, and we wanted to save them for other times. Furthermore, people who take jobs in banks have to be prepared to sacrifice weekends, late nights, and family life. Providence, however, came to our aid. Not long afterward, in fact, Andrea had to travel to Barcelona for work. I decided to go with him. It was almost like a little honeymoon. We stayed in Barcelona for almost a week, and I was able to explore every corner of that beautiful city, including the most remote areas and those normally only frequented by people who live there permanently.

I returned to Barcelona many times after, and sometimes with Carlo. I clearly remember the first time we arrived with him in tow. We were driving back from Valencia, the city where the Holy Grail is kept. According to tradition, this is the same cup that Jesus used during the Last Supper and which was subsequently used by Joseph of Arimathea to collect a few drops of the blood from the side of Christ. We had intended to go all the way to Girona, a little town which was the site of an important Eucharistic miracle in 1297. We had booked a hotel there for one night before returning home through France and into Italy.

Carlo had already been working on his website on Eucharistic miracles for a while. He wanted to take a picture of the monstrance located in the Museum of the Cathedral of Saint Mary, which, in addition to containing the largest Gothic nave in the Christian world, had held the corporal stained with the Blood that came out of the consecrated Host that was transformed into Flesh until 1936. Unfortunately, the corporal was destroyed during the civil war.

The distance between Valencia and Girona is almost 500 kilometers (about 300 miles). We decided to make a stop halfway, in Barcelona, which is less than two hours from Girona. It was early afternoon, and we parked the car near one of the main streets, la Rambla, which runs along the Gothic Quarter. Carlo very much wanted to participate in the afternoon Eucharistic celebration at the Cathedral of the Holy Cross and

Saint Eulalia, which is also famous for the geese kept inside one of its patios. We were a bit disoriented. We did not know which way to walk to get there as quickly as we could. Then a priest popped up behind us, and Carlo asked him in Spanish where the cathedral was. Carlo loved the Spanish language, and he had decided that he wanted to take courses to learn to speak it better in the future. The priest, smiling, answered in Catalan that he was going straight to the cathedral and that we should follow him. And so, thanks to this unexpected guide, we were able to arrive on time to attend Mass.

These were the typical treats, the little signs, that the Lord reserved for Carlo through his guardian angel. He was struck by the beauty of the cathedral. All the lights, the numerous wooden sculptures dressed in sumptuous clothing, and the twenty-six chapels that adorned the lateral naves left us at a loss for words. Carlo immediately fell in love with this beautiful city, with its almost surreal atmosphere, as though it was immersed in a never-ending party, and its triumph of colors and lights.

I remember you could smell Catalan foods in the alleyways. I am not sure why, but they made me think of the East. Along the street were stalls that sold sweets and other treats, including tasty churros with Nutella, which Carlo could not get enough of. I still make them today with my twins, Francesca and Michele, who, like their brother Carlo, absolutely love them. Of that day, I remember the sound of the voices of the passersby mixed with that of children playing in the streets and street vendors trying to sell interesting gadgets I had never seen in Italy. When Mass had finished, we left right away so as not to arrive too late in Girona, but Carlo made us promise that we would take him back to that beautiful city so he could visit it in less of a rush. He was glowing with happiness at having been able to attend Mass. He wanted to do so, and thanks to God, as he said, he was able.

4

The Bitter Cup

My memories of Carlo bounce around in my mind, jumping forward and backward in time. I can see them plunge down and come
back up, like seagulls diving into the ocean and coming back up to fly
high up into the sky. They bring up conflicting feelings. It is not easy for
a mother to remember her son who is no longer with us. However, the
certainty of his sanctity and the fact that his life was not spent in vain
bring me comfort.

Sometimes, memories come back suddenly, without even my trying,
like the waves in the ocean that come up and drag us under. Other times,
the sound of the lapping waves fills me with tenderness and helps me
focus on that which was my past and that of my son. I can see Carlo as
a child again, then as a teenager, and it all seems to come together in a
frame that is larger than me, but which has a precise meaning.

Of course, memories are often cuts that strike pain into a mother's heart. I am not always ready to endure them. Sometimes, the cup is bitter.

When Carlo died, I thought that over time the pain of his loss would be blunted. But that is not the case. Each minute of my son's life returns to live in me. And sometimes the wave of hurt is difficult to bear.

However, I have learned a defense mechanism. When a memory causes too much pain, I do not fight it. I let it overtake me, not bracing against it. In that way, bit by bit, it passes, and peace comes back.

The pain clearly expresses the hole that Carlo's absence leaves in my life. But all in all, it pushes me to look for him in heaven through prayer so that I can go back to living everyday life with certainty, comforted that he is distributing grace to many people, like he did when he was still among us and working for the good of both the poor in possessions and the poor in heart that he met along his journey. With the help of the Eucharist, his life was transformed into a highway to heaven, as he liked to define it. Another highway to heaven is the grace that he continues to spread to those who pray to him.

• • •

My pregnancy with Carlo was an easy one. Of course, I was often sick to my stomach. And I had heartburn which forced me to eat small amounts of food and skip dinner. But overall, it was a simple pregnancy. I had not yet started working and spent most of my time alone. My husband left at 7:00 a.m. to go to work. His office was over an hour from our house on the subway. He came back after eight in the evening. Sometimes, I went to meet him during his lunch break.

I had made friends with some mothers in the neighborhood where we lived. They were from different countries, and many like me had recently married and were staying in London because of their husbands' work. I was the youngest of the group. Many of these women had recently given birth and gave me good advice about where to go nursery shopping. Every so often, we took walks together and went to get coffee.

Until a few days before Carlo was born, I stayed very active. In addition to household chores (I did not have any help at the time), I found time to travel around the city to buy things for Carlo. I had no idea what a child might need, and I made my purchases very randomly. I bought a book that had some useful advice, but generally I followed my own instincts. There was no internet at the time. I did not have my mother and grandmother close by. Calling Italy cost a lot of money at the time, and I had to do so sparingly. No one gave me advice. I often found things in the city on sale for a very good price. This led me to accumulate things because they were "good deals." As a result, Carlo's dresser was overflowing with clothes that were not right for the season or the right size. My friends made fun of me and told me that not even famous rock stars had that many clothes. I later found people to give them to.

My purchases included one object that was truly anachronistic: a stroller from the early twentieth century, which I bought at a steep discount. It was so big that not even our highly expert nanny — Patsy from Scotland, who was barely taller than the stroller — was able to steer it. We had become the laughingstock of the neighborhood. And even though we lived in London, the capital city where you could feel comfortable in just about any situation, our stroller did not go unnoticed.

• • •

Starting right from his birth, I had the impression that Carlo was always one step ahead. He was precocious in everything. It was as though the hourglass that marked the passage of his life was running on fast forward. The words of the prophet Isaiah, when he writes that those "who wait for the LORD shall renew their strength, / they shall mount up with wings like eagles" (Is 40:31) perfectly summarize my son's life on Earth.

He developed a personal relationship with God starting at a young age. The Lord was his rock and his refuge. It was as if through natural grace, he knew that one can only reach the highest peak of the "mountain of holiness" — the place where heaven seems to bend toward earth — if he is deeply bound to God without anyone having to teach him. It was as though he were aware of the truth of the words of the Gospel that explain how no branch can bear fruit if it does not remain on the vine, nor can we bear fruit if we do not remain in God, because without him we cannot do anything. Just as he did with the people of Israel, who deserved to be free of their slavery in Egypt because they believed in him, he will do the same for everyone who asks for his help. "You have seen what I did to the Egyptians, and how I bore you on eagles' wings and brought you to myself," Exodus 19:4 tells us. Carlo dared to fly like an eagle and look into the future. He learned right away to see everything from the perspective of God and not from that of the world.

He often said that it is one thing to see a room from one corner or the other and another thing to see it from above. Only in this way can we see every aspect of it. To explain this, he used the example of a ball. If we take it apart, we can see that it is made of lots of different rings of different sizes, which if joined, form a sphere. The ball can be seen as a whole, therefore, only if all its parts are united. The same thing happens when we want to see the whole truth. If we look at it from the perspective of only one of the elements of which it is made, what we can see will be limited and partial.

• • •

Lots of photos of Carlo depict him with a backpack. I do not think this is a coincidence. Carlo had imbued the attitude typical of pilgrims, walking along a path toward a distant objective. However, he kept his roots alive, roots which tied him to the past but at the same time propelled him into the future. The true pilgrim must be full of a dissatisfaction that is not derived from bitterness or disappointment, but rather from hope, from a nostalgia for the infinite which provides justification for the departure. Carlo was a perfect pilgrim of the infinite, always engaged in a search for the absolute. But to begin this search, he always said you need to know yourself well so as to perform the exodus within yourself which allows you to go even more quickly toward God and toward others.

Carlo sometimes used the following expression: "The anti-self is the other aspect of the self, or better, of the 'myself.'" He said:

> Meeting the enemy is finding oneself with the anti-self, which
> is like the other side of the moon when it is not illuminated by

the sun. That is to say, within me is a dark place, an unexplored area where there are incredible surprises to be found. In order to make progress, I have to illuminate that part, remove the veils which do not allow me to see, and probe my "depths." This can be painful. Sooner or later, the anti-me must be confronted in order to find balance and harmony again and in order to re-purify.

Carlo believed, "Conversion is not a process of addition but of subtraction, less me to allow more space for God." And he often quoted this parable:

A man had a fig tree planted in his vineyard; and he came seeking fruit on it and found none. And he said to the vinedresser, "Behold, these three years I have come seeking fruit on this fig tree, and I find none. Cut it down: why should it use up the ground?" And he answered him, "Let it alone, sir, this year also, till I dig about it and put on manure. And if it bears fruit next year, well and good; but if not, you can cut it down." (Luke 13:6–9)

It feels like I can still hear his voice saying:

In the parable of the barren fig tree, God is telling us that he wants to see us bear fruit. He condemns ineffectiveness. He has given us extraordinary means, the sacraments, through his death on the cross, and he continues to support us, but he wants to hear us answer. All of revelation is a question that requires continuous answers from us. The sacraments that he has instituted are also a question. And the Eucharist is the biggest question of all. So, we need complete and attentive answers. We have to perform a metamorphosis on ourselves which means first of all freeing ourselves from a pagan, post-original-sin mentality. It is the mentality of the "down here" which prevails today, a mentality that is merely horizontal, materialistic, without ideals, and without any push upward.

For Carlo,

> Conversion means looking at things from the perspective of heaven, otherwise we risk seeing them as though we were looking through a small crack which prevents us from seeing a broader horizon. Today, we evaluate and we calculate looking toward objectives which do not go beyond death, where everything is aligned on the level of the self, where the ideal is to exploit existence for a kind of refined self-centeredness. If we look through the pages of history, if we examine the documents in the archive, if we look to the times before Christ, we find this: people who do not reach heaven.

So, let's get straight to work, Carlo would say! My son believed that:

> First and foremost, we must examine ourselves, scan ourselves. Look deeply at the condition in which we find ourselves. Weigh our virtues and vices, our strengths and our flaws. Calculate our merits and demerits. And all of this without excuses, without cutting corners, without making concessions. Once all of this is clear, we have to plan the correction. For example, a simple plan, which seems almost banal at first glance, is to get rid of one flaw every year and gain one virtue every year.

In our daily examination of conscience, we should be like Carlo and look at how much we have worked to make that correction or that gain:

> However, we must be sincere and staunch in our examination. We must be willing and decisive in our intention. And also try to re-supernaturalize our internal climate through prayer by meditation on the Word of God and assiduous recourse to the sacraments, especially Communion and confession, together with good spiritual direction where possible.

Carlo had read *Jonathan Livingston Seagull* by the writer Richard Bach.

He really liked it, and was especially struck by some beautiful words which are perfectly applicable to him: "The gulls who scorn perfection for the sake of travel go nowhere, slowly. Those who put aside travel for the sake of perfection go anywhere, instantly." And Carlo, we can state with certainty, was able to reach his destination, heaven, very quickly. Jonathan the seagull, like Carlo, was interested in other goals. "For most gulls, it is not flying that matters, but eating. For this gull, though, it was not eating that mattered, but flight. More than anything else, Jonathan Livingston Seagull loved to fly." This seagull was a lot like my son.

• • •

Of course, even though he was always looking toward heaven, Carlo also had to deal with this world, starting with his birth. It is said that being born and dying, even though they are natural for us, are the hardest things to confront. And it was not easy for Carlo to be born, either. My pregnancy went smoothly, but at his birth, Carlo gave me lots to deal with. I went into labor at around 5:00 p.m. on Thursday, May 2, 1991. My husband and I decided to go right to the Portland Clinic. I gave birth on Friday, May 3, at 11:45 a.m., just eighteen hours later. My contractions were long-lasting. Only at the end, when he saw that Carlo's head was crooked, did the gynecologist decide to use forceps to deliver him. Our doctor was able to deliver my son without putting him in any danger, even though he used a tool which can cause very serious brain damage if used incorrectly.

On that spring day in London, when I brought my firstborn into the world, the Portland clinic, as was their custom, sent Carlo's birth announcement to the *Times*, which I have kept until today. I would never have thought that that newspaper, which is very secular, would have written about Carlo not only at his birth but also multiple times after his death. It is said that every mother recognizes the cry of her child, and for me Carlo's was unmistakable. When he was hungry, you could hear his wails all the way in my room, which was on the same floor as the nursery. I knew with certainty that it was him, and a few minutes later, "the baby" (as the nurses called him) arrived in his mobile crib. I was sent home from the clinic after two days, and despite my lack of experience, I managed fairly well, especially because I was helped by a maternity nurse, Patsy, who was a gift from Carlo's great-grandmother.

In England at the time, an obstetrician also came by your house every week to weigh the baby and check that everything was all right. And despite the fact that Carlo measured 57 centimeters and weighed three and a half kilograms when he was born, he did not grow much initially because I did not have much milk. For this reason, they recommended that I feed him artificially and stop nursing him. The new milk gave him terrible colic, though. This worried us a lot until we started to feed him solids. I remember that every evening, as soon as my husband got home, he started to cry. In order to calm the baby, Andrea took him into his arms and started to walk around the edge of the room, alternating between singing songs and making weird noises, like "Banga, binga, bongo, bungu." We noticed that walking calmed him down, so we kept walking until around eleven in the evening, until he went to sleep. Andrea was very patient with his son, and often, when I did not have the nanny to help me, I let him give Carlo his bath, since he was much more meticulous than me.

• • •

Carlo was baptized May 18, 1991, in the church of Our Lady of Dolours on Fulham Road. The godfather was my husband's father, Carlo, and the godmother was my mother, Luana. I think that the name of this church was prophetic, because it already revealed somehow that we would also, like the Virgin Mary, drink from the bitter cup of the premature loss of a son. Carlo said that sooner or later we all go up Mount Golgotha, which is where Jesus was crucified. However, I can say that a parent who loses a child prematurely goes up Mount Golgotha early, while still alive, because such an event really causes you to die a little as well.

When I lived in Rome with my parents, our house was near Piazza Venezia. To get to my high school, which was on a side street off Via Veneto, I had to take two buses. The first brought me to Piazza San Silvestro. There, I changed buses and took another which brought me right to the school. Often, on my way home, when I had a bit of time, I would go into the Basilica of Saint Sylvester in Capite, where you can pray in a side chapel, isolated from the main church, with a beautiful statue of the grieving Mary with the dead body of Jesus in her arms. Right in front of the statue of the grieving Virgin was a relic, a skull that is said to be that of St. John the Baptist. This made the place even more special.

I always prayed to the Virgin Mary before exams or if I had a difficult oral exam coming up. I often went to pray to her, even with the little faith that I had, for people that I knew or that were experiencing great difficulty. This included my childhood friend Federica, one year older than me, who had a serious car accident and stayed in a coma suspended between life and death for a long time. Fortunately, in the end, she survived. When I think back to those solitary visits to the grieving Virgin, I can see that I had already been called, albeit with all my limits, to experience that same pain from which she had suffered. The grieving Mary has been a kind of connecting thread in my life. Her presence in my youth, then in London on the day of Carlo's baptism, was later like a premonition of something that I would also have to go through. And which I later experienced in the days of my son's illness and death. A "Stabat Mater" also awaited me.

Carlo believed:

> The Most Blessed Virgin, Mother of the Savior, went through each and every one of the phases of Jesus's existence on earth together with him, and she continues to go through each age of history today and until the end of time, holding the hand of those who trust in her with confidence and filial abandon, recognizing that she is a shining example and the facilitator of all grace. To say Mother of the Savior is to say Mother of Pain, of the Passion, of the Crucifixion, of the walk to the cross. Mary's was a motherhood of Calvary. She was a martyr, with a martyrdom that was bloodless but no less crucifying.

And it was precisely this sharing of pain with Our Lady of the Sorrows which led us to choose a bronze sculpture depicting a Pietà as decoration for the tomb where Carlo was initially buried in Assisi. We found the bas-relief in a shop that specialized in bronzes near Milan's Monumental Cemetery, among a series of broken, dusty iron scraps, and they sold it to us for a very low price. We were surprised that the price was so low, because if we had found such a beautiful item in other shops, we would have paid an arm and a leg for it. I attributed this discovery to a gift from my son. Even though our Calvary was short, it was no less intense. Seeing such a beautiful son, in the prime of his youth, like a field that fills with flowers in the spring, transformed by pain over the course of a few hours to the point where he no longer looked like himself, with a face swollen by hemorrhages and huge glands that distorted his features, was a great test of faith for us.

5

Nothing Will
Separate Us

Carlo felt a strong attachment with those that are no longer with us, with the deceased, starting at a young age. He always said that our relationship with them remains, even though it is experienced in a different way. There is a thread which connects us to them, a thread of love which continues for eternity. For this reason, it is right to converse with them, because the relationship is destined to last forever.

I came to understand this well when my father died. He passed away at age fifty-nine from a heart attack. There was a special attachment between Carlo and his grandfather. In fact, when he was still quite young, he had spent a lot of time with him and my mother in their house in Rome and at the seaside, which had reinforced their bond.

A few months after his grandfather's passing, Carlo told me that he had seen his grandfather dressed in blue. He said that his grandfather had asked him for his prayers because he was in purgatory, but also that he was all right because he had been saved. Carlo told me these things simply and with a disarming certainty. There was no doubt in his mind: His grandfather had spoken to him. Later, he told me that he experienced other signs through which God had made him understand that it was important to maintain a relationship with the dead, to pray for their souls, and to ask them to help us. Carlo's favored means for helping them was through the Eucharist and reciting the Rosary.

Many saints, such as Pius of Pietrelcina, have received confirmation from souls in purgatory that the most effective way to help them go to heaven is to have Masses celebrated for them. At Mass, Jesus offers himself to the Father because of his love for us. Carlo used to say that if we were to realize the infinite value of even a single Mass for eternal life, churches would be full to the brim.

The official writings of St. Pius of Pietrelcina include the story of being asked, "Father, can you tell me a bit of what purgatory is like?" He answered, "Souls in purgatory would like to throw themselves into a well of earthly fire because for them, it would be like a well of cool water." As Pope Francis writes in his encyclical *Laudato Si'*, we can find the entire universe and therefore also our dead within the Sacrament of the Eucharist. It unites heaven and earth, embracing everything and penetrating all of creation:

It is in the Eucharist that all that has been created finds its greatest exaltation. Grace, which tends to manifest itself tangibly, found unsurpassable expression when God himself became man and gave himself as food for his creatures. The Lord, in the culmination of the mystery of the Incarnation, chose to reach our intimate depths through a fragment of matter. He comes not from above, but from within, he comes that we might find him in this world of ours. In the Eucharist, fullness is already achieved; it is the living center of the universe, the overflowing core of love and of inexhaustible life. Joined to the incarnate Son, present in the

Eucharist, the whole cosmos gives thanks to God. Indeed the Eucharist is itself an act of cosmic love: "Yes, cosmic! Because even when it is celebrated on the humble altar of a country church, the Eucharist is always in some way celebrated on the altar of the world." The Eucharist joins heaven and earth; it embraces and penetrates all creation. The world which came forth from God's hands returns to him in blessed and undivided adoration: in the bread of the Eucharist, "creation is projected towards divinization, towards the holy wedding feast, towards unification with the Creator himself." Thus, the Eucharist is also a source of light and motivation for our concerns for the environment, directing us to be stewards of all creation.

Carlo used to say that it is mainly through Eucharistic adoration, which is nothing other than the adoration of God, that we find the entirety of creation. And he loved to remind us that by prolonging this holy practice for at least a half an hour, you can gain a plenary indulgence, according to the conditions established by the Church, which can be applied to oneself or for the dead in purgatory. He also said that even though it is not easy to achieve the main condition required, which is a complete lack of any sin whatsoever, including venial sin, we should not snub our noses at these graces which are dispensed freely because of the merits of Jesus Christ and of the saints, and the concession given to Peter — to bind and to loosen (see Mt 16:19).

Carlo also performed the so-called heroic act of dedicating all his good works and prayers to the souls in purgatory and to the intentions of the Virgin Mary who, since she is our mother, he said, intercedes on behalf of all those who address her, especially the neediest.

He loved to emphasize that our dead recall us to eternal life, to that which awaits us in the afterlife. They remind us that there is an after, they tell us how to live our everyday lives, and they help us avoid making the mistakes which can jeopardize our salvation. Many of them, he said, are in purgatory. They are suffering, and for this reason, they ask for our suffrage, because in this way we can speed up their entry into eternal bliss. Together, they provide us with an example of how we should live so that we in turn can achieve salvation.

After Carlo's death, three priests who did not know one another — one from Peru, one from Brazil, and one from Costa Rica — wrote that they had dreamed of Carlo telling them that he was especially praying not only for those who asked for his intercession, but also for those he had known in life and for souls in purgatory.

With this information, after my son's departure for heaven, I began to have Gregorian Masses celebrated at a cloistered monastery in continuous rotation, 365 days a year, as a gift for him. This holy work started with St. Gregory the Great, a pope and a great Doctor of the Church, and consists in the celebration of one Mass a day for thirty consecutive days for the soul of a single dead person. Pope Gregory ordered the prior of the monastery where he was staying to have a Mass celebrated for thirty consecutive days in suffrage of the soul of a monk who had not lived up to his vow of poverty. After the thirty Masses were celebrated, the soul of the monk, who had entered heaven, appeared to one of his brothers. The celebration of the Masses makes it so that Carlo can apply the work both to help the faithful who continue to address him in prayer as well as for souls in purgatory.

A few days after my son's death, I came across some reflections on purgatory in his notes:

> Purgatory is cleaning our robes down to the last stain. One enters into co-eternity dressed in white. As St. Catherine of Genoa wrote, "The Divine Essence is so pure and brilliant that the soul who has cognizance of a single imperfection prefers to pass through a thousand hells rather than to appear before the face of God with the stain of sin." But the point of purgatory is to eliminate the stain! The soul chooses this place to find within it the mercy needed to free itself from its wrongs.

Sin, which is a voluntary separation from the love of God, involves a crime and a punishment. The crime is remitted by the absolution for those who repent and approach the Sacrament of Reconciliation. The punishment is reduced through penitence or purgatory. And in this way, all punishments, all aches, all pains, all difficulties, all trials, all adversity, and all sicknesses are given meaning. God would not allow for them if they did not serve a greater good for the souls which he loves.

Souls in purgatory cannot help themselves. They must be helped, but they can intercede on our behalf. If we keep purgatory in mind, we get used to avoiding venial sin. We get used to atoning for our sins here on earth.

Carlo had mystical experiences regarding these ultimate realities. In particular, he was aware that life involves a continuous cycle of tests, which, if we dress ourselves in Christ, we can surely defeat. He liked to compare it to the *Labors of Hercules*, a work of Greek mythology that tells the story of the hero Hercules, who was born from a relationship between Alcmena and Zeus, the king of the gods. Hera, Zeus's wife, was very jealous of her husband and of the child, which she persecuted from the moment of his birth. She even placed two venomous snakes in his crib to kill him. But Hercules, possessing great strength, was able to kill them. We know that the devil also has waged, presently wages, and will always wage war against the human race until the arrival of the new heaven and new earth. Many will be subjugated by Satan, but we know that if we trust in Christ, we will emerge victorious.

We are like Carlo Collodi's *Pinocchio* — initially, we are all "puppets," but if we behave virtuously, respecting all of God's commandments because of our love for him, we can transform ourselves and become real men in accordance with his plan. The commandments are summarized in the law of love. God commands us to love him for himself and love our neighbor similar to our love of God.

But if God loves, why does he command? Because he is stating with all of his strength and with no room for contradictions, "These actions would separate you from what is Good." And if they are commandments, they involve my free will. In fact, love is not a feeling but rather our free choice — the choice of what is Good. As Carlo said, life would be truly beautiful if we were able to place God at the center and not false idols that the world offers us for "thirty pieces of silver" and which do not bring us anything but suffering and eternal death.

Our good Lord, the essence of love, asks each of us, personally, "Do you love me?" Earthly life is the opportunity for us to say, "Yes, I love you, help me love you." We have the freedom to accept and be filled with God's love, but we are also free to refuse, and if we refuse this highest good, what will remain for us in eternity? Only the company of those who think like we do. This is the essence of our freedom: to accept or refuse God's love.

For this reason, when we experience trials and difficulties, we must train our will to firmly desire and pursue what is good, always. And if we fall, we must throw ourselves immediately into the arms of Jesus, who conquered evil once and for all, for everyone, and for us as well.

With the Lord's help, we will win the battle and earn eternal happiness alongside God. If we lose, we risk eternal damnation, the result of a free and definitive choice to go against love, which separates us from God forever.

Carlo was quite struck by Sister Lucia of Fátima's memoirs, where she tells of how, during the May 13, 1917, apparition, she and the other two shepherds asked Mary if their two sixteen-year-old friends who had recently passed away were already in heaven. The Virgin confirmed that one was already in heaven, but the second would remain in purgatory until the end of time. Right after, the shepherds asked if they would also be brought to heaven, and the Virgin answered that Lucia and Jacinta surely would be, but that Francisco needed to recite many rosaries. One day, not long after reading this episode, Carlo told us, worried, "If Francisco, who was so good, so kind and simple, had to recite so many rosaries to go to heaven, how could I ever earn it, since in comparison I am much less saintly?"

The numerous writings which Carlo collected for his exhibition *Inferno, Paradiso e Purgatorio* included one to which he was particularly attached, from Saint Faustina Kowalska's *Diary*:

In a moment I was in a misty place full of fire in which there was a great crowd of suffering souls. They were praying fervently, but to no avail, for themselves; only we can come to their aid. The flames which were burning them did not touch me at all. My guardian angel did not leave me for an instant. I asked these souls what their greatest suffering was. They answered me in one voice that their greatest torment was longing for God. I saw Our Lady visiting the souls in Purgatory. The souls call her "The Star of the Sea." She brings them refreshment. I wanted to talk with them some more, but my guardian angel beckoned me to leave. We went out of that prison of suffering. [I heard an interior voice] which said, "My mercy does not want this, but justice demands it."

Starting when he was little, Carlo was animated by a strong desire for spirituality. In this regard, the presence and influence of our nanny, Beata, was important. She was Polish. She came with the aid of a friend of my father who owned a hotel in Naples. Lots of Polish students passed through during the summers, when there was the most tourism, to work and take a bit of a vacation. Beata stayed with us from 1992 until 1996, right before my son turned six. It was she who taught Carlo many notions of the Faith. She began to have him pray for those who were no longer with us, helping him to understand that there was full continuity between earthly and spiritual life.

I clearly remember the first time she came to our home. She had a bag full of holy cards depicting the Black Madonna of Częstochowa. Her presence was also important for me. The premature death of my father had left me unprepared to confront work problems which it had created. My faith was still what I consider immature, and Beata helped me to get through what had been a great tragedy for me, since I am also an only child, in a Christian manner. She had also experienced periods of difficulty, growing up during the Communist regime's persecution of Christians.

Beata and I spoke about Carlo often. She told me that he was a very precocious child who always asked "adult" questions. Carlo was, in fact, particularly curious. He was interested in the story of Jesus, and when he went to Mass with her, he was sad that he could not take Communion. With Beata, my son started to recite the Rosary. Some remember how he showed them his rosary beads at such a young age.

My son was social, full of energy, playful, open to everyone, and a great entertainer. He was easygoing and good-natured, but it was as if all of this was not enough for him. He had a thirst for the infinite, and he tried to imitate Jesus in everything. For this reason, he trusted in him, asking him for help to become a better person.

With us, he was always obedient. I can truly say that I never had any problems with him. He was always ready to do all we asked of him. With his eagerness to please, he sometimes did not even rebel against his classmates when they played tricks on him. I remember that Beata became angry with him because she wanted him to be strong and not allow other children to make fun of him. But Carlo answered that Jesus would not have been happy if he had reacted with violence. And he continued on his own path.

One day, we went to a supermarket. Beata and my mother entered while I stayed outside with Carlo in his stroller. He was about four. A girl with a lot of red curls came up to us with a blue ball in her hand. She came up to Carlo and started to throw it at him — partially to play and partially to annoy him. She also started to pull his blanket. Carlo remained impassive. Displeased, the girl started to make faces at him, sticking her tongue out and blowing raspberries. Carlo, unperturbed, looked at her sweetly and smiled. I can still remember today, so many years later, the stunned face of the little girl who could not understand how he could be so submissive.

Carlo had a strong character and knew exactly what he wanted. But he was basing his life on friendship with Jesus and always looked to him when deciding how to behave. Jesus was a fixed point of comparison in his life. He took inspiration from him. He felt his presence, that he was truly there beside him.

· · ·

His desire to be more like Jesus pushed him to be charitable with others, and especially with his friends and those close to him. His generous character greatly facilitated this. He had such a sunny disposition that transmitted joy and energy to everyone. He had a particular affection for the poor. Beata told me that even when he was little, when he encountered homeless people on the street, he went up to them to see how they were and to offer them kind words.

One summer, Beata told us that she had to stay in Milan and give up her vacation because she could not afford to take it. She had a three-year-old son, Konrad, and since she did not have a lot of money, she decided that he would also stay in Milan with her. When Carlo heard about her difficulties, he convinced us to invite her and her son to the country house we have in Cilento for the entire summer. He even wanted to leave Beata and Konrad his room so that they could sleep together. Beata still looks back at that summer with nostalgia today — how she went in to the bars and gelato shops with Carlo, who always greeted everyone with his characteristic Mediterranean sunniness.

One of his gifts was the ability to spend time with both kids his own age and with adults. I remember that he loved to play with Legos and make videos with a small camcorder, but if there was someone who could not afford to buy a toy, he was always ready to give them his. In addition, he was able to spend hours playing by himself without bothering us adults, simply drawing his favorite cartoons with some pencils and paper. His ability to wait and not throw tantrums also showed through when it came to eating. He never complained about food that was brought to the table, and even if he did not like it, he wouldn't make a fuss and ate it all. Even when desserts or special treats were served, he wanted others to take some first, and if there was any left over, it was then he took some for himself.

Carlo's interest in things concerning God did not come only from Beata's positive influence. Inside him was fertile terrain, ready to welcome divine grace and the urges of the Holy Spirit. It took me a bit of time to understand that he wanted me to follow him along this path of searching for Jesus. Early in his life, he did all the growing in friendship and in an intimate relationship with God by himself. My husband and I had not fully understood, and perhaps in that moment we were not able to accompany him and push him to correspond with divine grace. It was he who brought us all toward Christian worship. It was he who gave us a "wake-up call" and led us to follow Jesus through the difficulties and joys of life and make Christ the guiding light of our existence. Without

wow

Carlo, none of this would have happened, or at least not in the manner in which it did.

Carlo developed a passion for reading the illustrated Bible that his grandparents had given him, and for learning about the lives of saints. He and Beata often entered churches they ran across when they went out. He went to say hello to Jesus. When we took walks, he liked to pick flowers that he found in the fields and bring them to the church to the Virgin Mary. At four or five, he started to ask me to go into the churches as well and to go before the tabernacle with him to say hello to Jesus. It was the same kind of relationship. The path that Carlo was walking was clear by now, and he had already traveled well down it. At the beginning, I stayed back, and I could not understand the solicitations he made directly and indirectly regarding my faith. There were times when I struggled because I did not know how to answer his questions. I did not even know the difference between the Gospel and the Bible, and I knew next to nothing about many truths of the Faith. So, I decided to learn more about catechism and theology, initially because I simply wanted to be able to answer my son.

I asked a friend for advice on what to do, and she directed me toward a good confessor, a priest from Bologna, Father Ilio Carrai, who was considered by many to be another Padre Pio. It was spring 1995 when I went to Bologna for the first time to meet him. From that day on, I went to visit him once a month until he died on March 14, 2010. The first time I met him, he told me that he had been waiting for me for years, and that he had a mission to complete. I confessed, and he told me many things about my past. He talked to me about Carlo, explaining that he had been chosen by God for a special task, and he told me about things which all came to pass over the course of the years. I was very surprised by what I heard, but by then I had understood that with Carlo the surprises would never stop.

Father Carrai advised me to study theology to deepen my faith. I enrolled in the Theological Faculty of Northern Italy, where I started to take classes, but I did not finish my degree and never graduated, even though I took many exams. However, those lessons helped me better understand the mysteries of faith and answer questions competently that my son asked. Until this point, it had been Beata who read hagiographies of saints and Bible stories to Carlo. Father Carrai suggested that we parents also make ourselves familiar with the Holy Scripture and the catechism. So, we bought documentaries, books, and films on the main apparitions of the Virgin Mary, and on some saints.

• • •

My son often surprised me and piqued my curiosity. I watched him stop to pray before the cross after he lit candles. At home, sometimes, I saw him blow kisses to a statue of the Infant Jesus of Prague that had been given to him, or to the cross hung on a wall in our house. Once he even pretended to be a priest and went through the motions as if celebrating Mass. I remember how, when he was four, I gave him a gold chain with a medal with the scapular of the Virgin Mary of Mount Carmel. It had been given to me by one of my great-grandmothers on the day of my baptism. From that moment on, he never took it off, and he told me, "This way, I will always have Jesus and the Virgin Mary close to my heart."

He later gave medals to many people. The scapular was one of the devotions to which my son was especially attached. Near our house in Milan was a Carmelite monastery, and we often went to Mass there. Their church was dedicated to the Corpus Domini, which Carlo so loved. The time he spent with the Carmelite order sparked a desire in him to bring his scapular along, and he had one of the Carmelite priests bless it when he was seven years old. He alternated the cloth scapular with the gold one that he had been given.

Pope Saint Pius X had given permission to the faithful to substitute the cloth scapular with a medal with the Sacred Heart on one side and the Virgin Mary on the other where necessary. Scapular devotion began on July 16, 1251, when the Virgin Mary appeared to St. Simon Stock, prior of the Order of Carmelites. The Virgin Mary showed him the scapular and said: "Take this scapular. Anyone who dies wearing it will not experience the fires of hell. It will be a symbol of salvation, protection from danger, and a promise of peace." This great promise was confirmed about eighty years later, when the Holy Virgin appeared to Pope John XXII, telling him, "Those who have worn this holy garment will be removed from purgatory on the first Saturday after their death." At Fátima and Lourdes, the apparitions concluded with a vision of the Virgin Mary of Mount Carmel with a scapular in her hand. And the Virgin Mary confirmed to Sister Lucia that the Rosary and scapular are inseparable.

• • •

Carlo was an example for me, not only because of his love for the Lord, but also because of the great generosity and charity he showed toward others, which I am sure was fueled by Jesus himself. It was he who helped me to open myself more and more toward love for others, to understand that the initial intuition I had during a trip to India in 1991 could and must be the path that I would walk my whole life. When we arrived in India, my suitcases, which even had my initials on them, were stolen, with all my clothes. I had to manage with ugly garments I purchased for just a few rupees in a bazaar. That robbery was a great teaching moment. I am convinced the Lord wanted me to understand that the numerous pieces of clothing I had brought with me were completely superfluous. My "despoiling" had begun. The Lord had me undergo shock therapy.

My favorite saint has always been Saint Francis, he who loved Lady Poverty, who stripped himself of his father's garments so that he could be dressed with the cloak of the bishop of Assisi, which symbolizes dressing oneself in Christ and therefore starting on the path of conversion. I think it is no coincidence that this is the saint to whom we all feel most attached and attracted. I am convinced that it is heaven that organizes everything. I needed Saint Francis to help me be less materialistic and self-centered. And the fact that my son can be found today in the Sanctuary of Spoliation in Assisi provides me with further confirmation that my intuition was correct.

After the robbery, I continued my trip with the suit I had worn on the plane and the few items of clothing I had bought in the bazaar. I came to understand how stupid it was to spend so much money on articles of clothing that might even have been made right there in that place by designers that sold them for prices that are much higher than their true cost.

It was an important lesson for me — I was a bit spoiled and spendthrift. This episode taught me a lot about life and about style, which through Carlo's example later became the background of my life. The fact that I had touched such poverty, unimaginable in the West, with my hands, had seen so many Indian children who surrounded us and followed us in the hope that we would give them something at every point of artistic interest where we stopped, made me reflect a lot and turned my way of seeing the world upside down. You could say that I had an instantaneous spiritual metamorphosis which started my process of conversion.

• • •

My husband and I had a belated honeymoon a few months after Carlo was born. We decided to go without him. We left him with my parents in Rome. Carlo did not suffer from our absence. These weeks were a gift. My father was able to enjoy the presence of his grandson before leaving this world not long after. Those days together helped create a very strong bond with him which continued even after his death. After my father's death, in fact, my mother decided to come live in Milan and helped us to raise Carlo. For me, her presence was a grace. I could leave for work without worrying too much. I knew that my son was in good hands.

The same night my father passed away, a friend of my father's sister Aunt Rosaria, a spiritual daughter of Padre Pio who did not know of his death, dreamed that he told her that she had to go to Milan to help his daughter Antonia raise Carlo. I found this to be a beautiful dream, and it made me feel very safe. In the same way, the vision that Carlo had of his grandfather who had just passed away and the relationship of friendship and dialogue that Carlo was able to keep alive with him even after his sudden death were also signs. For Carlo, my father was still alive, even though he had moved to another dimension.

6

"The Eyes Are
a Window into
the Soul"

Carlo believed that every encounter he had was not random, but rather a gift sent from heaven. There was no event, word, or simple greeting that my son did not experience as a possibility for spiritual growth offered by God. He especially found his visits to places connected to Christian faith, where heaven had manifested, to be very important opportunities to make progress along the walk of sanctity.

We made many trips to various European sanctuaries. I remember one in France which included a stop in Paris. We were staying in the publishing neighborhood where the famous Saint-Sulpice church is located.

The church is popular among foreign tourists because it was cited in Dan Brown's best seller *The Da Vinci Code*. During our stay in this beautiful city, we went to Mass at Saint-Sulpice at 7:00 a.m. each day. One of the priests who officiated the Mass told us that people came from as far as America to make pilgrimages to see the "secret signs" that Dan Brown cited in his book, and he told us a bit about the story.

According to the author, there are various clues in Saint-Sulpice that provided confirmation for his insane theory that the Holy Grail was not, as the tradition has always held, the cup where the Blood of Christ was collected, but rather a person, Mary Magdalene. When we heard about this absurdity, Carlo and I laughed and laughed. My son and I often talked about the strange elements of the society in which we live, where truth often struggles to be heard and a dangerous kind of subjectivism reigns.

Of the things we did that trip, our visit to the Pompidou art museum made a particularly strong impression on Carlo. There, you can find many famous paintings as well as some objects that are just as original and provocative, such as Marcel Duchamp's famous urinal titled *Fountain*, which is a symbol of avant-garde subversion and *tout court* transgression. We laughed so much that our stomachs hurt. Some "intellectuals" looked at us scandalized because we dared to laugh at that "masterpiece."

Carlo and I always loved to exchange opinions and points of view on the things that happened to us. We had conversations on numerous topics not limited to those relating to faith. We loved to read what the daily newspapers and media reported, and my son, who had a great capacity for critical analysis, came to realize that many news articles were often ideologized.

Among the various churches we visited was one where a famous Eucharistic miracle occurred. It is located on the Rue des Archives and today belongs to the Lutheran Church. Numerous documents and works of art tell how during Easter of 1290, a nonbeliever who hated the Catholic Faith and did not believe in the true presence of Christ in the Eucharist was able to obtain a consecrated Host in order to profane it. He cut it up and threw it in boiling water. The Host began to hover before the man's eyes, and he was shocked. The Host then went to rest in the bowl of a pious woman who immediately brought it to her parish priest. The ecclesiastical authorities, the people, and even the king decided to transform the house of the profaner into a chapel where the Holy Particle would be kept. It was later destroyed during the French Revolution.

As our last stop in the French capital, we decided to go pray in the church where the body of St. Catherine Labouré, the visionary of the Miraculous Medal, is kept. We woke up early and had our taxi leave us at the beginning of Rue du Bac, where the church is located. While we were looking for it, we had a surreal experience. Rue du Bac is very long. We could not find the indicated address. We went in to various shops to ask, but no one knew anything. It was as if the place had never existed. This made us understand how little faith the Parisian French have. My son was upset because this was indicative of the process of de-Christianization which has been plaguing Europe for decades. Finally, we found it, and Carlo and I stayed for a long time and prayed. During the apparition Catherine experienced, the Virgin Mary had shown the saint the Miraculous Medal and the promises connected to it.

The church is also home to an urn with relics of the founder of the Daughters of Charity to which Saint Catherine belonged, St. Vincent de Paul, a great apostle of the poor and sick. History tells us that during the apparition, which occurred in 1830, the Virgin Mary showed Catherine a medal with gold lettering reading, "O Mary, conceived without sin, pray for us who have recourse to thee." Then, the medal turned on its own and the nun could see the other side. On the top was a Cross placed above an M for Mary, and on the bottom were two hearts, one crowned with thorns and the other pierced with a sword. The hearts represent that of Jesus and of Mary. Mary's letter M was intertwined with the first letter of Jesus' name in Latin, *Iesus*. The visionary then heard Mary say, "Have a medal struck upon this model. Those who wear it will receive great graces."

Carlo said that with this medal the Lord wanted to emphasize the special role that his mother, Mary, occupies in the economy of the salvation of the human race. I am convinced that through this apparition, heaven wanted to confirm that the Virgin Mary was not only the mediator of all graces but also the co-redeemer of mankind, but this is just my personal opinion. The fact that Mary's M is intertwined with *Iesus'* I and topped with a cross demonstrates that the Holy Virgin is associated with the redeeming sacrifice of Jesus.

In the following years, I often had conversations with my son centered around the importance of the sacraments. I remember one Sunday Mass in our parish church, Santa Maria Segreta in Milan. Carlo was about nine, and the parish priest had us renew our baptismal vows. After Mass, I saw that my son was very emotional, and I was struck by what he said about this sacrament. He told me that our time on earth was not enough to thank Jesus for having given us baptism, and that so many people do not realize what an infinite gift it is to receive it. He said, with regret, that many people seem to be more interested in the exterior aspects and the gifts that you normally receive on such occasions than in the sacrament itself, which gives us back the divine life lost because of original sin. He told me it was our duty to cultivate and correspond to the grace received through baptism, because in addition to being a necessary step toward receiving the other sacraments, it is also the gateway to heaven.

He had made the following reflection in some of his notes:

> We need to return to the intimate meaning of this sacrament, which is an instrument of salvation and a vehicle of grace. Baptism eliminates the sin that we have inherited from our predecessors Adam and Eve, caused by the sin of disobedience toward God, also known as original sin, which has infected and continues to infect all of humanity. But it does not heal the wounds that this sin left behind and which continue to tip us toward evil. Since this sacrament is also the door that allows us to access the others, which are the instruments that the Holy Trinity uses to give us grace, and so that we may fully heal this wound, it automatically becomes the door that gives us access to salvation.

Canon law legitimately and correctly fixes the maximum period for the administration of baptism to the first weeks of life. What happens today, however? It is put off for months, if not years. This means depriving young lives of sanctifying grace and condemning those young ones to a

kind of spiritual asphyxia. To be reborn and forgiven, we need to let ourselves be immersed in the water, just like Jesus did in the Jordan river. We
need to emphasize the holiness of the human being, on which the Holy
Spirit casts its gaze, resanctifying it.

Carlo said:

> The narration of the Baptism of Christ is almost as succinct as
> a telegram, but very dense. So, Jesus is baptized. Heaven opens.
> The Holy Spirit descends. The voice of the Father confirms that
> he is the Messiah: "You are my dear Son with whom I am well
> pleased." As you can see, this event has a near infinite value in
> the history of humanity. Jesus has himself been submerged in
> the Jordan river and heaven answers as stated above. Up there
> and down here. Heaven and earth. Jesus, who has himself been
> baptized by his precursor, is the humility which forms the basis
> for Messianism. The Savior places himself at the level of the sin-
> ners. He publicly joins the crowd and demands to be baptized.
> Massive humility. Immolation of one's image on the highest lev-
> el. Assimilation with the sinner in a condition of extreme sim-
> plicity. He joins the people who demand forgiveness. He throws
> himself into the purifying water. He does not hide. He does not
> escape. He does not run away. Quite the opposite. … And heaven
> answers. An event narrated with extreme simplicity, but excep-
> tional. Heaven opens. "The dove" descends. A voice is heard. It
> is not a performance. It is not drama. It is not an allegory. It is
> divinity which enters into time and assumes a human voice in
> that corner of Palestine. That voice declares that Christ is the
> Son of God. He is the object of divine satisfaction. We have read
> and heard this story, and we have made it a habit. It runs over us.
> It runs away from us after we read it. It reaches the level of a …
> little tale. We should pause. We should underline. We should take
> it in slowly. Heaven opens, that heaven which has been closed al-
> most for eternity, and speaks. Christ, who has just been baptized,
> is explicitly and solemnly identified as the Son. Son, so of the
> same divine nature. Do we think about this? Here we are before

all of eternity, with all its solemn expressions in time. We are listening to a fundamental truth: Christ is God and man. There is the entire Gospel. There is the basic truth. ID. Passport for redemption. These lines summarize the operation of salvation. The human race is in the trinitary line of co-eternity. By now, the operation of salvation is in effect. The fullness of time is in all its splendor. They are words-center. They are word-substance. It is the *Verbum Aeternum* which assumes human nature in order to redeem. The sole, triune God reveals himself to us in his Second Person.

Carlo loved to read the Gospels. Every day, he concentrated on a small passage which became the compass he used to guide his day. He believed the Gospel was also a gift from God. Once again, everything was a gift for him. One of his favorite parables was that of the sower. He believed it was important for the seed to bear fruit to the fullest extent and not to allow it to shrivel up due to the thorns of life. He loved chapter twelve from the Gospel of John, where Jesus discusses the fact that if the kernel of wheat does not die, it does not bear fruit.

I remember one time when this parable was recited during a week-day Mass in our parish church. Soon after, Carlo went to write down some reflections. He said that the more we are able to die to ourselves each day over the course of our lives, the more possible it will be to be reborn in Jesus. I found the following reflection in his notes:

Jesus talks about a kernel of wheat which falls to the earth and remains alone if it does not die. I dare say that we are all this grain of wheat, in the sense that we are all in the lowest position, like a kernel of wheat, but a kernel so precious that the Lord expects all that you can imagine from it. We have a great resource within us that is known as the spirit or soul, and it is the main component of our organism, because we consist of a soul and a body. But the soul is simple, and that which is simple is not decomposable, not complicated. So, our soul is not made for time or space. Right now, as long as we live, we are enclosed in a trap, in a cage, which we call space-time, on which we are dependent, because time and space make existence difficult for us. However, we have the spirit, which since it is simple, is immortal, and since it is immortal, it does not have to remain in time and in space. That kernel of wheat which we all are is placed deep into the earth in order to mature, develop, and arrive at the "level of the soul," which does not want time or space but rather is made for eternity.

But in addition to being this kernel of wheat, we are also reason, and we need to collaborate in the development of this kernel. In order to promote this development, which allows the kernel to become a stalk and grain, we need to practice two virtues: humility and simplicity. Humility which is truth, humility which is reality, humility which does not consist in scorning ourselves, but rather in feeling that we are beneath God. God, and then us. On the other hand, the word humility comes from the Latin word *humus*, which means earth, so the humble man is one who comes from the earth, stays low, keeps himself low. If we feel that we are beneath God, then we are in proportion. And when we are in proportion, then we are humble. It is humility which makes us stay in our place. And it invites us, and it brings us to make use of our resources — resources that we should not scorn and which we should cultivate for the glory of God. Simplicity is the virtue of not complicating, as the Latin word *simplex* tells us. It consists of two parts: *sim* and *plex*. *Sim* means just once, and *plex* means to bend. The opposite of the word "simple" is "complicated," which comes from the Latin word *complicare* and means to bend together, or to wrap. So "complicated" means being bent onto oneself, made less simple, confused, difficult to understand. So, simplicity is the art of not doubling over, of not complicating, but rather of leaving everything open, available for the glory of God and for the good of our brothers. These two virtues allow the kernel to come out from Mother Earth, develop, and become a grain. This grain becomes flour, this flour becomes bread, and this bread becomes the type or semblance needed for the holy Eucharist. When Jesus talks about a kernel

of wheat, he is thinking of himself, as consecrated and transubstantiated Bread, and us, as people who live off of this Bread, and
exist in this Bread, and bring themselves to eternity with this
Bread. So let us ask Jesus: O God, make me a productive kernel,
an efficient kernel, an effective kernel. Jesus, make me a kernel of
wheat so that I can reach your Eucharistic reality, through which
I truly and really live.

Carlo always said that our life is a gift, because, as long as we are on this
planet, we can increase our level of charity toward God and toward our
neighbors, and the higher the level it reaches, the more we will enjoy the
eternal beatitude of God. He was deeply convinced that we do not realize
that each minute that passes is one less minute that we have to sanctify
ourselves, and we should not waste time with things that God does not
like. Rather, we must make time our ally. He said that in making himself
flesh, Jesus showed us how best to use our time. Through him, eternity
came down into time, giving us even now the possibility of living in the
trinitary dimension in communion with the One and Triune God, in the
so-called time of God, Kairos, time par excellence that brings us, here
and now, into the co-eternity of God.

He realized that although life is an immense gift, it is also a test in
which we can accept God's love and his will for us, or refuse. He was
deeply convinced that the sacraments are the greatest aid in helping us
resolve to place God at the center of our lives and orient our will toward
what is good. Once, he told me:

Our Objective should be the infinite, not the finite. It is important, however, to know that we should not scorn or come to hate
earthly things, as though they were the antagonists of God. The
words written by Trappist monk Thomas Merton are significant
in this regard. In his book *Seeds of Contemplation*, he emphasizes, "Detachment from things does not mean setting up a con-
tradiction between 'things' and 'God,' as if God were another
thing and as if creatures were his rivals. We do not detach ourselves from things in order to attach ourselves to God, but rather

we become detached from ourselves in order to see and use all things in and for God. This is an entirely new perspective which many sincerely moral and ascetic minds fail utterly to see. There is no evil in anything created by God, nor can anything of his become an obstacle to our union with him. The obstacle is in our 'self' … in the tenacious need to maintain our separate, external, egotistical will. It is when we refer all things to this outward and false 'self' that we alienate ourselves from reality and from God. It is then the false self that is our god, and we love everything for the sake of this self. We use all things, so to speak, for the worship of this idol which is our imaginary self. In so doing, we pervert and corrupt things, or rather we turn our relationship to them into a corrupt and sinful relationship. We do not thereby make them evil, but we use them to increase our attachment to our illusory self."

One of Carlo's favorite flowers was the rose. He said that the beauty of the body is like that of a rose. It lasts a short while and is destined to fade away quickly. For Carlo, a person's exterior beauty was comparable to a sandcastle built on a beach. As soon as the waves come, it disintegrates, and nothing is left except a pile of sand, just like what will happen to us after death. We are dust, and to dust we will return. Physical beauty flowers, and then time takes it away without pity. Afterward, nothing is left. Spiritual beauty, however, never deteriorates and will only become greater if we are faithful collaborators. Carlo found all of these efforts to remain aesthetically young and beautiful to be completely useless. For this reason, he used to say, "Everything fades, anyway. … What will make us truly beautiful in the eyes of God is only the way in which we loved him and how we loved our neighbors."

The amount of unhappiness with which so many people confront the problem of aging, sinking into a deep existential crisis, provoked great pity in Carlo. He had met so many people like this, and he always asked the Lord to help them heal their insecurities. Carlo said that true handicaps are internal, not physical, because physical handicaps will end, but internal handicaps will last for all of eternity and will be decisive in determining the degree of eternal beatitude we will enjoy. My son could see the holiness of a soul through the brightness of its gaze. He always asked me jokingly if his eyes were still bright. He often cited a passage from the Gospel of Matthew where Jesus says, "The eye is the lamp of the body" (6:22). Many said that my son's eyes were particularly bright.

Carlo loved cloistered monks and nuns. He said that their eyes were almost always bright, and when he spent time with them, he felt a feeling of lightness, as if his soul had been lifted. He built a special friendship with the Romite nuns, who had hosted him in their convent during his first Communion. He asked me to bring him to visit to ask for their prayers. He felt that they were like "guardian angels on earth." Carlo was very much in tune with the cloistered nuns, who he regarded as sisters who helped him to grow in love for Jesus. The words that are written on the entrance hall of their convent, "*Dio mi basta*" ["God is enough for me"], made a strong impression on him. Each time he went to visit them, he asked them to help him pray for the conversion of sinners and for the freeing of souls from purgatory. This spiritual bond bore a lot of fruit. The Romites were with him through the various phases of his life. They accompanied him in prayer during his confirmation, which he received on May 24, 2003, from the hands of Msgr. Luigi Testore, and before and after his departure for heaven, and they continue to pray for the many who ask for their prayers.

It was not only the Romites who had a place in his heart, but also other cloistered nuns, such as the Poor Clares of Assisi and the Urbanist Poor Clares of Spello. He placed a lot of faith in the prayers of the contemplatives and asked them to help him become "saintly." I remember that a nun had taught him a brief prayer which he often repeated: "Wounds of Jesus, mouths of love and mercy for us, speak to the Holy Father about us and obtain an intimate transformation for us."

He said that when he spent time with them, he felt that his soul was content. In addition to the cloistered nuns, Carlo was very fond of the Little Sisters Disciples of the Lamb, a religious congregation founded in France. On July 16, 1983, the Community of the Lamb was also recognized by Father Vincent de Couesnogle, who was master of the Order of Preachers at the time, as a "new branch on the tree of the Order of

Preachers." The Little Sisters Disciples of the Lamb, pilgrims, women of prayer, and poor beggars, in the model of Saint Dominic and Saint Francis, have the charism of going to the poorest of the poor so that all might receive the light of the Gospel and of the Lamb Jesus, and spend many hours in Eucharistic adoration. Carlo met them for the first time in Assisi, where we had a house at which we spent the summer holidays. They came to ask for something to eat, and, after asking permission, he invited them to lunch. They came to our house while they were making a pilgrimage to Assisi in August 2005. They asked for bread, as they did each day at lunch time. Carlo opened the door for them. He brought them in and invited them to eat with us. They had a problem with their computer, and he solved it for them right away.

Carlo saw consecrated monks and nuns as special people who had generously given everything to find "Everything." For this reason, he was convinced that Jesus could not refuse anything in their prayers. They had chosen to live only for him, so God would not let their requests go unsatisfied. In addition to the prayers of the consecrated, Carlo considered parents' prayers for their children to be very important. He urged them to support their children in their walk of friendship with Christ, and he told us, "If one day these kids were to become lost on the path that leads to God while growing up, the Lord will remember the prayers that they recited together with their families, sooner or later, and will lead them back to the flock."

He used to say that God would always listen to a sincere prayer from a mother or father, said with faith and devotion, sooner or later.

• • •

Carlo was aware that, unfortunately, we live in a narcissistic society, which places more emphasis on taking care of your physical appearance than your interior life. The origins of narcissism are relevant here. Ovid clearly describes — and anthropomorphizes in the character of Narcissus — the flaw that all those who in loving themselves too much bend inward toward themselves while forgetting God and their neighbor. In the myth, Narcissus is the son of Cephissus and the nymph Liriope. Impervious to love, he did not return the deep passion of Echo, and for this reason he is punished by the goddess Nemesis, who made him fall in love with his own reflection in a pool. Narcissus died consumed by this vain passion and turned into the flower that bears his name. If we do not pay attention, the same thing could happen to us, spiritually. Carlo was struck by the fact that there are people who waste hours of their life trying to become more beautiful because of great vanity and never go to Mass because they have no time left to dedicate to prayer. He said, "Why do people worry so much about the beauty of their body but never worry about the beauty of their soul?"

This misplaced love of self was something Carlo talked about. He cited a sentence that he had heard his guardian angel tell him in an inner locution: "Not love for oneself, but the glory of God." The human "I" — the "I" enclosed within itself, that is — is at the origin of pride and therefore of every sin.

It is the enemy of God and attacks his universal and absolute dominion. It is the enemy of men because it incites one against another due to a difference in interests. It is the enemy of each man because it brings each man further from the true good, dragging them toward evil and robbing them of peace and rest. If you annihilate the human "I," and all its thoughts, desires, and actions are directed towards God without bending back towards itself, God will be loved, adored, and served. Then everything else will be loved because of love of God. He will be loved when he comforts man and when he strikes him, when he caresses him and when he wishes to test him, when he attracts him with sweetness and when he seems to push him away.

If the human "I," the haughty and prideful "I," is annihilated, man will spend his days in constant innocence and in an unalterable peace, because nothing can disturb him internally or externally. The annihilation of haughtiness, of pride, and of disordered love must be the constant task of every true Christian and of everyone who wants to follow in the footsteps of Jesus Christ. And it is extraordinarily necessary to begin this fight right from the beginning of the spiritual life. My son used to say that it is Jesus himself who commanded us to reject ourselves and take up our cross and follow him. Only if we can annihilate this human "I" will all crimes on earth disappear and all men live in fraternal relationships, dividing the resources of earthly life between them without envy. It is at that point that everyone will help one another, and each will see another "self" in his neighbor.

Carlo believed that a good exercise for understanding one's level of humility and internal freedom was to see how tolerant we are to the criticism, whether just or unjust, that we receive. The degree to which it disturbs us serves as a thermometer that will reveal how high our disordered love for ourselves is, and how much more we must work to rid this grave spiritual flaw, which, if unresolved, will prevent us from progressing on the path of holiness. When we are freed from disordered love and attachment, we can love everyone, including ourselves, due to love of God.

He wrote soon after his first Communion, "To always be united with Jesus: this is my life's goal." To achieve this ambitious plan, he believed it was fundamental to eliminate everything that could somehow bring him further from God. He wrote the following in this regard: "Conversion is nothing other than lifting one's gaze upward. All you need is a simple movement of the eyes."

Despite the fact that he interpreted these words metaphorically, and when he said them, it was with an attitude somewhere between serious and facetious, you could clearly understand that this was his cutesy way of stating a great truth. Even though it seems like it should be simple to put that plan into action, in reality, the facts demonstrate that it is very hard to detach oneself from worldly things and attach oneself to those of heaven. Carlo said:

Conversion is ceasing to plummet downward and beginning to climb upward. The further we have fallen, the harder and more strenuous the climb back up. What is important is to turn around. Step by step, day by day, keep going forward without ever stopping. The higher we climb, the more we see things with the right perspective, in their entirety and totality. The higher we climb, the more we enter into the atmosphere which surrounds co-eternity. We breathe the Air of Infinity. Eternal life becomes

RE READ ?

our habitat. Co-eternity becomes our ID card. Co-eternity = eternity together. Together with whom? With the Holy Trinity. We are immortal. Thought is irrefutable proof of this. Thought, in its unchanging reality, is independent in principle and fact from everything from which it is composed. What is composed can by nature be decomposed — because ... it is temporary, provisional, its being is connected to space and time. Thought, however, is simple, un-decomposable, endless, immortal. It is not connected to time or place. God, the One God, unique and Triune, is Eternity. The immortal divides eternity — that is, it is co-eternity. Co-eternal not in principle but in fact, for grace. Our person cannot avoid confronting the problem which is commonly and vulgarly called "the afterlife," and more scientifically and precisely called co-eternity. Co-eternity is the kingdom of the On High, the domain of the On High, the dominion of the On High, the principle of the On High, and the fact of the On High. In order to reach the On High, we have to climb. If you set the On High as your personal destiny, as direct participation in what is outside time and outside space, then the climb or ascents become part of the tools used to arrive at the concretization of the On High. Climbing in the clear and precise sense of making the On High our daily plan, a twenty-four-hour project, a plan for our existence. Climbing is placing ourselves at the disposal of the On High, and so perfecting ourselves for the On High, making ourselves suitable for the On High, making ourselves candidates for the On High, raising ourselves up to the On High. The mystical aspect is the sublimation of existence turned toward the On High.

Carlo believed that only when we become completely free from sin and from each attachment that distances us from God will we be able to achieve true peace and happiness. There is a great difference between a person who spends his time thinking of material interests and situation sand concerns himself with worldly pleasure to affirm his own sense of self, and that of a person who often thinks of our good Lord, who concerns himself with pleasing the Lord first and foremost, and who does not think of worldly things except as means for reaching heaven. The life of the latter will surely be more noble and more beautiful. What keeps us from living in this way with God and being joyful and pure in his presence are worries, false fears, and futile curiosity. We should concern ourselves with making more space for supernatural things in our lives. When we truly decide once and for all not to give too much importance to terrestrial things and to place our trust only in God, we will be truly happy and at peace with ourselves and with creation, like a clear sky with no clouds.

One part of Carlo that always made an impression on me was that he did not want any "stains" to mark his soul. He had clearly understood that confession was what he needed to reach this high objective. He said that together many small stains make a big one, and in the end no white space is left. When he taught catechism to children, he always taught the following story from the life of St. Anthony of Padua, to whom he was devoted:

> One day, a great sinner came to him and decided to change his life and to make all the evil acts he committed right. He got down on his knees before him to confess, but he was so moved that he was unable to open his mouth, and tears of repentance slid down his face. At that point, the saintly friar suggested that he go back and write down his sins on a sheet of paper. The man obeyed and came back with a long list. Father Anthony read them out loud, then he gave the sheet of paper back to the repenter who knelt before him. How the penitent sinner was shocked when he saw that the paper was wiped clean! His sins had disappeared from his soul and therefore also from the paper.

Carlo would recite Psalm 50, where King David, who has repented of his sins, asks God for forgiveness. "Wash me thoroughly from my iniquity. … Create in me a clean heart, O God, / and put a new and right spirit within me."

He confessed every week, usually with a retired priest who served in our parish. This priest told me that Carlo was a boy of exceptional transparency and clarity. He wanted to improve in all aspects, both in terms of love toward God and in terms of love for his neighbor, starting with his parents. He wanted to perfect his friendships with those his age, with his classmates, with his teachers. He also wanted to work harder to dive deeper into various school subjects and informatics in addition to topics related to faith. Carlo approached the Sacrament of Reconciliation to thank the Lord for the gifts he had received and to improve and overcome even the smallest imperfections that prevented him from climbing higher up the mountain of holiness.

He often used the following metaphor to describe the residue that sin leaves on the soul: "The smallest flaw keeps us anchored to the earth, just like balloons that are held down by a string that you hold in your hand."

He loved to play with the kites on Mount Subasio in Assisi, and he often compared the soul to an kite. The kite needs wind to take flight, just like our soul needs the Holy Spirit. He used another analogy to show how we need to confess:

> In order to rise, a hot air balloon needs to remove weights, just like how the soul needs to remove the little weights of venial sins in order to rise up to heaven. In the case of a mortal sin, the soul falls back to earth, and confession is like the fire that makes the hot air balloon rise up again. We need to confess often because the soul is very complex.

There was another phrase that he often repeated that clearly reveals the importance Carlo attributed to spending time before God: "If people truly realized how lovely it is to be in God's grace, respecting his commandments, they would do everything so as not to commit grave sins and would work as hard as possible to help those who live far away from God." He often cited Saint Jacinta of Fátima, who used to say, "If men knew what eternity is, they would do everything to change their lives."

• • •

Carlo was aware that many people prefer to consult a psychologist or motivator rather than go and confess. He said that unhappiness is born from sin and from distance from God. The only solution is to abandon sin to begin a new life in the grace of God. The psychologist will speak of difficulties, mistakes, problems, feelings of guilt, and trauma, but never of sin, of the relationship between man and God, or of a friendship that is no longer there and which we want to recover. Carlo said that Christ is manifested in confession and that we reconcile with the Father through the Holy Spirit. The fruit of the Sacrament of Penance is peace. Carlo felt the need to explain that confession is also called the sacrament of mercy, because it reflects God's love for us — the love of he who died on the cross to save us and redeem us. Since eternity, he has thought of each of us individually. Carlo said that through this sacrament, it is as if a ray of light filters through the consecrated hands of a priest and tears down the shadows in which we are enveloped by sin. Mercy is the movement of light in the shadows.

He also said that where possible it is important to confess regularly with the same priest. He believed it was fundamental to have changes recommended at each confession and to have achievable goals. He said that you have to look at the priest with eyes of faith. The confessor is like a doctor for us. In fact, it is through him that God heals the wounds which come from sin. The only obstacle to a good confession is the "I." When we confess our wretchedness, we demolish the "I," and the mirror of our soul becomes pure, with no shadows, and God reflects his own image through this mirror since no obstacle presents itself to him.

Carlo never told lies, and he would refer to the following story about a spiritual daughter of Padre Pio:

> The father, as we all know, did not want us to tell a single lie, not even as a joke or for something unimportant. In order to keep the commitment I made in confession, I started to ask for help from my guardian angel. When I found myself in difficulty because someone asked me something I did not know or which I could not answer, without resorting to a lie, I asked him for advice.

He prayed to God to ask for help in keeping the baptismal innocence that we should all jealously guard. We should ask the Lord to help us always remain in God's grace, like the wise virgins of the Gospel who had already prepared the oil when the groom arrived and were not caught unprepared.

7

The Poor, the Weak, My Closest Friends

Carlo recognized the living presence of Jesus in the poor and the sick, and he especially saw the crucified Christ in those who were suffering. In these people, he vividly perceived the presence of the Lord, and for this reason he tried to perform any concrete act of charity that he could for them, because helping them was equivalent to giving relief to the crucified Jesus.

When he gave them a blanket or sleeping bag, in his mind he returned to the night of Jesus' birth, when everything was refused to him. Carlo felt that doing something for the poor meant doing it for Jesus personally. When he came into contact with human suffering, he found himself directly projected onto Calvary in the presence of Christ on the cross.

Saint Francis's and St. Anthony of Padua's examples of performing acts of charity toward the poor greatly encouraged Carlo to do the same. Everything he did, he did with passion. His enthusiasm was infectious. He was always trying to improve himself and continuously worrying about his neighbors, especially those in need. Sometimes, it seemed like he could not rest when he saw a beggar or a person with problems. If he could, he would give the shirt off his back to help them.

He believed these people were comparable to the Holy Family of Nazareth, who could not find a place to sleep except in a stable. He wrote the following in this regard in one of his meditations:

> The Lord Jesus was made incarnate by choosing a poor girl of only fifteen as a mother and a poor carpenter as a surrogate father. When he was born, there were nothing but refusals on the part of people who did not know where to put him, and in the end, they found him a stable. If we think carefully about the stable in Bethlehem, it was surely better than many houses of today where the Lord is still refused and often even insulted because he is received in an unsuitable manner. A poor girl of fifteen and a poor carpenter were the parents of God, who chose poverty and not luxury.

When Carlo heard about the Opera San Francesco per i Poveri, an organization run in Milan by the Friars Minor Capuchin, it opened his eyes to a new world of apostleship and charity. They have soup kitchens where they give food to thousands of people and provide aid to the needy, providing extra services as well. He was inspired by this organization and wanted to do something himself to help the homeless and beggars that the friars served every day.

We often met with Father Giulio Savoldi, vice postulator and confessor of the venerable Friar Cecilio Maria Cortinovis, the friar caretaker and founder of this organization for the poor located on Viale Piave. Father Savoldi told me he had never seen a kid that was so sensitive to poverty and the suffering of others. He met Carlo when he was about five. Carlo brought all the money he had saved in his piggy bank to give to children in need. The Capuchin told me that he had been quite struck and moved by this child who was so small and generous, with such a bright face open to everything that was beautiful and good. He immediately intuited that a special soul was hidden within him — a soul that wanted to help soothe the pain of those who were less fortunate than him in many ways.

Carlo wanted to help those who were in difficulty, and he told me that when he was older, he wanted to create an organization to help those who had no place to call home and nowhere to go because there was not enough space in the food kitchens and shelters. One of his greatest wishes was to build shelters where each person could have their own space with cabinets where they could keep their things.

• • •

I remember when we had recently bought a little house in Assisi where we went on vacation with our dogs. Once, while taking them for a walk, we passed the little Santo Stefano church and Carlo noticed a beggar sleeping on the ground in a public garden. Starting that day, he reminded my mother to prepare extra food to bring to the poor man every evening. Additionally, when he could, he gave him money.

He did the same for the homeless that slept near our house in Milan, or near the Arch of Peace near Parco Sempione, which had not yet been closed and was a favorite place of theirs. Together with Rajesh, he arranged to bring them food. With his allowance, he bought insulated dishes and small thermoses, and each time he saw that there was a homeless person there, he went outside and brought him or her part of his dinner, some fruit, some cookies or bread, and hot drinks. When he could, he gave them clothing.

Once, he asked me if he could go with Rajesh to a store in the city center to buy sleeping bags to give to the poor with the money he had saved up. These homeless people often slept on cardboard boxes in front of Santa Maria Segreta Church. Of course, I gave him permission and some extra money. I felt proud to have a son that was so generous and altruistic. St. Teresa of Calcutta used to say that you can do good right at home; you do not have to take a long trip to do so. I can see the saint's words perfectly realized in Carlo.

On multiple occasions, we went to visit a poor eighty-year-old man in the hospital. This man had no one left who cared about him. We met him because he always asked for money in front of our church. In the beginning, he lived in one of Milan's homeless shelters, but since long-term stays are not allowed, he had to move constantly from one place to another. Finally, he was able to get public housing assigned by the city. He had heart disease and diabetes and spent a lot of time in the hospital when his illnesses worsened. He often called us at home, and Carlo and I went to visit him and deliver things he needed.

Carlo loved to bring relief to the ill by entertaining and cheering them up. He made a habit of helping the poor and least fortunate and gave money when asked on the street. Once, he bought food for two Roma children. He took them to the supermarket to go shopping. He had called me to ask for permission, and I gave it.

Two other beggars who were friends of Carlo could not find work, and they often stayed in front of our church near the time of afternoon Mass. After Carlo's death, I spoke with them. They told me they remembered Carlo with great nostalgia because he was so nice, kind, and polite. Every so often, he gave them some money and took interest in their problems.

One of the two beggars had a friend named Giuseppina that he met in a shelter. She was depressed and was letting herself die in the garden between our church and the Marcelline Sisters' Istituto Tommaseo. She had been sitting on the benches for three days. You could see bloodstains on her body. No one paid any attention to her except Carlo, who asked me to help him get treatment for her. We were able to convince her to go get treatment at the Fatebenefratelli Hospital, where they kept her for forty days. We often went to visit her. Finally, she was also able to get public housing.

• • •

I remember another poor man who begged in front of our church. He was about fifty. He could not find work, so each day he waited for the people to leave the two Masses that were celebrated at 6:00 and 7:00 p.m. to ask them for some change. Carlo went to one of the Masses every day with me or my mother, and when he left and saw him, he would give some money and talk with him. Once, when the man needed a bicycle, he convinced me to give him a used one.

Carlo helped many homeless over the course of his life. These included some Muslims who were left without work and without hope. For a time, we went to help serve meals at the soup kitchen run by the Missionaries of Charity in Baggio. It was mostly used by immigrants, mostly of Muslim faith, and Carlo made friends with some of them. Many begged in the area near the Duomo, and since we often went to Mass there, as soon as they saw us, they came toward us and greeted us warmly. On multiple occasions, we invited some of them to come eat a sandwich at McDonald's with us. Among them were some who were very young, for whom we had a particular soft spot.

• • •

Grandma Luana once told me of a time when she went with Carlo to Parco Solari for their usual walk. Carlo must have been around six, and he had made friends with a little boy. Our dog Chiara was with them because one of my son's favorite games was throwing rocks so that Chiara would bring them back. Carlo's friend joined him, and together they started to play with Chiara. Carlo's grandmother sat on a bench and made friends with the boy's Filipino nanny. The children often met in the local public parks and played together.

Once, the nanny arrived with red, swollen eyes. Carlo did not fail to pick up on this, and he immediately asked her what was wrong. She told him that in the Philippines her family's house had been destroyed by a typhoon, that here mother was hurt badly, and that she was distressed because she did not have money to send her so she could get proper care. When he returned home, Carlo immediately went to work to find money. He asked his grandmother and me and took all of the money from his piggy bank. I was touched by his generosity, and so I decided to contribute as well, telling him I would give him one less present for his birthday, but I would help the nanny. He happily brought the Filipino girl the money he collected. The girl embraced him and started to cry, saying that Carlo was the only one who had helped.

Carlo also made a strong impression on the father of his good friends Mattia and Jacopo from Assisi. When Carlo went out with them, as soon as he saw a poor person, he ran to give his allowance. This attention toward the poor was so deeply rooted in Carlo his friends said they had gotten used to the fact that as soon as he would see someone, he would run to give them money and stop to talk.

For a long time, we had a woman who would come to help us iron our clothes. She was from the Mauritius Islands. She was with her daughter because her husband had left her, started a new family, and stopped helping her financially. To keep the respectable standard of living she had before her husband left, she took on various jobs. She often finished work late, and Carlo was worried because she would take the subway at night. She lived in a bad neighborhood, and it was not safe for a woman to walk around at night. Moreover, her daughter was waiting for her at home, and Carlo felt involved in the problems of this young woman who was often alone. For this reason, he helped her fold laundry and iron the simpler items, especially when she had to mend a garment or shirt, so that she would finish work earlier. The woman grew fond of us and started to come visit, with her daughter. Although her daughter was older than Carlo, she was happy to play with him. She was also interested in computers, just like my son, and together they had fun creating little newspapers and websites.

Carlo always took the side of the weak. It was his natural attitude. There was not a single classmate in difficulty who did not find a safe haven in him, a place to take refuge from the attacks of the others. Just like he loved the poor, he loved the meek, the weak, the disabled. He advocated for them without fear of judgment of his peers. He was happy to lend a hand to all his peers, whether to help with homework or computer problems.

Once, he stepped in to defend a classmate who had disabilities that were not immediately evident. He arrived in class to find a young substitute teacher, unaware of the young man's problems, and started to make fun of him due to the difficulty he had in expressing himself. Carlo took up the classmate's defense and told the woman about his young friend's problems in private. The teacher apologized to Carlo many times and immediately stopped picking on him. As a Chinese proverb reads, "The wise man puts a dash of salt in everything he says and a bit of sugar in everything he hears." And Carlo was just like that — he tried to make excuses for others and let things blow over, even when he had been offended or the person was in the wrong, and he never spoke poorly of anyone.

• • •

Once, we went to see my parents at the seaside, and on our way home, after we had parked, we crossed a square where an elderly man was getting a bit of air on the bench. There were some kids who often mocked him because he was homosexual, and when my son realized this, he intervened immediately and told them off in a stern voice, telling them that everyone must be respected, no one should be discriminated against, and only God has the right to judge people, whoever they are. From that moment on, the man and Carlo became friends, and each time he saw Carlo, he rushed over to greet him.

In Assisi, we had a woman who helped us with household chores. She had become friends with Carlo and often confided her problems to him. She was upset because she had a husband who drank a lot and sometimes became violent. I remember that Carlo began to pray and ask the Lord to free the woman from that situation. Miraculously, soon after, her husband stopped drinking.

Carlo obtained many graces especially by praying to the Virgin of Pompei and by offering Masses to help those in difficulty. He worried a lot if he saw people that were far removed from God, and he immediately started to pray for them. He said that if Providence had placed them near him, it was so that he would say prayers of intercession for them. He obtained healing for many sick people, including a woman who was not only sick but also far removed from faith. She had not been to church in over forty years. I remember that Carlo started to pray for her, and soon not only did she heal, but she converted. She started to go to Mass again every day and to live a holy life.

• • •

Due to the example of my son and his testimony, Rajesh also decided to become a Catholic. Carlo had made him fall so deeply in love with Jesus that it sparked in him a desire to receive all the Sacraments of Christian Initiation and to start to recite the Rosary. A strong bond took hold between Rajesh and Carlo. Rajesh was almost like a nanny to him. He was a point of reference for Carlo, a sort of playmate, to the point where Carlo started to call him, "my trusted friend Rajesh."

He still keeps Carlo alive today in people's hearts by talking about his experiences with him. Carlo often played with Rajesh, who liked to play as an actor in little films he made. He loved to play the role of international spy, like James Bond, a role that suited him. Carlo enjoyed recording him with his camcorder, and they would laugh and laugh together. This is what Rajesh wrote about Carlo:

> Given how deeply religious Carlo was and the great faith that he had, it was normal that he often tended to give me lessons on Catholicism, since I was Hindu, from the priestly Brahmin caste. Carlo said that I would be happier one day if I became closer to Jesus, and he often taught me using the Bible, the *Catechism of the Catholic Church*, and stories of the saints. Carlo knew the catechism almost by memory, and he explained it so brilliantly that he was able to excite me about the importance of the sacraments. He was very talented at explaining theological concepts that even adults were not able to explain. Little by little, I started to take his advice and the things that he taught me seriously, to the point where I decided to get baptized as a Christian.
>
> Carlo taught me what an authentic Christian life looked like and was an exceptional example of morality. I got baptized because Carlo infected me and struck me by his deep faith, his great charity, and his purity, which I always considered to be out-

side of the realm of the normal, since such a young, beautiful, and rich boy would normally prefer to live a very different life. Carlo was such a great example of spirituality and holiness that I felt the desire to become a Christian and to be able to receive Communion arise in me.

He explained to me the importance of approaching the Eucharist every day and of praying to the Virgin Mary with the holy Rosary while trying to imitate heroic virtues. The boy always told me that virtues were mainly acquired through an intense sacramental life, that the Eucharist was surely the culmination of charity, and that through this Sacrament, the Lord turns us into complete people, made in his image.

He cited the words of the sixth chapter of the Gospel of Saint John the Apostle, which he knew by heart, where Jesus says, "He who eats my flesh and drinks my blood has eternal life, and I will raise him up at the last day" (v. 54), and afterward he explained that the Eucharist is the heart of Christ. Once, he told me about the importance of devotion in the practice of the first Fridays of the month devotion to the Sacred Heart of Jesus and … devotion to the Immaculate Heart of Mary. He said that "the Heart of Jesus and the Heart of Mary are inextricably joined' and that when we take Communion, we are also in direct contact with the Virgin Mary and the saints in heaven. "God is very happy if souls approach his great gifts of the Eucharist and … confession often."

He explained and prepared me to receive the Sacrament of Confirmation, telling me that it was very important. He told me that when he received the Sacrament of Confirmation, he had felt a mysterious force envelop him from within and from that point on, his Eucharistic devotion had grown. When I received the Sacrament of Confirmation, I also felt the same thing. The thing that struck me most about Carlo was his great purity and his faithfulness to daily holy Mass. Carlo had such a luminous vision of the Catholic Faith that he was able to infect everyone with the serenity and kindness with which he presented the truth of faith.

When he was a bit older, Carlo accompanied Rajesh on various occasions to renew documents or visit the doctor because, since he was a foreigner, he was sometimes treated poorly in public offices. Carlo was very patient in teaching him the secrets of computers, which he found to be a real challenge. Of course, Carlo did the same for me and my mother.

He was very generous with others, but with himself, he was always frugal and somber. It took me a lot of effort to buy things for him because he never wanted anything. I remember at the beginning of the school year, I always tried to buy him at least two new pairs of shoes. He was always opposed to the idea. He only wanted to have one, and he did not want new ones until the current pair was totally worn out. He said that many people in need could be helped with that money. He avoided fashions and was very understated in how he dressed. He always tried to maintain a low profile.

• • •

Carlo's charity manifested itself not only toward his friends and classmates, but, as is evident in much of this recounting, toward anyone with whom he came into contact. People told me how along his bike ride from home to school, he stopped to greet all the doormen, who were mostly foreigners. He made friends with everyone, providing words of encouragement and solidarity for them. He made no distinction in terms of religion or nationality. For Carlo, all the usual "walls" of indifference or suspicion, which many of us build, especially those of us in cities, came crumbling down. He saw a Jesus to love in everyone. Many marveled about the fact that a young man from a well-off family would stop to chat with those people.

In addition, he did not fight or ever offend anyone, even when he would have had serious reason to do so. He was a bearer of good will because he wanted everyone else to work to recuperate the humanity that so many seemed to have lost.

• • •

His care for others showed through in how he looked at them. He was chaste, careful to pare away what was superfluous from his life, and never materialistic. He would say: "It is important to always look after ourselves. Only in maintaining purity of heart will we be able to accumulate the proper treasure in heaven which will serve us for eternity." He loved to quote Jesus from the Gospel of Matthew when he says, "For where your treasure is, there will your heart be also" (6:21). He would comment:

> With these words, Jesus wanted to show us that those who are united with him tend by nature to sail toward the only safe port which is found only in heaven. So, what is the proper treasure that we should accumulate, stock up, and capitalize on? That which will make us safe, which will make us feel protected. It is a treasure that can withstand any impact, repel any assault, venture into any enterprise. What is important is to accumulate the right things — those which lead us to this safe port. Secret charity, secret prayer, secret fasting, sacraments lived well, and the reciting of the holy Rosary are doors which open onto our union with God. They are the realities which will ensure this safety. Various angles, various lenses, various facets, but just one objective: existence organized and spent for co-eternity. If we mortify ourselves, if we help ourselves, if we pray, if we accumulate for what is "Up There," the problem of existence and the fear of living will surely resolve. If we walk the right path, if we clarify our aims, we will identify the destination. If we constantly direct ourselves toward the beyond and always keep the words of Jesus in mind, we will overcome the challenge for eternity.

He explained that in addition to being poor materially, we must also be poor in spirit. He liked to meditate on the Beatitudes in this regard:

> Jesus got up on the mount: he raised himself up. He removes himself from the crowd. He does not remove himself from an

individual person. The mountain is up. The crowd is down. Jesus looks up to attract the down to him. He gets up and then he sits down.

That is, he places himself in a condition of rest, of taking a break, but also of teaching. So, he sees the crowd and distinguishes the individual people. He rises: he leaves the down behind and goes to the up. He sits down: he stops, pauses, rests, takes a breath, takes position. The picture is completed as the disciples come near. The master has his favorite audience. Master + disciple = school. Now he can teach. We are at the famous "Sermon on the Mount." Eight teachings, each introduced by the word "blessed." Who are the "blessed"? The poor in spirit, those who mourn, the meek, those who hunger and thirst for justice, the merciful, the pure in heart, the peacemakers, and the persecuted. Not included are: the rich, the famous, the erudite, the clever, the economists, the politicians, the entrepreneurs, the craftsmen, the merchants, the doctors, the lawyers, the soldiers, and the professors. There is poverty, mourning, meekness, justice, mercy, purity, peace, and persecution. A group of entities which covers the fields of custom, feeling, detachment, idealness, comprehension, honesty, calm, and endured aggression. Blessed people, blessed situations, blessed realities.

He liked to quote the words with which Jesus gives us the plan for being able to enter heaven: "Blessed are the poor in spirit, for theirs is the kingdom of heaven" (Mt 5:3).

In his notes, I found the following written in this regard:

Who are the poor in spirit? They are those who have the soul of the poor. But what does it mean to have a "soul of the poor"? It means experiencing detachment from earthly things. It is not scorn for things, which are also creatures of God, but rather a superiority, a knowledge of how to handle them, how not to remain attached, not to be controlled by them. "The soul of the poor" is the temperament or character of people who live what is above. This is why Jesus states that the kingdom of heaven belongs to these people. That which is above is theirs from the moment when that which is down here no longer affects them at all. Those with "souls of the poor" are not miserly, not covetous, not ravenous. They do not LOVE wealth as though it were the main character. Poor, not like people from the lowest class or of low quality, but rather of a superior "race." Superior in terms of feelings, in terms of appreciation, in terms of desire for more and better. The kingdom of heaven is that which is above. The kingdom of heaven as a homeland, environment, mentality. The soul of the poor is the spirit of the above.

Jesus himself proved this. He did not want anything. He supported himself with his services. He was the guest of others. A perpetual pilgrim. Jesus truly had a "soul of the poor." He lived in nature. He lived naturally. He lived off of sun and rain, of dust and dirt. "Soul of the poor" is a beautiful expression. It clearly depicts the attitude of those who are disciples of Christ. Soul of the poor: nothing on the inside, everything on the inside. Soul of the poor, free, autonomous, unbound from everything that could mean ownership. You can see the superiority, you can see the grandeur, you can see the purity. Yourself is enough for the kingdom of heaven. The rest is just surplus. Because the kingdom of heaven is yours.

Poor: not rich, not affluent, not well to do, not beggars, not destitute. Poor: without tantrums, without distinctions, without satisfactions, without gratifications, without superfluities, without … Detached from riches, from possessions, from honors, from offices, from satisfactions, from recognitions. Poor: not terrestrial, not from down here, not of this time, not of this moment. In summary: the poor man is he who does not make of his existence an opportunity for affirmation, an instrument for climbing, a vehicle for his career, a situation of enjoyment, but a reality that is always and entirely and everywhere directed towards co-eternity.

These "poor men" are people who use themselves as a trampoline for eternity, who use the "I" as a lever for the up above, who are not empty or delusional, or anything else, but rather consecrated in God without conditions or reservations. Theirs is the kingdom of God. The kingdom of God, or co-eternity. The kingdom of God, or association with the Trinitarian family. The kingdom of God, or the entity or reality in which the Lord is King, is Master, is everything. He is the one Triune God. With this and through this Beatitude, Jesus wants to create a reality which he calls "the poor man." As you can see, with this Beatitude, this term has lost its pejorative meaning forever. Jesus institutes the "poor" as a category. Jesus gives the poor the characteristic of having a necessary trait for conquering the kingdom of heaven. This is worth emphasizing: "evangelical poverty" is not your usual poverty. Evangelical poverty is the status of the Christian who has detached from what he knows of what is terrestrial and provisional. Evangelical poverty has its treasure in heaven. Here, treasure means both the container and the supernatural assets within.

8

My Son Is Holy?

One of the questions often asked of me when I go to the various organizations that invite me to speak about my son is, "What it is like to be the mother of someone (declared) blessed." Unfortunately, many think that having a special son automatically makes us special ourselves, but this is not the case. Each person has his or her own free will, and we must each sanctify ourselves. Carlo can intercede, but he cannot do the work of sanctification on our behalf.

My son used to say that the sanctification of a soul is first and foremost the work of God. He determines, in accordance with his will, what aid to offer each of us. But we have full freedom when it comes to the use of these means. We can use them or abuse them and gain much or little from them. We have the primary responsibility. Carlo used to say that God gives everyone numerous opportunities for doing good. And life itself, through the suffering and joy experienced, contributes to our sanctification. And the Lord gives us more graces based on the generosity and gratitude with which we greet them and make them bear fruit. Our progress towards eternity depends in large part on our cooperation with these interior graces.

However, these gifts from God require effort on our part, such as fulfilling the duties of one's state of life, praying well, mortifying oneself, and sacrificing oneself for love of others. Some will make a generous effort, others a mediocre one, and still others minimal. As St. Thérèse of Lisieux wrote, "To pick up a pin for love of God can save souls. ... Our Lord does not look so much at the greatness of our actions, nor even at their difficulty, as at the love with which we do them."

The more intense and pure the love with which we do things, the more it will please God. Carlo did everything in Jesus, for Jesus, and with Jesus. He was able to transform his ordinary life into an extraordinary one by welcoming St. John Paul II's invitation to open wide the doors of our hearts to Christ and not to be afraid to take risks for him. As Jesus teaches us in the parable of the talents, we must make the most of the abilities the Lord has given us and not hide them. More is asked of those who have received more, and surely having such a special child is an obligation to work even harder.

On this note, I think it is important to explain why the Church decided to propose Carlo as a model to be followed. Of course, the call to holiness is for all Christians. In the Book of Leviticus, God urges us to be holy because he himself is holy, and Jesus also invites us to be perfect like the Father, who is perfect in heaven. In the collective imagination, a saint is someone who performs extraordinary miracles. But in the eyes of the Church, it is not wonders that reveal a person's holiness. In fact, these are considered *gratiae gratis date*, or gifts given freely by God that do not provide any merit to the individual, because they are operated by the Holy Spirit. What determines a person's holiness is the way in which the person lived with a righteous and constant desire to do good and, therefore, lived the three theological virtues (faith, hope, and charity) and the four cardinal virtues (prudence, justice, fortitude, and temperance) in a heroic manner. The Dominican school catalogues about two hundred virtues, but all the others depend on these first seven.

The virtues help prevent us from committing venial sins voluntarily. After a candidate has been declared venerable, if he or she performs a miracle that is inexplicable through science and to the theologians, he or she will be declared blessed, and if another is performed, he or she will be proclaimed a saint by the Church. We must acquire the virtues on our own. No one can help us do so except ourselves. This is why Carlo used to say, "Of what use is it for a man to win a thousand battles if he is not able to win against himself and his own corrupt passions?"

He often repeated these words of Jesus, reported in chapter 7 of the Gospel of Saint Mark, when he says, "Nothing outside a man which by going into him can defile him; but the things which come out of a man are what defile him. … Are you also without understanding? Do you not see that whatever goes into a man from outside cannot defile him, since it enters, not his heart but his stomach, and so passes on?" Swedish writer August Strindberg wrote the following in this regard: "[The heart] is divided into two large chambers: In one lives the good, in the other the evil — or, with a word, there sits an angel on one side of the wall and a devil on the other. When they chance to be at odds with each other — which happens quite often — there is unrest in the person and he fancies the heart will burst."

My son taught catechism to children for a few years, and to help them progress spiritually, he created a kit for becoming a saint. He wrote:

> I want to tell you a few of my very special secrets which will help you quickly reach sainthood. Always remember that you, too, can become a saint! First, you have to want it with your whole heart, and if you do not have the desire yet, you must ask the Lord for it with insistence.
>
> Try to go to Mass every day and take holy Communion.
>
> If you can, try to spend a few minutes in Eucharistic adoration before the tabernacle where Jesus is truly present. In this way, you'll see how your level of holiness increases!
>
> Remember to recite the holy Rosary every day.
>
> Read a passage from holy Scripture every day.

If you can, confess every week, even for venial sins.

Make promises often to God and the Virgin Mary to help others.

Ask your guardian angel, who must become your best friend, for help.

Carlo was deeply convinced that to the degree which a soul makes a continuous and generous effort out of love for God, maintaining a faithful correspondence with grace and deciding in its heart to never refuse God anything, giving of itself without reservations to become that which it should be in the mind of its creator, from that moment and forever God will spread an ineffable peace within it that will fill it up and inspire within it a deep detachment from the things of this world.

In this regard, Carlo and I often reasoned that present-day society could be defined with the term "anti-Christic," in the sense that it contains an attitude of exaltation of the human "I" taken almost to the extreme. We have already gotten a taste of how this "anti-Christ" — one who places himself in opposition to Christ — might be with figures such as Nero, Napoleon Bonaparte, and Hitler. Then in the twentieth century, with the arrival of the 1968 protests, a way of thinking began to develop that deliberately erased God. Instead of saying, "Not I, but God," like Carlo, a choice was made to switch the words and say, "Not God, but I." Simple tweets, for better or for worse.

When I think back to discussions with Carlo, I realize he was a profound young man, equipped with the analytical capabilities of a university professor. I could even perhaps define him as a true prophet, who knew how to go beyond the boundaries of the era in which he lived and project himself into the future. He was able to perfectly understand the transformations that we are experiencing today. In the words of philosopher Ludwig Wittgenstein, "his time" has arrived: "If someone is merely ahead of his time, it will catch up to him one day."

In our society, social networks dictate the law and people become enslaved by them. So many compete to have as many contacts as possible, basing their happiness on the views and likes they receive, and become depressed if they do not gain a large following. We have gone back to the times of the ancient Romans, where, with a "thumbs up" or "thumbs down," the life or death of a person was decided. Ours is nothing more than an ill-concealed culture of discarding, where the weakest are eliminated.

This way of living life is not far from the absurd yet possible story described by Franz Kafka in his novel *The Metamorphosis*. In the novella, the main character, Gregor Samsa, feels useless and underappreciated by everyone. One morning, he woke up and "discovered that in bed he had been changed into a monstrous insect" which is eventually swept away without pity, like you do with a bit of dust. The risk that we run today is that of winding up, metaphorically, like Gregor Samsa. Some people have even committed suicide because they felt "bullied" and misunderstood by the internet and the world.

Carlo was a true and effective influencer of God, as we would say today, and not an influencer of worldly things. Ours is a society that, whether deliberately or not, most often directs itself toward false divinities which presume to replace God. We are all deeply affected by the world of cinema and all it proposes, whether for better or worse. This has created a mentality in many of us which is that of the Hollywood star system. Mainly through the media, this system tends to place all kinds of people on a pedestal — singers; actors; soccer players; influencers who mostly plug transient, earthly things that are destined to become dust; advocates of false values or wrong ideals, often far from the Christian worldview — and to venerate pseudo-gurus and avatars who are not mystic but rather often outlandish.

Many do not ask themselves even for a moment whether God exists or not. Others evade the question and many deny him. Numerous people think they can solve their problems by replacing their innate and primitive need for the Absolute, which is part of their DNA, with inconsistent idols. All of us, whether we want to admit it or not, have been created for eternal life and to love and serve God. Many people go to astrologers, seers, and fortune-tellers thinking that they will find the solution to their existential anguish instead of praying to their creator. Superstition has infiltrated itself everywhere. It is striking to see how many people seem to anthropomorphize science, technology, and culture, almost reaching the point of idolizing them, without ever healing their own insecurities. As sociologist Zygmunt Bauman, who developed the theory of the so-called liquid society, clearly describes, "The most technologically advanced generation in human history — which is ours — is also the one most afflicted by feelings of insecurity and powerlessness."

9

Humility, the Teacher

A t school, Carlo distinguished himself for his work ethic and obedience. His secret was to remain in constant contact with the Father. He always said, "Praying is just conversing with God." In this sense, I can truly say that he was always praying. His relationship with God was continuous.

In addition to reciting the Rosary every day, he loved to pray with the psalms and the Liturgy of the Hours. He was able to carve out moments of deep silence and meditation despite his young age. On this note, it gives me pleasure to quote the beautiful words with which Mother Anna Maria Canopi, OSB, the founder and first abbess of the Mater Ecclesiae Benedictine Abbey on San Giulio Island on Lake Orta and who recently died, described Carlo and his love for prayer:

Everything of value is born from silence. What is silence? It is hard to put it into words, because silence is not spoken with words. Only by having the experience can we understand what it is and its importance.

There are moments in which silence is like an atmosphere that surrounds us and penetrates us intimately, providing a sensation of fullness and not of emptiness, one not of absence but rather of presence. Who has not tried to find himself outdoors, in the middle of the countryside or on the top of a mountain at sunrise or sunset or, even more deeply, in the night below a starry sky? It is as if everything were suspended in a silence pulsating with life, a silence in which you can perceive the harmony of the cosmos. In a certain way, that is the experience of the presence of God.

This can be felt even more deeply when you enter a deserted church and your gaze goes to the tabernacle and, to the side, the flame of a lamp indicates the Eucharistic presence of Jesus. Then, in the silence, you communicate with a You that is truly present through compliance with an overwhelming condescension of love that deeply touches our hearts and fills them with emotion, with gratitude, and with blessed joy.

This is certainly the experience that young Carlo Acutis had. Beginning with his first Communion, he made the Eucharist the center of his life, or rather, an encounter of living friendship with Jesus, to the point of saying that the Lord is truly present in the world through the Eucharist, just as, during the time of the apostles, the disciples could see him walking through the streets of Jerusalem in the flesh.

In his life, full of serious dedication to studies and many friendships, meetings with classmates, and various activities, he placed the Eucharist at the forefront. Daily Mass was a priority for him, as was Eucharistic adoration. And through the Eucharist, he was internally molded into the meek Lamb, and he learned, without even noticing that he was doing so, true silence, the silence which always says yes to God's will, without rebelling, without asking for explanation, but rather embracing it with love.

The first gift he received from his mother is significant. It was a little lamb with white fur to which he was always attached. It is significant that on the day of his first Communion, in an unusual twist, he found a little lamb on the street. This almost foreshadowed what awaited him, and for us it is like a symbol of how he lived his life, becoming himself a Eucharist, a silent offering.

In his daily stops before the tabernacle — an appointment which he awaited and prepared for — silence meant sitting heart to heart with Jesus, in a reciprocal giving of oneself to the point of becoming one single entity. This is the mystic silence with which divine love is expressed.

Carlo, who had a very sociable and affable personality, absorbed goodness and joy which he communicated to others from these intimate, silent encounters with the Lord. You could say that all of his interior beauty and the goodness and kindness with which he related to others were the fruit of his long sessions with Jesus in the silence of love and adoration.

All the saints and great men who have distinguished themselves in science and art were educated in the school of silence. They learned to be quiet and listen, to reflect and meditate, humbly trying to learn the truth.

If we are always noisy and chatty, if we speak without thinking, we cannot become mature and wise people. There is an ancient proverb that says, "The wise man says few, well-thought-out words. The chatty man falls on the ground with no direction."

There is also a silence that is not good, which is not true silence, but rather mutism or quietness. It is that which separates us from others when we feel offended or we dislike someone or we are not interested. It is a self-centered, un-Christian attitude, because Jesus tells us to love everyone, even our enemies.

We also need to learn to tolerate offenses. Carlo was an example in this regard during his life. Even though he died so young, he learned from the school of "offenses," such as when, for example, his classmates made fun of him because he went to Mass or for the "unfashionable" way he dressed. And Carlo demonstrated himself, as always, to be a diligent disciple who knows how to make lemonade from every lemon. He knew how to stay silent, not defend himself, not take offense, and earn — despite his "differences" — the respect and friendship of his classmates as well as many adults. In this way, [in] his life [he] became an evangelizer, much more so than his "word," which incidentally, he did not fail to appreciate. On the contrary, he tried to make the most use of it, including through the most modern means of social communication.

Jesus himself, who is the Word of God incarnate, experienced this silence of humility, of patient tolerance, of selfless love which desires only to communicate goodness and peace. He especially loved to spend his nights on the mountain alone in the silence of intimate communion with the Father, therefore gaining from the Father what he would later say to the apostles so that they would transmit it to the Church and to all peoples.

Mary, the Mother of Jesus, is also a model of humility and contemplative silence, and so was Saint Joseph, who was chosen by God as the caring guardian of Mother and Child.

Discovering the beauty of silence is like finding the key for growing in every virtue.

For every moment of existence, there is a silence which helps us to live it well, in simplicity, and in peace. There is the silence of joy, adoring silence, the silence of humility. There is also a silence for times of trial, a silence woven from fortitude and faith, which makes us embrace suffering, whether physical or moral, without crying out and without complaint. This is what the holy Scripture urges us to do: "Be still before the Lord, and wait patiently for him" (Ps 37:7). In the Hebrew text, the words "be still" are expressed with the same verb which reappears in Psalm 131, that of the tranquil and serene child in his mother's arms. This silence is not spontaneous in us, nor is it a heroic effort, but rather a gift of the Spirit. And Carlo revealed himself to be full of it in the hour of his sudden illness, which he accepted like a meek lamb, allowing the Lord to bring his plan into action through him. "It had been years since I last saw a patient in that condition," one nurse said, "and I kept asking myself how he could keep himself from complaining about the pain, since he had swollen arms and legs that were full of fluid." And when he was asked one day, "How do you feel?" Carlo answered with his usual calmness. "Good, as always!" Half an hour later, he fell into a coma. …

It has been said that Carlo flew up towards heaven "on eagle's wings." He could not have flown so high if he had not known how to say, in his hour of suffering, that he felt "good," in a deep sense, because in God's will, we always feel good. But from where did this ability to say "Yes, good" come? Certainly, from his contemplation. He had inebriated his soul and his chaste senses by focusing the gaze of his heart on the blue of the sky and listening to the harmonies of silence full of divine Presence.

Each of us can and must become a place of "sacred silence," as occurs during liturgical celebration. When Pope Paul VI went to the Holy Land on pilgrimage in 1964 and visited Nazareth, recalling the life of the Holy Family with emotion, he said: "The lesson of silence: May an appreciation of this stupendous and indispensable moment of spiritual opportunity return to us, deafened as we are by so much tumult, by so much noise, by so many voices of our chaotic and frenzied modern life. The silence of Nazareth teaches us recollection, reflection, and eagerness to heed the good inspirations and words of true teachers, it teaches us the need and the value of preparation, of study, of meditation, of a personal and interior life, of prayer." All of this is even more necessary in our times, where silence is made almost impossible by the excessive clamor of mass media and a social and familial lifestyle that is becoming more and more exterior, superficial, and often alienating.

It is said that words are silver and silence is gold. The weight of a person, or in other words his value, is proportional to his capacity for silence. True silence, in fact, leaves space for grace to work under the strong and sweet guidance of the Holy Spirit, the

Spirit of Truth and Love, of communion and peace, of holiness
and joy.

Mother Canopi references the insults that Carlo received during his life.
He did not pay them any attention. Like the three Persons of the Holy
Trinity, there was an ever-flowing movement of love in him. Through
prayer, he learned how to remain united to the love of God, and this was
enough for him. "Prayer is the language of heaven," he used to repeat. "As
we increase our capacity to love, we become ever more righteous and
pure, and we are able to state freely, 'God is my everything.' Alone, we are
not able to add even an hour to our life, nor can we procure the graces we
need for ourselves. We always have to ask God for them."

He thought that in order to get closer to God it is important to
truly free ourselves from all created things. The simpler the prayer, the
more profound, he said.

Monsignor Poma, the parish priest of Santa Maria Segreta, was
a perfect witness for recounting some of my son's traits. He especially
wanted to emphasize that Carlo had an attitude that was, as far as possible, from the desire to

be the best and create a starring role for himself, even though he
had an excellent alacrity and pleasantness in conversation and
in how he addressed people. He was somber in life and in his as-
pirations. Those who remember him today discover with growing surprise a "pleasing justice" with clear Christian roots. … He
loved to spend time alone with his thoughts and in conversation
with God. In this he was very meticulous and capable. It was his
way of not forming ideas about his future that were too vague. It
came spontaneously to him to end certain conversations with a
quick "if it is God's will." I was not familiar with his "devotions"
in detail (he was bothered even by the idea of showing off his
spiritual secrets), but when it comes to his intense relationship
with the Eucharist, there I can state with certainty … Carlo lived
every moment of his existence with intensity but without ever
backing away from his duties. Despite the small trials typical of

the life of a teenager, he confronted everything with optimism and joy and an attention that was always directed upward.

Monsignor Poma defined Carlo with the following adjective: unforgettable. He recounts:

> His gaze, first and foremost, which was so frank and accessible, a gaze that by itself was a great smile at life, the gaze of a boy with nothing to hide and a great desire to communicate. Within me, I can still hear, with a precision that moves me, the tone of his voice when he talked about and asked questions about this. It was a transparent voice, with nothing to hide and the desire to confirm what he was thinking and the plans which push life forward. In my memory are the observations, the arguments, the evaluations which Carlo presented to me from time to time. It was an interview, but without putting on airs and without timidity. … Carlo was a clear grace, through whom I could see that it is not difficult for a smart and healthy young man to marry the Gospel and celebration, justice and good humor, and intelligence and amiability in his life. Yes, because Carlo was a boy that was so sweetly unaware of his uncommon character traits and just as comfortable in all of the fields of play of his humanity: at home, at school, at youth group, in friendship, in his relationship with God. Grateful to everyone, but a pawn of no one. Always polite, but firm in his convictions. He was able to find time for God, and he did not mind setting aside even the things that were his favorites and which provoked spontaneous interest to do so. Carlo was happy when he paused before God. Then he got up, and he took the secret of that which the Lord asked of him with him. It is a great gift to be able to live in clear and serene sobriety. It is an extraordinary gift when a young man perceives this right from the morning of his life.

Carlo's elementary school English teacher told me that my son was a very positive and generous child — polite, always smiling, and sensitive in his relationships with adults and his classmates with whom he was kind and friendly without exception. The teacher told me that he was full of enthusiasm and passion. He loved to make suggestions to improve the lessons, and many remember how he raised his hand and, with his unmistakable lisped "r," addressed the teacher in English ("Teacher!") so that he could tell her some fact about the Anglo-Saxon world. In the classroom, he was among the first to lend an intelligent and discrete hand to those who were having trouble.

His teacher also found him to be a polite and generous child. She writes:

> He almost never got into the "usual" trouble for his age and never let his classmates drag him into any kind of "mischief." My co-workers also noticed him because he was always tidy and elegant. … In other words, a true budding gentleman. As he grew up, he showed that he had a truly good heart, and he always wanted to help anyone who needed it. I noticed that he did not want to show it off, though. … Carlo was very shy. When I complimented him on his kindness, he would tell me that he had not done anything special. … But, actually, it was he who was special! He was loved and sought after by his classmates. Sometimes, he played peacemaker in the little fights that broke out among them every day, and … he was great at it. There was a friend of his that had notable difficulties, both academically and socially. Carlo took him under his wing, and with infinite patience, he helped him every single day. Sometimes, I told him to go play with his other classmates, to "let go" a bit of this friend who was a bit clingy and sucked up so much energy, but he would not let up, and he stayed by his side and helped him. When he went to middle school, I often ran into him at recess. He greeted me cheerfully and kindly asked me: "How are you? Do your new students drive you crazy like we did? If you need anything, let me know. … I'm happy to come lend a hand!"

When my father died, I had to take over his business, and I started to travel a lot. We decided to have a girl spend afternoons with Carlo and help him with his homework. Her name was Elisa. After Carlo's passing, she confided in me that she had always been struck by his exceptionally good heart. She said that Carlo was very obedient, and unlike many boys of his age very responsible. He started to study and do his homework without anyone making him. She considered him to be an exceptional boy who knew how to care about the physical and spiritual well-being of the people he came across.

When she met Carlo, Elisa had some problems with her boyfriend. My son realized this. He tried to console her and pushed her to eat, since she had lost a lot of weight due to the stress. He wanted her to be calm despite the delicate situation, and he always offered her something, whether it be candy or little treats.

Elisa was struck by my son's spiritual maturity. Sometimes, after Carlo finished his homework, he asked her to take him to Mass. They went together, and this simple gesture helped bring Elisa back to the Faith.

On multiple occasions, she told me about how Carlo was always ready to help his classmates. Especially after school in the afternoons she saw him help the kids that had problems becoming part of the group, or those who did not join in because they were shy. He was quite sensitive and immediately realized when someone was going through a rough patch. This was the case with a classmate whose parents were separating and was having problems with bulimia for this reason. His complete readiness to help others showed in his behavior. He was always ready to give of himself, to play his part, and to help even before he was asked.

He was also helpful with the nuns, especially the older ones who worked in reception. He gave them little cotton balls which they use to make doilies that were sold to benefit their missions.

At school, he was considered to be a well-adjusted, polite, prudent child more mature than his age would suggest.

Carlo did not care about having designer clothes or accessories. He always swam against the current when it came to his minimalism. He could not stand those who bragged about being from a higher social class. He said that a person's worth is directly proportional to his level of charity or generosity. He was deeply convinced that those who had more economic means also had more responsibility because they should help those less fortunate to the extent that they were able.

In practice, he could not abide any form of social injustice, because, he said, all people are creatures of God. He spoke to everyone, and he always had words of encouragement and solidarity for each person he encountered. He did not make distinctions when it came to religion or nationality. He saw Christ, to be loved, in everyone. On Christmas, he bought gifts for everyone, including teachers and service staff, with his savings.

He often brought a classmate who had motor difficulties and learning disabilities, that others marginalized, home with him. He tried to support him, and when he was in class he helped him become part of the group, to the point where that boy only wanted to play with my son.

Of course, Carlo was an energetic child, but he never lacked respect and politeness when it came to others. He did not like to fight or argue, but rather preferred to remain in holy silence. He was a force for good.

Sister Miranda Moltedo, principal of the institute where Carlo attended elementary school and an art teacher, told me that Carlo was really a very good kid. She had never heard him say a bad word. He was not argumentative but rather diligent and obedient when it came to teachers' instructions. He never had to be scolded. She also told me that for his age and during the years when she knew him, he already possessed the Christian virtues to a heroic degree in child form. For example, he hid his social status, while most of the children, even in elementary school, bragged about the wealth of their families.

Sister Isa Velante, the religion teacher, said that Carlo was a "very generous" boy. If a classmate asked him to lend him something, he was always happy to give it to him without ever asking for it back. Sometimes, a nun or teacher had to intervene to remind the classmate that he had to return what Carlo had lent him. If she could not remember a passage from the Bible, she would ask Carlo, who always knew everything.

Another nun at the institute, Sister Maria del Rocío Soria Ratia, was charged with watching the kids during recess. She remembers that Carlo loved to joke around. Sometimes, she played soccer with the kids. Carlo would go up to her and enjoyed telling her that, sooner or later, she would become a famous soccer player.

Carlo was very curious. He wanted to get to know things and understand them, and he made an effort to do so. He liked to talk to the nun about important things, about religion, Islam, and the relationship with other religions. He was able to give serious and profound answers and was attentive and an active participant. She remembers him as a transparent, sincere boy. He said what had to be said without fear and without aggression.

• • •

Many agreed that my son was an intelligent young man, very gifted in some subjects, and, most of all, humble and ready to defend the weaker and marginalized. He was even a cheerful jester on certain occasions. He infected others and allowed others to infect him with their vivacity. Sometimes, an excess in this area led to notes being sent home, because with his uncontainable voice combined with the gestures he would make with his body, he would disrupt lessons. He had a deep sense of humor and was able to defuse even the most difficult situations. He always tried to cheer up those who were sad or discouraged. He once said something about those who abandoned themselves to depression and distrust: "Sadness is looking toward oneself, happiness is looking toward God."

Carlo was the opposite of unhappiness. I never heard him complain or grumble. On the contrary, he was always positive and optimistic, even in the most difficult of situations. He was full of energy and considered life to be an immense gift. He wanted to taste it with gusto in each moment, because, as he said, "each moment that passes is one less moment that we have to sanctify ourselves." He liked philosopher Blaise Pascal's meditations on this topic: "The Stoics say, 'Retire within yourselves; it is there you will find your rest.' And that is not true. Others say, 'Go out of yourselves; seek happiness in amusement.' And this is not true. Illness comes. Happiness is neither without us nor within us. It is in God, both without us and within us."

• • •

At the age of fourteen, for the 2005–06 school year, we enrolled Carlo in the classical lyceum at the Istituto Leone XIII in Milan, run by Jesuit fathers. Here, he was able to demonstrate one of his most appreciated qualities: a gift for computers. The fathers greatly contributed to the development of his talents. They immediately understood that Carlo's spiritual stature was special. The parish priest, Don Gianfranco Poma, also immediately understood that Carlo was an extraordinary young man. He told me this openly.

I often met people who were immediately enlightened by and attracted to my son, who was sort of a magnet. It seemed that people realized unconsciously that Jesus was present in Carlo. They were attracted to him because, whether they were aware or not, they had the desire to encounter Jesus in their hearts.

In Assisi, when Carlo was eight, we ran into a nun that we had never seen before. She stopped us and told us that Carlo had a special mission in the Church. I do not know how it was possible, but that was exactly what she said.

• • •

For various reasons, we had always been close to the Jesuits. This was why we decided to enroll him at Leone XIII. In the year that he moved up to Leone, we decided to pass through Manresa in Catalonia, Spain, where Ignatius of Loyola lived for eleven years, during one of our trips. This is where Ignatius made his conversion from a noble knight with a hot-blooded temperament to a friend of the Lord, placing himself entirely at his service to respond to his love. It was in Manresa that Ignatius began to write the *Spiritual Exercises* with the clear intention of helping others have the same experience of salvation through a personal encounter with God.

In the footsteps of this saint, we went to Montserrat, another place connected to the saint's conversion, where there is a sanctuary dedicated to the Virgin Mary where she appeared many times, performing graces and miracles. In February 1522, Ignatius arrived at the Benedictine monastery in Montserrat, outside Barcelona. It was the eve of the feast of the Annunciation. He spent the entire night there, and at the end of it, he symbolically placed his sword and dagger at the altar of the Virgin Mary to mark the beginning of a new life in Christ, donning the habit of a pilgrim.

Carlo was especially touched by this place, which, in addition to the nature park that surrounds it, is full of unique views of formerly rocky mountains smoothed by the wind and containing shades of pink. We concluded our visit in Barcelona, where Carlo was enchanted by the basilica of the Sagrada Familia by architect Antonio Gaudí, whose canonization cause has begun and was nicknamed "God's Architect" by contemporaries.

Carlo agreed:

> True originality consists of returning to the origin, which is God. ... Creation continues incessantly through the mediation of mankind. But man does not create ... he discovers. Those who look for the laws of nature as a support for their new works collaborate with the creator. Copiers do not collaborate. Because of this, originality consists in returning to the origin.

The Sagrada Familia was built to, as you can read in the records from the laying of the first stone on March 19, 1882, "Awaken sleeping hearts from their tepor. Exalt the faith. Warm charity." Carlo really liked Gaudí. One day, he told me he had received a little sign from him. In fact, he had prayed to him to help glorify Jesus, who makes himself truly present in the Eucharist, turning himself into our food and drink. My son admired him deeply. He was the only architect of the modern age who dedicated himself to an enterprise that had not been attempted in centuries: the building of a cathedral, dedicated to the Sagrada Familia, built solely and exclusively using the offerings "*de los pobres.*" He himself died very poor. He was an ascetic and a mystic. The entire text of the Gospels can be found on the stones of the Sagrada Familia. It is a book for the entire world. For those who have faith, for those who know how to read with their hearts and minds, but also for those who are far from it.

In the central portico of the Nativity facade reigns a sculpture that depicts the birth of Jesus, who is the apex of God's love for us. The three doors represent the three virtues: hope on the left, with the Massacre of the Innocents and the Flight into Egypt; faith on the right; and charity at the center, because it is the greatest, the virtue which, as Saint Paul says, remains even after death and will grant us the degree of eternal Beatitude that we will enjoy. Angels sing above the image of the Holy Family, as the Gospels recount. Carlo said that at such a deep moment of crisis for the institution of the family, this holy architect represents the divine response to so much devastation.

While society destroys the family, Gaudí reconstructs it metaphorically through the temple of the Sagrada Familia. Carlo himself cited the prophetic words of Sister Lucia of Fátima, one of the witnesses to the apparitions of the Virgin Mary in Portugal in 1917, on multiple occasions: "A time will come when the decisive battle between the kingdom of Christ and Satan will be over marriage and the family. And those who will work for the good of the family will experience persecution and tribulation. But do not be afraid, because Our Lady has already crushed his head."

Father Roberto Gazzaniga, SJ, in charge of pastoral ministry in the Leone XIII school and later dean of the same institute, draws a complete picture of Carlo:

> Carlo enrolled in the Istituto Leone XIII, a school run by the Society of Jesus, in the 2005–06 school year, choosing to attend the classical lyceum.
>
> A student in gymnasium IV B, he immediately stood out, with evidence and discretion, due to his profound human qualities. Right from the start of school, he acted as though he had known the school for a long time, with a cordiality, familiarity, amiability, and smoothness that was not common among new students. He felt at home at school, and classmates, teachers, and staff were happy to talk to him, helped along by the welcoming attitude and gentlemanly, spontaneous, and refreshing manner which characterized him. Carlo's time at Leone XIII was marked by enthusiasm and participation, and he easily laid the groundwork for becoming

friends with his classmates and feeling like they were his friends, something which was very important to him.

It is important to note that Father Gazzaniga also noticed the attention that Carlo paid to the underprivileged:

> At the time, the attention that he directed toward those that he perceived to be "a bit left out" stood out. Some young men and women need more time to get familiar with a new school context with new classmates. Right from the first day, Carlo made himself an ally to those who were struggling most to find their place within the new reality of their class and the institute with discretion, respect, and courage. A few months after he was separated from his life on earth and from his classmates, we asked them about some of Carlo's characteristics that had made an impression on them and listened to their answers. Several of them emphasized his delicacy in noticing who was having difficulties right from the first couple of days of school and his willingness to stay by their side and help them integrate into the class, encouraging them not to make the situation worse and trying to help break the ice of resistance and silence. Many classmates were grateful to Carlo for his ability to create and facilitate relationships and to inject confidence and build closeness without being invasive.

Father Gazzaniga found Carlo's vitality in his relationships with his classmates to be very special:

> I was soon struck by his ability to be present and to make others feel present. He happily walked around the hallways throughout the two floors of the high school during the mid-morning break, looking to connect with both students and faculty. He was often joined by classmates who, had he not stepped in, would have spent the break at their desks or nearby, waiting for the bell alone. He had an ability to take initiative and get people involved

that was respectful, lively, and very youthful in his exuberance. Various adults were impressed by his natural and notable ability to take initiative with courtesy and not with overfamiliarity. Our longtime custodian recounts with emotion the sensitivity with which Carlo would walk through the poolside door and stop by during the break expressly to say hello to the people at the reception desk when he had not done so earlier in the morning. It was a spontaneous gesture which was often repeated with true enthusiasm, and it made an impression, because kids often decide whether to say hello based on their mood.

Carlo's sunny disposition and search for direct connection did not breed indifference. He was a kind young man who was always forming bonds with others. I have always been surprised by the fact that his innate qualities and capacities, which went much beyond the average, did not become a target for jokes or pranks. Often, when one student excels, the students around him are very good at "bringing him back down to size" with little gibes, hints, and sneers. At an age which is characterized by strong contradictions and intense competition, it is not easy for a teenager to recognize the superior value of another or the richness of the talents which have been received and acquired. This is another element which makes Carlo great in my eyes. Carlo's goodness and authenticity overcame the little games of revenge which tend to lower the profile of those who are gifted with exceptional qualities. He certainly lived his value of transparency. Carlo never hid his choice of faith, and even when it came to conversations and verbal disagreements with classmates, he started from a place of respect for others' positions but never forgoing the clarity of stating and bearing witness to that which had inspired his Christian life. When one of my fellow brothers went to Carlo's class to propose an after-school group called "*Comunità di Vita Cristian Life CVX*" ["CVX Community of Christian Life"], Carlo immediately stopped him in the hallway afterward, saying, "I am interested in that evangelical itinerary that you presented." He was the only one in his entire class to take a position and declare his genuine interest in the club.

Father Gazzaniga also emphasizes the unanimous comments from Carlo's school friends:

> When I asked his classmates about "Carlo's gift," I remember that the echoes of his presence, the traits that had made the strongest impression and formed part of the students' memories and experiences were his joyfulness, vivacity, generosity, desire for friendships, and ability for self-discipline — "I never saw him get angry even when he was provoked." A young man who dedicated time to many different interests without ever neglecting his duties, smiling, kind, able to have good relationships with everyone — "If you were in a bad mood and spent time with him, it would fade away" — contagious in his optimism, and interested in societal problems and politics — "During a phase of growing up where attention to oneself and to one's own little world often prevails, his kindness and his welcoming attitude, including when it came to inviting friends into his own home, gave you the feeling that he was never just listening to listen, but rather was really interested in people." In particular, his classmates — and not only his classmates — were struck by his spontaneity, helpfulness, and trustworthiness. When I needed someone to help with the volunteer work that the Leone students performed, Carlo offered to work on various volunteering proposals with a professional software called Dreamweaver, which took him a considerable amount of time over the summer to design, program, and implement. During the meetings of the volunteering committee, which consisted of some parents, everyone was deeply impressed by the energy, passion, and inventiveness that Carlo employed to create a CD in order to spark students' interest and help them make the decision to volunteer. The mothers were enthralled by Carlo's approach, by his leadership qualities, and by his kind, lively, and efficient manner.

The Jesuit concluded by emphasizing the aspect of faith and of the search for God in Carlo's life:

> The last time that I saw him was on the Saturday before his presentation on volunteering that he was preparing to show the students, which was planned for October 4, 2006. I found him to be receptive to the indications that I gave him, ready to revisit some of the work that he had did with a sense of freedom and of searching for what is better, which should not be taken for granted in a young man. When his work was presented by a classmate in his fifth year, he ended the presentation by saying that it had been created by Carlo, and the sound of spontaneous and intense festive applause that we heard brought him joy and a bit of embarrassment. We will not forget his love for life and for people or his manner and approach, which were so personal, transparent, and wonderful. All of us are convinced that it was the flow of a crystalline and festive interior life which merged love for God and for people in a joyful and true fluidity which did not fail to impress. How many times did I, as a priest and someone who works in youth ministry, delight in seeing Carlo and in recognizing his positive influence on his classmates? I was and am persuaded that he was just like yeast in bread dough — it does not make noise, but it makes things grow. Now more than ever, he is like the grain of wheat which has come into the earth to bear the fruit of life. You could point to him and say, "Here is a young man and a Christian who is happy and authentic." "Carlo is a gift," and his name is pronounced with respect and deep nostalgia. Carlo is here, and at the same time, we miss him.

Carlo loved everyone and was loved by everyone. Once, he got a nine out of ten on an essay for school, perhaps one of the highest grades in the class. However, he was almost disappointed, because two of his friends who were at the top of the class had started to cry because Carlo had gotten a higher grade than them. He marveled at their reaction and told us that he had spent time consoling them, telling them that the teacher had given him too much credit and that he did not deserve it. Envy was not a feeling that was familiar to Carlo, and in his own way, he always tried to help everyone find success in their studies and spiritual life.

He did have friends who went to nightclubs, used drugs, and drank a lot of alcohol. On various occasions, they would invite him to come along, but Carlo hated nightclubs. He had very strong signs from his guardian angel alerting him to the danger of these places. He told some cloistered monks about these signs and had asked us to join him in praying for this intention.

Rajesh recounts how Carlo was not happy when he was asked, "But do you have a girlfriend?" He was convinced that middle school was too early to think about these things. Unlike him, many of his friends had gotten an early start on romantic life, which often takes away the purity and youthfulness which should characterize boys and girls of that age. He loved to cite the example of St. Maria Goretti in this regard. My mother was also convinced that his was an extraordinary, almost heroic purity.

• • •

Carlo's religion teacher told us how he shared the Church's position on abortion and passionately defended the value of unborn life. During religion class, there was an animated discussion, and Carlo was the only one who stated that he was against abortion. He was not afraid to go against the current, and he firmly stated his ideas without wanting to impose them on anyone else. Carlo was formed directly by Jesus and his mother, Mary, in silence and in prayer, even more so than by the books he read. His docility toward the Holy Spirit greatly facilitated his walk of faith and allowed him to free himself toward elevated spiritual horizons without losing his healthy contact with his family, his friends, and activities related to his responsibilities.

During the school year, he participated in various sports: karate, kung fu, tennis, volleyball, soccer, skiing, swimming, athletics. He pursued them all with dedication, but without the competitive spirit that young men and women normally possess. What was important to Carlo was to be able to share in moments of joy with his friends. He saw sport as a means for cultivating friendship, sharing, and personal growth. As French writer Jean Giraudoux wrote, "Sport consists in delegating to the body some of the highest virtues of the soul." Carlo was convinced that sports were an effective means of developing willpower, with which you can achieve great goals, but he was not interested in having a perfect physique but rather in health, so he did not dare to participate in dangerous sports.

I remember he worried a lot about my health because I was a bit overweight. He hid desserts from me that I would have eaten had I found them lying around the house, and he took me on walks so that I would lose weight. He did the same with Rajesh, who was diabetic. Carlo was able to control himself. Even though he said he had a sweet tooth, he did not ever snack and he controlled his portions. When he was around eight, he had gained a bit of weight. At the seaside, we had gone overboard, eating lots of pizzas and ice creams and so on, and when we came back from our vacation, he started to moderate himself on his own and was immediately able to lose weight. He already possessed the virtue of temperance, which for a child of his age should not be taken for granted. In this regard, he made small sacrifices to help souls in purgatory, for example, giving up snacks, desserts, and fruit. He made little sacrifices to the Virgin Mary, who had expressly requested this in her many apparitions over the course of the centuries. He also made sacrifices by not watching his favorite movies. He never wanted to see violent or vulgar films. He loved cartoons and documentaries about animals. If he saw questionable or sexual advertisements on TV, he covered his eyes and immediately left the room, or asked us to change the channel so as not to watch harmful programs.

I have to say that I was astounded to have a son whose main interests were God, the Virgin Mary, the angels, and the saints. When I compare him to myself as a child and to my childhood friends, he seems like an alien, a boy from another planet. One of his elementary and middle-school classmate's mother, a writer for a famous Italian newspaper who I greatly admire, realized how pure he was. On various occasions, she was able to see when she spoke to him how Carlo was convinced that living a Christian life spread great values and helped people become better and more altruistic. Even when it came to the Christian proposition regarding moral life, Carlo was not afraid to express his convictions when it came to purity and premarital sex. One day, he told her that he was deeply convinced of the beauty of spending an engagement chastely, just like he was very decidedly opposed to abortion.

He expressed his ideas with conviction, but always with respect, sometimes even jokingly so as to avoid too serious a tone which could offend. Father Ilio, his spiritual director, bore witness to Carlo's convictions when it came to values regarding life and morality. He told me once that Carlo was very upset because some of his classmates declared themselves in favor of abortion, masturbation, and premarital sex. He expressed his opinion of opposition and told him that his friends had reacted with much perplexity and resistance.

• • •

Despite the fact that his studies took up a lot of time, he would spontaneously spend time with adult volunteers preparing children for confirmation. He was still in middle school and asked us for permission. We agreed, as long as this commitment did not interfere with his academic performance. He cared deeply about these responsibilities, and when he could not go because of school commitments, he was disappointed.

Carlo dedicated lots of time to others. With a computer programming student, he took over the website of the parish of Santa Maria Segreta in Milan. He could create computer programs using the most complicated programming languages, to the point where two of our friends who were professors of computer science marveled at his abilities. Starting from a young age, Carlo showed an interest in science, and in computer science in particular. He liked to dress up as a chemist, with a pair of fake glasses and a badge that his father had given which had "Computer Scientist" written on it. When he was nine, he started to read computer science textbooks usually used in college courses. He was great at organizing and programming, and he could build websites and web pages. Many, family and others, marveled that a boy of his age could program without ever having taken courses in the computer languages C, C++, Ubunto, or Java yet knew how to use logarithms like he did. Because of his computer talents, family, friends, and classmates started to go to him for help. He tried to put this interest of his at the service of others. During his eighth-grade final exam, he prepared presentations of their projects for many classmates on the computer.

Carlo was naturally drawn to technology, just like most kids his age, and also to games. When he was younger, new electronic games such as Gameboy, PlayStation, Gamecube, and Xbox started to come out. One Christmas we gave him a Gamecube, which was in the shape of a black cube. We laughed a lot about the fact that that same year, a Nativity scene in the form of a black cube with cats drawn on it for Christmas was presented in front of the Basilica di San Francesco. It looked just like Carlo's toy. Even though he liked video games, he set a limit of not more than one hour per week for himself. He had read that many children, especially in the United States, had wound up in hospitals with seizures due to excessive use. My son had always wanted to remain unattached to these systems, computers included.

Soon after Carlo's death, the historical committee addressing the cause of his canonization went through the entire internet history on his personal computer, which went up to the day before he was admitted to the hospital. They did not find a single website out of place. Most sites were about faith.

This righteousness and purity was also surely manifested in his favorite hobbies, which like computers, he used to do good. I heard Carlo urge his friends so many times to live a chaste life and not fall victim to the perverting influence of demons. He said that his guardian angel had told him that the devil brings many, many souls to hell through pornography and sins of impurity. When she appeared in Fátima in 1917, the Virgin Mary also told the three shepherds Francisco, Jacinta, and Lucia, "Many souls go to hell for sins of the flesh."

The *Catechism of the Catholic Church* warns, "Pornography … does grave injury to the dignity of its participants (actors, vendors, the public), since each one becomes an object of base pleasure and illicit profit for others. It immerses all who are involved in the illusion of a fantasy world. It is a grave offense" (2354).

· · ·

Pope Francis dedicated three paragraphs to Carlo in the apostolic exhortation written for the closing of the synod for young people that took place in the Vatican in 2019:

> I remind you of the good news we received as a gift on the morning of the resurrection: that in all the dark or painful situations that we mentioned, there is a way out. For example, it is true that the digital world can expose you to the risk of self-absorption, isolation and empty pleasure. But don't forget that there are young people even there who show creativity and even genius. That was the case with the Venerable Carlo Acutis.
>
> Carlo was well aware that the whole apparatus of communications, advertising, and social networking can be used to lull us, to make us addicted to consumerism and buying the latest thing on the market, obsessed with our free time, caught up in negativity. Yet he knew how to use the new communications technology to transmit the Gospel, to communicate values and beauty.
>
> Carlo didn't fall into the trap. He saw that many young people, wanting to be different, really end up being like everyone else, running after whatever the powerful set before them with the mechanisms of consumerism and distraction. In this way they do not bring forth the gifts the Lord has given them; they do not offer the world those unique personal talents that God has given to each of them. As a result, Carlo said, "everyone is born as an original, but many people end up dying as photocopies." Don't let that happen to you! (*Christus Vivit*, 104–106)

The secretary of the Pontifical Academy of Martyrs, of which I have been curator since 2000, asked Carlo to help him create a specific section on the Vatican website (vatican.va) dedicated to martyrs. He dedicated himself to it with great passion. Carlo was very struck by the story of Jesuit priest Anton Luli, of Albania, who went to prison for seventeen years under the Communist regime. This was followed by eleven years of forced labor and a ban on ministry. He made a moving speech during the Special Assembly for Europe of the Synod of Bishops, which began on November 28, 1991, before an audience that included St. John Paul II.

Carlo listened to his full story on a tape that a Jesuit priest had given him so that it could be transcribed and posted on the website. Here is one excerpt:

> I learned what freedom is at eighty years of age, when I was able to celebrate my first Mass with the people. The years spent in prison were truly terrifying. During my first month, on the night of Christmas, they made me strip and hung me from the rafters with a rope, so that I could touch the ground only with the tip of my toes. It was cold. I felt the icy chill moving up my body: It was as though I were slowly dying. When the freezing cold was about to arrive at my chest, I groaned desperately. My torturers heard, they kicked me mercilessly and then took me down. They often tortured me with electricity, putting two electrodes in my ears: It was an indescribably horrible experience. That I remained alive is a miracle of God's grace. I bless the Lord who gave me, his poor and weak minister, the grace to remain faithful to him in a life lived almost entirely in chains. Many of my confreres died as martyrs: it was my lot, however, to remain alive, in order to bear witness.

We had the fortune of meeting Cardinal Ernest Simoni, a living saint, who touched the world and Pope Francis when on September 21, 2014, in the cathedral in Tirana, Albania, in the presence of the pontiff, he recounted the violence and oppression he underwent for twenty-seven years during Communist dictatorship. He was arrested on Christmas evening 1963 while celebrating Mass in Barbullush, Albania, and sent to solitary confinement with a sentence for eighteen years. His torturers ordered his fellow prisoners to make note of his "forseeable anger" against the regime, but only words of forgiveness and prayer left the priest's mouth. His death sentence arrived soon after, but it was commuted to twenty-five years of forced labor in the dark tunnels of the Spac mines and later in the Scutari sewers. Even in this savage situation, he never lost his faith and never stopped his ministry. He was even able to secretly celebrate Mass every day and hear confessions of the other prisoners, becoming a spiritual father to some of them and even distributing Communion, with a host cooked secretly on a small burner and resorting to the juice of grape seeds in lieu of wine. He was finally freed on September 5, 1990. As soon as he left prison, he forgave his torturers, invoking the Father's mercy for them. He was careful to specify that his nomination as cardinal was a way of recognizing all martyrs and Catholics who were persecuted in his homeland.

When I think of these heroes of the faith, the words of Carlo come to mind. He told people who complained to look for those in worse situations than we are, especially the example of the martyrs who were able to bear heroic witness in their faith and acts, becoming "living Gospels."

Carlo believed that if we have God in our hearts, nothing can trouble us, because through him thorns turn into flowers and clouds disappear from the sky, which becomes clear and serene. Like mountains reflected in a calm, peaceful lake, so will God find his own image mirrored within us if when he looks inside us, he finds us calm, serene, and confident in him.

• • •

Carlo's academic growth continued on pace with his spiritual growth. When he was old enough to enroll in primary school, we decided to have him attend the Istituto San Carlo in Milan, which is one of the schools of the diocese. After two months, however, we moved him to the Istituto Tommaseo, operated by Marcelline sisters. In addition to being closer to home, the school was less disorganized and competitive compared to the Istituto San Carlo. He spent eight years with the Marcelline sisters. Then we moved him to Leone XIII. I remember that Carlo was upset when he learned that he would have to leave San Carlo. He did not say anything to us, however, as was his style. He loved his teacher and had bonded with his classmates. He shed a tear when he had to say good-bye to everyone. He tried to hide it from me so as not to sadden me, but it did not escape me.

Carlo immediately adapted to the new school, however, due to his open and sociable personality. He fit right in. He was very happy and always in a good mood. He liked to play with the other children, who immediately took an instinctive and sincere liking to him. For a while, his liveliness created problems because he could not keep quiet in class, but he soon learned how to behave and control himself. He worked to improve this flaw and gave himself an examination of conscience every evening, sometimes grading himself and taking note of his goals, especially when it came to his relationship with God, his neighbors, and prayer.

According to his teachers, he was very intelligent. He learned quickly, even though not at the top of the class when it came to grades. That he had taught himself many things stunned many adults. For example, he decided to play the saxophone at school instead of the recorder, which he did not like very much. He learned to play it immediately, on his own, without the help of a teacher. If he set himself a goal, he worked toward it with great diligence. He was tenacious and strong-willed.

He loved good food and started to cook on his own. He often put himself to the test with new recipes that sometimes were complex and normally the work of the best chefs, but they turned out well.

He loved to read the newspapers that his father passed him, and they often talked about the news together. This sparked in him to try his hand at journalism and writing, and he became a gifted writer. One of his favorite games was making up fantasy stories, such as that of Pomodorin Laden, a pseudonym of Bin Laden. In this metaphorical story of his, he was able to defuse and scale down the terrible situation caused by international terrorism through a lens of faith.

He truly possessed the virtue of obedience to a heroic degree — something that is rather rare today, given the planetary disobedience which can be seen in every field, including that of religion. He told me, in 2003, that he had dreamed of angels with trumpets spread across a blue sky that slowly began to fill with menacing clouds. Not long after, the scene changed, and Our Lady of Fátima appeared above Piazza San Pietro, which was full of a multitude of people enveloped in a gray light. Our Lady said, "Difficult times await Christianity because of disobedience."

• • •

He said we are made for our neighbors and not for ourselves. This is why my son found it prudent and wise to get help and advice from the people that God has placed near us for guidance and support. Carlo said there are no obstacles for those who constantly abandon their hearts to the Lord. His meekness and humility deeply convinced us that Carlo was a truly special and holy young man. He wrote the following regarding humility:

> Jesus wanted to make humility the basis for Christian asceticism. Humility is also the basis for the other virtue which he so often preached: charity. Humility is the virtue which allows us to live in society, which brings people closer, which converts. What is humility? It is recognizing that everything that one is comes from God. It is recognizing that everything good that one has comes from God. ... The virtue of humility is a typically Christian virtue. He first lived it and brought it to earth. Many say that Jesus was born poor, that he was placed in a manger ... and for this reason, he was of humble birth. But this is not why Jesus was born humble. The joining of divine nature to human nature was the gesture of the most sublime humility. That is why he could say, "Learn from me, for I am meek and humble at heart." After his baptism, Jesus is driven to the desert for forty days. It comes as a surprise, taken and driven off. No reaction. No conflict. No rebellion. He lets things happen. He is extraordinarily meek and submissive. This is also because this was all part of his plan. Throughout the entire arc of his so-called public existence, during his various travels from place to place, where he was followed, chased, thrown around, suspected, envied, attacked, insulted, not believed, and abandoned, he puts what he taught into effect: "Learn from me, for I am meek and humble at heart." Meek and humble: gentle, sweet, helpful, modest, obliging, respectful, tranquil, calm, balanced, a good example. The first capital vice, pride, has no place in him. He makes humility,

a virtue which is almost unknown before this point, the basis for his asceticism, the basis for his morality, the essence of his spirituality. Learn from me, that is starting from me, for I am meek and humble at heart. In Hebrew, "at heart" means "in my mind," because they also called the kidneys, the place where our most profound decisions are made, the heart. "I love you with all my kidneys."... And it is only God who can inspect our most hidden thoughts and feelings. "I am he who searches mind and heart, and I will give to each of you as your works deserve" (Rv 2:23). The decisions which will merit or fail to merit the prize of eternal life start from our hearts and our kidneys. The kidneys/ heart are where our secret thoughts and hidden desires and sensibilities lie. All our thoughts start in the heart. All our decisions start from here, whether good or bad, and this is why Scripture urges us to guard our hearts innocently and not allow anything to enter them that does not please God: "Keep your heart with all vigilance; / for from it flow the springs of life" (Prv 4:23). Jesus says, "Nothing outside a man which by going into him can defile him; but the things which come out of a man are what defile him" (Mk 7:15).

When God speaks to our hearts, this means that he speaks to our will, to our mind, to our conscience. For the Bible, the heart is the center of the person which makes decisions in accordance with God's will. In the book of the prophet Jeremiah, we find the following words: "I will give you shepherds after my own heart, who will feed you with knowledge and understanding" (3:15). And later, "Righteous, are you O LORD, when I complain to you" (12:1). We should all repeat this constantly! Wanting to argue with God comes only from evil. So, [if] I am meek and humble at heart [it] means that I am humble in mind. This is the manifesto of the initial and original virtue invented by Jesus and followed by his religion. This virtue is humility.

Carlo continues in his notes:

The ability to feel that evil comes from us and good from God. The ability to not judge our neighbor but judge only ourselves. Effectively, it is this virtue of humility, which came down from heaven with Christ, which is the fundamental, basic, and central virtue of Catholic spirituality. Humility which Jesus exercised with his Incarnation. The humility that he lived was not so much the fact that he was born in a manger but rather that he walked through the grueling passageway that is called Incarnation. Since Jesus went from the Infinite, his substance, to the finite, his condition. This exhausting passage from the infinite to the finite is humiliation. And it is the continuous example of humility that he gives us with his Incarnation that he lived for an entire generation, more than thirty years, and that he suffered and offered in the continual exercise of humility. So, we Catholics must dedicate ourselves to living this humility, or rather this fundamental virtue through which we bow before God, we bow before our neighbor, and we dive into charity, which is nothing other than practiced humility. Because each lack of charity is a lack of humility and vice versa. The world feeds on pride. The world has haughtiness as its essence. Because if we were truly humble, the Lord would bow before us and grant us grace. Because each grace which is not granted is an act of pride which is performed. And a grace which is granted is an act of humility which is performed. "Learn from me, for I am meek and humble at heart." "Have this mind among yourselves, which was in Christ Jesus, who, though he was in the form of God, did not count equality with God a thing to be grasped, but emptied himself, taking the form of a servant, being born in the likeness of men. And being found in human form he humbled himself and became obedient unto death, even death on a cross. Therefore God has highly exalted him and bestowed on him the name which is above every name, that at the name of Jesus every knee should bow, in heaven and on earth and under the earth, and every tongue confess that Jesus Christ is Lord, to the glory of God the Father" (Phil 2:5–11).

10

Sister Earth

Carlo was especially attentive and sensitive when it came to animals. One day, we were walking by a pet shop near Viale Piave in Milan and saw a little black dog with a white spot on its chest. It started wagging its tail. It was a little mutt, a cross between a mix and a Pomeranian. It was love at first sight. We went into the store so that we could see her up close. She was so cute and friendly that we could not resist adopting her. We called her Chiara, in honor of one of our favorite saints from Assisi. This name later created problems for us. When we walked her in Assisi, many nuns would glare at us when they heard the dog's name. My husband suggested that we call her Ara. She immediately became a constant playmate. Carlo would hide and she would look for him. He threw things and she brought them back. It was as if the only thing she could not do was speak.

She suddenly became pregnant when she was already fairly old. Carlo was not yet eleven. We thought that it was the Lord that allowed it. We went to the park to take a walk and let her loose. At that moment, a dog that had been following us for a while without us noticing approached, and in an instant, she was pregnant. We did not even have time to turn around and call her to us before the "misdeed" had already occurred. She gave birth to four little puppies. One of these, Poldo, who became one of his favorites, was born a few hours after the others. Carlo had just gotten home from school when he was born. My son played obstetrician and helped with the birth. Initially, we had found a family for each of the puppies. All of his friends wanted one, and many came to our house to see them. However, two of them decided to give them back to us, and so our family grew. In total, we had three dogs, Poldo, Chiara, and Stellina, and two cats, Bamby and Cleopatra.

These animals were the main characters in one of Carlo's favorite games: writing screenplays, playing director, editing, and adding soundtracks to the movies he made. Every so often, he invited his friends to come see the movies with plenty of popcorn, Coca Cola, and other treats available. You can imagine the kids' laughter as they watched evil cats try to conquer the world and get rid of all the dogs on the planet, who were the good guys. Chiara was "Supreme General Rat," Stellina "The Cannon Dog" because she ate a lot and was quite chubby, and Poldo "Captain Dummy." Cleopatra was a black cat and played the part of the evil general. Finally, the merry cast was joined by Briciola, who became the biggest of stars, the unmentionable, terrible "Dog of the Seven Demons." She got the nickname due to her menacing look, like a miniature Doberman, and for her unmistakable growl and way of chewing on things.

This special dog arrived in our home in early 2005. Carlo and I saw her in a shop behind the Duomo. Our walks through pet stores were dangerous. Near them, we were like Ulysses with the sirens, who had to have himself tied to the mast in order to resist their songs. It was very difficult to convince my husband to agree to another dog. I remember that he asked the Lord in prayer whether it was his will. He then said that he really felt that God was happy that Carlo would have that dog as well, and so we got her.

They told us that she was a miniature pinscher. The shopkeeper had even convinced us to buy her a little coat in a cashmere blend which was on sale, telling us that she would not grow anymore and that these dogs really suffered in the cold and loved the heat. When home, the other dogs were rather confused, almost nauseated, when they gave this little animal which resembled a miniature Rottweiler the once over. Obviously, the shopkeeper pulled a trick on us, because Briciola grew quite a bit and became a sort of "little calf," as a priest friend of ours called her.

We were frequently taking road trips in Europe at the time, and we were able to convince my husband to bring Briciola with us. The first stop on our trip was Lourdes. Grandma Luana carried the dog in her purse so that no one would notice her. Her Mary Poppins-style bag allowed us to visit various places without being disturbed. Briciola even had the privilege of visiting the Lourdes Grotto, and I am sure that the miraculous water we had her drink helped sweeten her character.

When Carlo got to the Massabielle Grotto, he renewed his vow to Mary to faithfully recite the Rosary every day, and he consecrated himself to her Immaculate Heart.

I remember that after he drank the miraculous water, he spent more than an hour absorbed in prayer. We were all struck by the long lines of candles on the side of the grotto which shone and illuminated the surrounding area as the sun went down, creating a surreal atmosphere. To think that each of these candles represented the story of a person, of his or her secret desires, hopes, and deepest fears, was truly moving. How much pain, but also how much faith, shone around that place. We also lit our candles.

The next day, we visited the places connected to Bernadette Soubirous, especially the Moulin de Boly, the wretched house where the shepherdess was born. She spent her childhood suffering from terrible asthma attacks in an environment that was unhealthy but calm and full of love.

Through the Lourdes apparitions, Carlo came to understand the Virgin Mary's invitation to penance and sacrifice and to make it his own. He would often tell the story of Bernadette and the visions she had at the Massabielle Grotto in order to invite everyone to follow the recommendations of the Immaculate Mary. Bernadette, an illiterate teenager and poor daughter of the people, was chosen by heaven for her profound simplicity and humility. This made a strong impression on Carlo and surely contributed to his spiritual growth.

From February 11 to July 16, 1858, the Virgin Mary appeared to fourteen-year-old Bernadette eighteen times. The visionary said that she had seen a woman dressed in white wearing a white veil and a blue belt with a yellow rose on each foot. Among the messages that the Virgin Mary gave her was a promise that Bernadette would not be happy in this world but rather in the next. She urged her to live a life of sacrifice and prayer, and especially to recite the holy Rosary. Three times, she said, "Penance! Penance! Penance!" and asked her to eat grass and dig a hole with her hands from which miraculous water would emerge. This water led to, and continues to lead to, many healings and conversions.

Mary revealed that she was the Immaculate Conception to Bernadette, who said, "She raised her eyes to heaven, clasped her hands, which had been outstretched toward the earth, in prayer, and told me in local dialect, '*Que soy era Immaculada Conuncepciou.*'"

Bernadette did not know the meaning of the words and struggled to remember them. She herself said that as soon as the apparition had ended, she ran away and continued to repeat them to herself for the whole journey continuously so as not to forget them so she could faithfully repeat them to the parish priest, on whom this made a strong impression. She did not know that this theological expression referred to the holy Virgin and that four years prior, in 1854, Pope Pius IX had defined the dogma of the Immaculate Conception.

Carlo wrote the following regarding the Immaculate Conception:

Mother of God. Creature transformed into the infinite. In giving herself to God, delivering herself to God, she finds herself the Mother of God. Now we have one of our own who has been elevated, sublimated, "celestialized." Mother of God: three words, four syllables, eleven letters, a poem. The universe must have gasped. The entire universe was in some way involved. And heaven, the Angels, the Archangels, the Thrones, the Dominations, the Virtues, the Sovereignties, the Principalities, the Cherubs, and the Seraphims must have also perceived the event. It is us, the superficial, the ignorant. We must feel that we are a part of this blessed situation. She who was preserved from original sin, overshadowed by the Father, maternalized through the work of the Holy Spirit, is one of us. We cannot say the words "Holy Mother of God" with an air of habit and familiarity and superficiality. We have to think of them in a theological manner, in a spiritual manner. Mother of God: Being with a being. The Infinite with the finite. The Eternal with time. The Creator with the creature.

From Lourdes, we continued our journey and went to Spain. For our first stop, we stopped in Burgos, where there is a beautiful cathedral and the Carthusian monastery of Miraflores. Here the monks receive prayer requests and celebrate Gregorian Masses. Carlo bought a rosary that was made by the monks with pressed rose petals, which still has its perfume today.

The next day, we went to Mass and continued our journey toward Madrid. In our trunk were ten-liter tanks of holy water that we had bought in Lourdes. They were clearly visible and attracted the attention of some Spaniards, who started to laugh kindly when they saw us. They were probably used to seeing tourists come from Lourdes with lots of bottles.

We had a lot of fun in Madrid. We were struck by the beauty of the city. When we got to Puerta del Sol, we found a little red jacket for Briciola in a small shop with a picture of a black bull, which is one of the symbols of Spain. With this jacket, the dog looked like a true miniature bull, and we laughed a lot about this.

Of the museums we visited, the Monasterio de las Descalzas Reales, where the Poor Clares still live, sticks out in my memory. We brought the dog with us on our guided tour. On the phone, they had told us that we were not allowed to bring animals, but Grandma Luana did not want to leave her in the hotel all alone, so she decided to take the risk and bring her hidden in her bag. The tour of the monastery museum was quite long. It felt like it would never end. During his descriptions, the guide sometimes stopped and left long pauses where he invited us to meditate. Inevitably, Briciola started to make little grunting sounds, and, mortified, Carlo, his grandmother, and I took turns pretending to cough compulsively. Carlo had a lot of fun filming all the scenes with his camera, and here the film *Panico al Museo* [*Panic at the Museum*] was born.

• • •

One day at the beach in Palinuro, Italy, Umberto, Carlo's cousin, was with us. They were both around thirteen and recently made friends with some kids from Naples. While they were all playing together, on our land, one of them threw a rock at a lizard for fun and killed it. Carlo was very upset, and it looked like he might cry. I tried to console him by telling him that by now the lizard was in heaven with Jesus. He was very angry because he said that the lizard was a defenseless creature who had never harmed anyone.

Another time, my son and I went to his friends Jacopo and Mattia's house in Assisi, and their cousins were also present. The cousins started to play around, annoying their uncle's dog with a broom. Carlo became angry and took the broom away, telling them that they should not hurt animals for fun. We still have a picture of him with the broom in hand.

When we were in Assisi, we would go to the town pool, and in addition to helping the lifeguards clean the pool, Carlo would also play "lifeguard" for the insects that fell into the water and risked drowning.

Another time, we were in Assisi and staying in a hotel near the Church of Saint Peter. Carlo, Grandma, and the dogs were all there. In the evenings, we went to walk the dogs before going to bed. As soon as we got to the yard in front of the Church of Saint Peter, we let the dogs off leash so they could run a bit. As soon as the dogs were let off leash, they ran off and jumped into the abyss. We were convinced there was nothing we could do. However, Carlo prayed to Jesus, trusting that he would protect them. And he did. We walked down the street, and when we walked under the arch of Saint Peter's gate, we turned to reach the lower level on which the wall stood. We were amazed to find the dogs safe and sound, wagging their tails and happy to see us. This episode was a clear sign of how the Lord listened to Carlo's prayers. That same evening, I heard a voice tell me, "Jesus saved them for Carlo."

• • •

Carlo's love for nature, which for him was a reflection of God's love for man, brought him close to Saint Francis. It is no coincidence that Carlo's favorite poem was the "Canticle of the Creatures," in which the poor man praises God for the beauty of creation.

Sometimes, Carlo looked at the sky and at beautiful landscapes and became emotional, remembering the words of Psalm 8:

> When I look at your heavens, the work of your fingers,
>   the moon and the stars which you have established;
> what is man that you are mindful of him,
>   and the son of man that you care for him?
>
> Yet you have made them a little less than the angels
>   and you have crowned him with glory and honor.
> You have given him dominion over the works of your hands;
>   you put all things under his feet,
> all sheep and oxen,
>   and also the beasts of the field,
> the birds of the air, and the fish of the sea,
>   whatever passes along the paths of the seas.
>
> O LORD, our LORD,
>   how majestic is your name in all the earth! (vv. 3–9)

Before Carlo, I had never met a child capable of being amazed at the beauty of a sunset or the majesty of a mountain landscape. One summer, a relative who came to visit us in Assisi was complaining about how all mountain landscapes were the same and nothing changed. From that point onward, when someone showed a lack of appreciation for nature, Carlo would jokingly say to us: "It's all the same; it's all the same. What changes?"

Carlo loved creation and being in nature. One of his favorite hobbies during our walks was to build crosses with the wood that he found on the ground and spread them along the street. He liked the idea that someone might find them and remember that Jesus was crucified for love of man.

• • •

In the summer, Carlo would run cleanup "operations" to get rid of the garbage we would find on the walks we took with our dogs in the Umbrian mountains. We found all sorts of things above Mount Subasio — broken glass bottles, pieces of glass all around that could be dangerous and hurt someone, rusted caps and cigarette butts, wastepaper and picnic materials, even syringes used by drug addicts. Carlo would bring along gloves and a trash grabber he had asked for as a gift. He did the same thing at the seaside over the summer. He put his mask on and went to pick up the pieces of plastic that the tide sometimes brought in along the shore.

His cousins recall how Carlo would yell at them when they left the tap open with the water running or the light on when they left a room. He would jokingly call earth the "spinning garbage can" because he said that with our compulsion toward waste, sooner or later, we would wind up buried in trash. As Albert Schweitzer put it, "Man has lost the capacity to foresee and to forestall, he will end by destroying the world."

Carlo found the indifference toward environmental disasters, and of which man is the first victim, to be the reflection of a human race that was getting further and further from God and which refuses his love. Carlo thought the damage to creation was an alarm signaling the disrespectful position that man has taken regarding nature. He said that our society is no longer capable of recognizing the vestiges of God in the nature that surrounds us.

We know what Saint Paul tells us in his Letter to the Romans: "We know that the whole creation has been groaning with labor pains together until now" (8:22), while awaiting the complete Redemption which will reestablish and complete the entire harmony of creation in Christ. He "unite[s] all things in him, things in heaven and things on earth" (Eph 1:10). The Gospel of Mark tells us what Jesus commanded: "Go into all the world and preach the gospel to the whole creation" (Mk 16:15).

Since the Greek word *ktísis* means both creation as an act and the creatures and realities that have been created, we can infer that the proclamation of the Gospel is addressed to all creation. We could say that there is a planetary vocation to meet with God. Human beings are not the only protagonists in the story of salvation — rather, all of creation participates in this salvific dynamism. Again, Saint Paul in his Letter to the Romans: "Ever since the creation of the world his invisible nature, namely, his eternal power and deity, has been clearly perceived" (1:20).

If Carlo were alive today, he would be in absolute agreement with Pope Francis's approach to these environmental questions described in his encyclical *Laudato Si'*. Here, the pope calls us to adopt an approach to integral ecology rooted in the knowledge that everything is connected. Integral ecology involves the interactions between the natural environment, society and its cultures, institutions, and the economy. In this interconnection, we must dedicate particular attention toward restoring dignity to those who have been excluded by taking care of nature. Pope Francis writes:

> It is essential to seek comprehensive solutions which consider the interactions within natural systems themselves and with social systems. We are faced not with two separate crises, one environmental and the other social, but rather with one complex crisis which is both social and environmental. Strategies for a solution demand an integrated approach to combating poverty, restoring dignity to the excluded, and at the same time protecting nature. (139)

When we went to Turin to visit Carlo's grandparents, we passed by the Fiat factory on our way to the hill where they lived. In front of the factory were shacks where Roma lived. Carlo was scandalized by the fact that these poor people had to live in those conditions and said that every town should have to organize designated areas with all necessary services.

The environment where we live is closely connected to man, who God chose as its protectors. Even though lifestyles dominated by technology appear to create a better life for people, giving them the illusion that they have the key to happiness in their hands, they also lead to an increasingly worrying degeneration of the relationship between man and earth. As the philosopher Günther Anders wrote that today "technology is our fate." It risks becoming like the fire that Prometheus stole from Zeus in mythology while convincing himself that he had solved all his problems. If not used well, it can work against mankind — just think of the atom bomb, which is a true Pandora's box.

Carlo had spoken to us about this topic. He realized that technology had the potential to dramatically improve people's lives, but it depended entirely on how we use it. My son was very clear in his opinion that we could say we improved our human condition through technology only if we leave a better world for future generations — that is, if the material well-being acquired can be maintained while preserving the natural capital we have received. For this reason, technology must enable material progress within a sustainable circular economy.

As Pope Francis writes in *Laudato Si'*:

> The earth's resources are also being plundered because of short-sighted approaches to the economy, commerce, and production. The loss of forests and woodlands entails the loss of species which may constitute extremely important resources in the future, not only for food but also for curing disease and other uses. Different species contain genes which could be key resources in years ahead for meeting human needs and regulating environmental problems. (32)

But a better world will be measured not just in terms of material well-being but on the degree to which people answer their vocation — that is, the reason they were created. We are called to love the God of Love himself and our neighbors through love for God. Technological progress is a solution and not a problem if it is used by people for good. And in the end, the responsibility lies in the hands of each person. It is of no use to complain about what others do if we do not first use our ingenuity to perform virtuous acts. Taken together, virtuous acts build a virtuous and therefore sustainable society. Being blind before the apocalypse, as Anders would say, indifferent and accustomed to environmental upheaval, has created a de-humanized society which seems to only think of consuming.

Pope Benedict XVI emphasized this in one of his homilies:

> And there are so many kinds of desert. There is the desert of pov-

erty, the desert of hunger and thirst, the desert of abandonment, of loneliness, of destroyed love. There is the desert of God's darkness, the emptiness of souls no longer aware of their dignity or the goal of human life. The external deserts in the world are growing, because the internal deserts have become so vast. Therefore, the earth's treasures no longer serve to build God's garden for all to live in, but they have been made to serve the powers of exploitation and destruction.

Arne Naess, the Norwegian philosopher who originated the deep ecology movement, states:

> Essentially there is at present a sorry underestimation of the potentialities of the human species. Our species is not destined to be the scourge of the earth. If it is bound to be anything, perhaps it is to be the conscious, and joyful, appreciator of this planet as an even greater whole in its immense richness.

A few days after his death, I addressed Carlo in prayer to ask him to send me a sign regarding a doubt that always made me uncomfortable and worried. I was in anguish around the idea that animals might end up in nothingness after their death. The Church has never defined the answer to this question in an exhaustive manner. Since I had many animals over the course of my life, I found consolation in the idea that after my death I would find them all there again, just like Pope St. Paul VI assured a child who was dejected following the loss of his much-adored dog. I told Carlo, "If animals all also go to heaven after their death, come and find me in a dream with my dog Billy from when I was a child, who I loved very much." I made this request in secret, convinced that my son would send me a sign. And the answer came promptly. Note that I did not mention this request to anyone else. A few days later, my aunt called me from Rome and told me she had dreamed of Carlo and my dog Billy.

A second confirmation to me as to animals' survival after death came from the doorwoman in the building in Milan where we lived. The woman had lost her beloved dog, which had been hit by a car. She was in despair.

The same night, she dreamed of Carlo playing with her dog. This reassured her greatly, and she immediately wanted to tell me about it. In 2019, Briciola, Carlo's dog, went to heaven. I was very attached to her, especially after Carlo's death, because she had become a kind of living relic for me. Carlo also sent me a clear sign on this occasion: Briciola appeared to me in my dreams in the arms of a priest, on the same night that the dog had passed away. Additionally, when Carlo was alive, he was sure that animals would not wind up in nothingness.

• • •

Carlo confided in me while we were in Assisi that when he looked at creation — nature, the sky, the stars, the animals — he became emotional because it made him think of God and his greatness. "For from the greatness and beauty of created things / comes a corresponding perception of their Creator" (Wis 13:5).

I would like to conclude this chapter by quoting these marvelous verses which Giacomo Leopardi wrote in his poem "The Infinite":

> But sitting and gazing, endless
> spaces beyond it, and inhuman
> silences, and the deepest quiet
> I fake myself in my thoughts; where almost
> my heart scares. And as the wind
> I hear rustling through these trees, I, that
> infinite silence, to this voice
> keep comparing: and I feel the eternal,
> the dead seasons, the present,
> and living one, and the sound of her. So in this
> immensity drown my own thoughts:
> and sinking in this sea is sweet to me.

11

An Angel Will
Walk Before You

Carlo was always devoted to angels.

Starting when he was little, he would pray to his guardian angel every day and experience the concrete help that was his answer. His relationship with these messengers of God began very early. Reading about angelic manifestations in the lives of the saints contributed greatly toward reinforcing his faith in these celestial messengers. When Carlo was about seven, we took a cultural trip in Italy with his grandmother. We visited Florence, Pisa, and finally Lucca to see the artistic beauty in which our country is very rich.

We stayed with nuns in the center of Florence, near the Church of Sant'Ambrogio. This place is special because it has been the setting for two Eucharistic miracles, occurring in 1230 and 1595, respectively. The first took place on December 30, 1230. A priest named Uguccione did not realize that there were a few drops of consecrated wine which had been left behind in the chalice after he had celebrated Mass. The following day, when he returned to celebrate Mass in the same church, he found drops of condensed, incarnate, living Blood in the chalice. The Blood was immediately collected in a crystal vial.

The second miracle occurred on Good Friday in the year 1595. A lit candle accidentally fell to the ground and set the side chapel, known as that of the Tomb, on fire. People immediately ran to put the fire out and were able to save the Most Holy Sacrament and the chalice. In the general confusion, six Particles fell from the pyx containing several consecrated Hosts onto the burning carpet. Despite the fire, they were found intact and joined together. In 1628, the archbishop of Florence, Marzio Medici, found them to be incorrupt after examining them and had them placed in a valuable reliquary. Each year, during the Forty Hours of Prayer celebrated in May, the two relics are displayed together. Carlo was already fascinated by these Eucharistic wonders, and he liked to visit these holy places.

In Lucca, we went to the tomb that contains the remains of Saint Zita in the Basilica of San Frediano. Saint Zita is the patron saint of the city but also that of housewives and maids. At the age of twelve, she began to work as a maid for the Fatinelli family, and she lived and worked in the house until her death. Many miracles were attributed to her intercession, performed while still alive. She was often visited by angels, and Carlo wanted to go to this church to pray to her and ask her to help him to build an even more special relationship with his guardian angel.

One of the miracles for which Saint Zita was the protagonist was that of the "coat." One evening, before Christmas Eve Mass, while leaving her home to go to Mass, she ran into her master. He was worried about the cold, and for her not to become sick he insisted Zita wear his coat, which was lined with fur. Arriving at the southern door of the church, she saw a badly clothed poor man suffering from the cold. She was moved to pity and lent him the coat, asking him to give it back at the end of the service because it belonged to her master. Zita was so deeply immersed in prayer that she did not realize that everyone else had left and she remained alone in the church. When she went outside, the poor man was no longer there. She returned home in despair over the loss of the coat. Her master was still awake, and when he saw her without his coat, he began to scold her. Soon afterward, they heard someone knocking on the door of the house, and a very beautiful young man turned up with the coat in his arms. The mysterious character thanked the woman in front of her master for having defended him from the cold and immediately disappeared in a halo of light. He was an angel, and from that moment onward, the southern entrance to the basilica was known as the "Angel's door." The miracle is depicted on the stained-glass window above the capital of the door. Dante Alighieri himself, a contemporary of Zita, cited her in the Divine Comedy multiple times, even before she was officially canonized.

We stayed in Lucca for the night, and the next day we went first to the church where the remains of Saint Gemma are held and then to visit Casa Giannini. This is where the saint was taken in after the loss of her parents and where she spent the rest of her days. Carlo was moved while listening to the stories that one of the nuns who lived in the house museum told about the relationship between Gemma and her guardian angel. The nun told us that Gemma's guardian angel scolded her because she was sometimes distracted during Mass, or because she sometimes became too attached to objects, as was the case with a gold watch that she had been given as a gift.

When the nun saw Carlo's devotion to the saint, she gave him permission to sit on the same chair where Gemma normally sat. The nun told me that Carlo reminded her of a little angel. Soon afterward, she also had us visit Saint Gemma's bedroom, where the desk that the saint used to store the letters that she wrote to her spiritual director, Father Germano, who lived in Verona, still stood. In the night, her guardian angel came to collect the letters and brought them immediately to her director. Saint Gemma never used ordinary mail because her guardian angel acted as a mailman for her.

Carlo was also very impressed by St. Pius of Pietrelcina's devotion toward angels. In 2001, we made a pilgrimage to the Shrine of the Virgin of the Rosary of Pompei, and from there we continued to San Giovanni Rotondo to visit Saint Pius. There, we met a taxi driver who was a spiritual child of Padre Pio and he told us about how the saint often asked him to bring some people who were especially blighted by the devil directly to the Sanctuary of St. Michael the Archangel. Carlo asked me to bring him to visit this sanctuary, which I was happy to do. He marveled to see that it was not outdoors but rather within a very deep grotto. He was impressed by this sacred place, and from that moment he made it a habit of reciting the Rosary of the Angels, dedicated to the nine choirs of angels, while we were on vacation. The devotion consists of twenty-seven Hail Marys and nine Our Fathers dedicated to the angelic hosts.

Saint Pius, who Carlo adored, also had his guardian angel as a faithful companion. Starting when he was a boy, the angel guided him along the path of goodness and directed him toward the roads that lead to heaven. "If you need help, send me your guardian angel," he would tell the faithful. And he kept himself very busy night and day listening to the messages of the many angelic creatures that brought him messages from people around the world. In a letter dated April 20, 1915, and addressed to Raffaelina Cerase, the saint urges her to love the angel: "Make it a good habit of always thinking of him. By our side is a celestial spirit who does not even abandon us for a moment from our cradle to our grave." Padre Pio's guardian angel often helped him translate letters that he received from faithful scattered around the world. On this note, Father Agostino, his spiritual director, wrote in his diary: "Padre Pio does not speak Greek or French. His guardian angel explains everything to him and he answers appropriately."

Based on the experiences of these saints, Carlo learned to seek out his guardian angel so that he would help him overcome his main flaws. He said that these angels do not enter places where sin is regularly cultivated, such as certain nightclubs. When we agree to sin, we no longer enjoy their protection because this involves indulgence and spiritual compromise. For Carlo, it was important to build a relationship with his guardian angel because these faithful messengers are a special and unique gift God gives to each person. By building this personal relationship, we can benefit from his inspiration. If we deprive ourselves of the special protection of our guardian angel, it will unfortunately be easier for the devil to get to us. Guardian angels guide us from the moment of our conception along the entire walk of our lives and then accompany us to heaven, where we can enjoy the presence of God with us forever. If, after death, we go to purgatory, we will still benefit from their assistance and intercession, but they will not come with us if we go to hell. Padre Pio said that if we could see the devils that surround us with our eyes, we would not be able to see the light of the sun. In the places in which our soul feels edified and closest to God, it is because the holy angels are particularly present.

Carlo said that our attachment to sin and persistence in committing it not only separate us from communion with God and with the angels, but also leave us open to the power of evil and the various consequences of spiritual disorders, including vexation and possession by the devil. Many physical and psychological diseases are caused by diabolical influence. The way in which Satan can bring spiritual devastation to the soul is to have it fall into the trap of superstition, divination, and magic, which are sins against the First Commandment, or sins of idolatry. Together with other sins, including that of impurity, it is the way in which the devil binds souls to him and impedes spiritual progress.

According to Carlo, during exorcisms the Devil claims victory through abortions, pornography, immorality, betrayals of the family, and New Age practices which are spreading through the world, because they become an arbitrary substitute for God's commandments and for Jesus' teachings. All souls that are close to God have always had to wage spiritual war, which is often brutal. I myself can bear witness to experiences with my guardian angel through the soul of a priest who was favored with many mystical experiences, including the opportunity to converse with his guardian angel and that of others. On many occasions, I sent my guardian angel to that of this priest, and although he lived many miles away, he received my messages and answered my questions. Through this priest's guardian angel, I received many useful pieces of advice for my spiritual journey and for various situations.

12

"In the End, My Immaculate Heart Will Triumph"

Carlo always had a great devotion to the Eucharist and the Virgin Mary. He would say:

> Each time that we address the Mother of God, we place ourselves in direct and immediate contact with heaven. It is almost as if we enter. In calling her "full of grace," in invoking her in this manner, we attest to our filial faith. We believe in her in this way. We hope that she is the giver of all things good. Of every Grace. We say, "Pray for us" — that is, we invite her to use her status to meet us

halfway. We address her knowing that she is *Omnipotentia Supplex* (omnipotent for intercession). Her intercession is assured. Her intervention is taken for granted. Her prayer is infallible. The human race, through Mary, was given supernatural dignity. God associated himself with a creature, a mother. A mystery!

Carlo considered the places where the Virgin had revealed herself, either through the performance of miracles or to guide her children toward true life, to be very important. It is for this reason that before dying he had begun to create his exhibit on the "Pleas of Our Lady," which we later finished. The last trip we took with Carlo was in 2006, to Fátima and Spain, during the 750th anniversary of the Eucharistic miracle that occurred in Santarém, Portugal. Therefore, before arriving in Fátima, Carlo wanted to visit this holy place. He cared deeply about it and was very happy to receive medals commemorating this prodigious event as a gift as well as many photos that he could add to his exhibit.

Two miracles occurred in Santarém, in 1247 and 1340, respectively. The first miracle occurred after a young woman, afflicted by jealousy of her husband, went to a witch. The witch suggested that she go into the church and steal a consecrated Host. The woman did so, hiding the Host in a linen cloth, which became immediately stained with blood. Terrified, she ran home. When she opened the napkin to see what had happened, she saw that the Blood was coming directly out of the Host. Confused, she placed the particle in a drawer in her bedroom, but beams of light began to emerge from it. Her husband became aware of her misdeed and immediately informed the parish priest, who came to their house to reclaim the Host and return it to the Church of Saint Stephen in a solemn procession, accompanied by many religious figures and laypeople. The particle bled for three days. It was later placed in a magnificent beeswax reliquary.

In 1340, the second miracle, a priest opened the tabernacle and found the wax vase broken in many pieces. In its place was a crystal vase with the Blood of the Host inside, miraculously mixed with the wax.

After the visit, we continued to Fátima, where we met a nun friend of ours together with the then postulator of the Cause for Beatification of

Francisco and Jacinta Marto, Father Luis Kondor. He took us to visit an exhibit full of unpublished photos regarding the apparitions of the Virgin Mary which had occurred in Fátima in 1917 to the three shepherds, Jacinta, who was seven years old, Francisco, who was nine, and Lucia, who was ten. He told us that Sister Lucia, the oldest of the three, who later became a nun, had seen the statue of the Virgin Mary in the convent cry soon before she died. Carlo had had many signs from the shepherds of Fátima. He had also dreamed of Francisco, who asked him to offer reparation and sacrifices so that the people would love and honor the Eucharist more. A few days after the death of Sister Lucia in 2005, Carlo dreamed of her. She told him that the practice of the first five Saturdays of the month could change the destiny of the world. Another time, when he was around eight, he saw Our Lady of Fátima during a procession in church. She stopped in front of him and gave him her heart. She placed it in his chest. She told him to consecrate himself to her Immaculate Heart and to the Sacred Heart of Jesus.

Carlo and I were very struck by the story of the shepherds. He was very moved when he read the story of their life written by cousin Lucia in her memoirs. As the Virgin Mary foretold on June 13, 1917, the two siblings, Francisco and Jacinta, died soon after, in 1919 and 1920, respectively, due to the Spanish influenza pandemic. In answer to Lucia's request, "I would like to ask you to bring us to heaven," the Virgin Mary responded:

> Yes. I will take Jacinta and Francisco soon. But you are to stay here some time longer. Jesus wishes to make use of you to make me known and loved. He wants to establish in the world devotion to my Immaculate Heart. I promise salvation to those who embrace it, and those souls will be loved by God like flowers placed by me to adorn his throne.

The death of a young person is not always met with faith, and soon after Carlo's premature death, I discovered that many of his classmates and friends were angry with God. In particular, one of his close friends told me that she had a ninety-year-old grandfather, and she could not understand why Jesus did not have him die instead of Carlo. I understand that it is not always easy to understand God's plan, but we know that every-thing is in service of bringing good to those who he loves.

The Book of Wisdom tells us:

But the righteous man, though he die early, will be at rest.
For old age is not honored for length of time,
nor measured by number of years;
but understanding is gray hair for men,
and a blameless life is ripe old age.

There was one who pleased God and was loved by him,
and while living among sinners he has taken up.
He was caught up lest evil change his understanding
or guile deceive his soul.
For the fascination of wickedness obscures what is good,
and roving desire perverts the innocent mind.
Being perfected in a short time, he fulfilled long years;
for his soul was pleasing to the Lord,
therefore he took him quickly from the midst of wickedness.
Yet the peoples saw and did not understand,
nor take such a thing to hear,
that God's grace and mercy are with his elect,
and he watches over his holy ones.

The righteous man who has died will condemn the ungodly who
    are living,
and youth that is quickly perfected will condemn the prolonged
    old age of the unrighteous man. (4:7–16)

God will always make good emerge from what is bad. Heaven reasons in terms of eternal life. There is an episode regarding Jacinta's mother that is meaningful in this regard, and it can help us understand why we cannot judge events only through the framework of time, which is always limit-ed, but in the key of eternity.

Sister Maria Godinho, who took care of Jacinta for a period while the young visionary was hospitalized, asked the girl's mother one day whether she would have liked her daughters to embrace religious life. She was speaking especially of Teresa, who was fifteen, and Florinda, who was sixteen. Jacinta's mother answered almost in fear, "May God look after them!" Jacinta was not present for this conversation, but not long after told the nun: "Our Lady would like my sisters to become nuns. My mother does not want this, and for this reason, Our Lady will bring them with her to heaven." In fact, not long after, the two sisters also died of pneumonia. The Virgin Mary probably brought them immediately to heaven because she knew they would have made decisions that ran contrary to God's plan for them.

My son was convinced that the beauty of life does not depend on its length but rather whether we are able to make God the most important part of it. He believed that was what made a "successful" life. He said that "loving God above all else" should be the ideal "goal" for everyone's life. Carlo believed that if we were able to achieve this high objective, we would receive the keys to open the gates that lead to heaven directly from God.

Carlo used to say that heaven reasons differently than we do. For example, in the Kibeho apparition in Africa, the Virgin Mary gave the following message to Nathalie on May 15, 1982: "No one goes to heaven without suffering. … A child of Mary does not reject suffering." The apparition was recognized in 2001 and made a strong impression on Carlo. Here, the Virgin Mary asked that the rosary of her sorrows, known as the Rosary of the Seven Sorrows, be recited every Friday. She promised that those who recited it would be given the graces necessary to repent for their sins before death. Carlo recited it often. He liked to meditate on the suffering of Mary. He was also devoted to the Rosary of Our Lady of Tears.

The Virgin Mary also revealed herself to the young Estelle Faguette in 1876 and cured her of an incurable disease. In one of her apparitions, after Estelle asked her to bring her to heaven right away, the Virgin answered:

Ungrateful one, if my son restores you to life, it is because it is necessary for you. What has he given to man on earth more precious than life? In restoring you to life, do not believe you will be exempt from suffering; no, you will suffer; you will not be free from sorrow. This is what makes life meritorious. If my son has allowed himself to be prevailed upon, it is on account of your resignation and your patience.

In 1918, the Virgin Mary asked Jacinta if she wanted to stay on earth for a little while longer to offer herself and save other sinners. The girl generously accepted this test due to her love of God, but like the Virgin Mary had foretold, she died alone in the hospital without the comfort of loved ones, suffering greatly from pneumonia and from the operation she had had to have on her ribs without anesthesia. Just like Jesus, who was hit with a spear to the ribs, little Jacinta also had to endure a very painful wound to her ribs which assimilated her to the Passion of Christ.

Suffering is a way of expiating sin from the world if united with the suffering of Jesus and Mary. The long hours he spent contemplating the Crucified and Risen Christ, and his most holy mother at the foot of the cross (see Jn 19:25), led Carlo to dig deeply into the mystery of human suffering, the origin of evil and, most of all, the meaning and value that Christian faith gives to man's great questions regarding death, suffering, sickness, and his final destiny.

Carlo looked at the teachings of the Word of God with a healthy realism when it came to evil, the sins committed by man, and what he termed the "disorder which this has brought to personal, family, and social life." In effect, we are shown in the first few pages of Scripture how Adam and Eve's disobedience to God's commandments radically changed the destiny and life of every man and woman — of the whole human race. Before sinning, they possessed sanctifying grace and the preternatural gifts of integrity, immortality, impassibility, and infused knowledge. Then, after the original sin, disorder, effort, sickness, and death came into their lives. Carlo said, concerning this:

Mysteriously, each moment of suffering has two faces: It is the consequence of a previous disorder which caused it and the purifying action of the Mercy of God, perfectly united to his Justice. In fact, God, in his infinite wisdom, set it up so that evil, the fruit of sin, or rather of rebellion toward God, contributes to the good of those who love him, through their purification and sanctification.

St. Ignatius of Loyola wrote, "If God causes you to suffer much, it is a sign that he has great designs for you, and that he certainly intends to make you a saint." Then there is the famous story of St. Teresa of Ávila, who was caught in a sudden storm while returning to her convent and fell off her horse into a puddle of mud. She told Jesus, ironically, "If this is how you treat your friends, it is no wonder you have so few!"

Unfortunately, the path that leads to sainthood is difficult. "Enter by the narrow gate; for the gate is wide and the way is easy, that leads to destruction, and those who enter by it are many" (Mt 7:13). No less indicative of this is the heroism of the stigmatized Blessed Alexandrina Maria da Costa, who spent fourteen years bedridden living on only the Eucharist. She said the Lord had appeared to her and had given her a plan for her life of "loving, suffering, and repairing." The Virgin Mary herself had obtained the grace of accepting this plan of immolation for her. "Our Lady has given me an even greater grace: first abandonment; then complete conformity to God's will; finally, the thirst for suffering," Alexandrina said. It is certain that when Carlo became ill, he was very much aware of the examples of these saints who welcomed suffering, knowing that everything leads to good if offered to God with faith and confidence.

Carlo believed that the mercy and justice of God, which redeem man from the consequences of his sin, are inextricably bound. God does not abandon man in his situation or disorder. He does not leave him alone, but rather continuously knocks on his heart to give him grace and his reconciliation. All human suffering, including that of the innocents, is an effect of original sin, a disorder that deprives humanity from the "blessed life" God had planned for earthly paradise. This blessed life, eternal beatitude, is not a dream which has failed forever. Believers know that with their obedience to God's commandments and their patience and meekness in the face of situations in life that may be happy, but also sometimes sad and tragic, they are on a path that leads to the blessed life that Adam and Eve lost but Jesus Christ won back with his passion, death, and resurrection.

There are two women: the first, the one who represents disobedience to God's commandments, of saying "no" to God's plans, is Eve; the second, the one who represents saying "yes" to God's providential plan, is the most holy Mary. Eve was born without original sin. Mary was conceived without original sin in view of the passion, death, and resurrection of her son Jesus. In these two women, Eve and Mary, we can see the situation that we men and women of the third millennium are experiencing. We also have the freedom to choose good or evil and therefore to walk the path that leads to eternal life or eternal death.

By virtue of the Mystical Body, of which Jesus is the head and we are the limbs, each good work we perform, each prayer we say, and each sacrifice we make will be for the benefit of all members of this body. The reverse is also true — each evil act we commit and each missed opportunity to do good works is to the detriment of all. As Saint Paul says in his Letter to the Colossians, "Now I rejoice in my sufferings for your sake, and in my flesh I complete what is lacking in Christ's afflictions for the sake of his body, that is, the Church" (1:24).

Christ also calls us to cooperate in the redemption which he performed once for all in dying on the cross for our salvation. The *Catechism of the Catholic Church* reaffirms:

> The Eucharist is also the sacrifice of the Church. The Church which is the Body of Christ participates in the offering of her Head. With him, she herself is offered whole and entire. She unites herself to his intercession with the Father for all men. In the Eucharist the sacrifice of Christ becomes also the sacrifice of the members of his Body. The lives of the faithful, their praise, sufferings, prayer, and work, are united with those of Christ and with his total offering, and so acquire a new value. Christ's sacrifice present on the altar makes it possible for all generations of Christians to be united with his offering. (1368)

In her apparition at Fátima on August 19, 1917, the Virgin Mary urged the shepherds to pray and offer sacrifices: "Pray, pray a great deal and make sacrifices for sinners, for many souls go to hell because they have no one to pray for them." Carlo obeyed her words to the letter and always felt guilty because he said that he did not make enough sacrifices and pray enough for those who were far from God.

Scripture also emphasizes that suffering and tribulations are a source of grace for oneself and for others for those who love God: "For one is approved if, mindful of God, he endures pain while suffering unjustly" (1 Pt 2:19). According to the *Catechism of the Catholic Church*:

> The forgiveness of sin and restoration of communion with God entail the remission of the eternal punishment of sin, but temporal punishment of sin remains. While patiently bearing sufferings and trials of all kinds and, when the day comes, serenely facing death, the Christian must strive to accept this temporal punishment of sin as a grace. He should strive by works of mercy and charity, as well as by prayer and the various practices of penance, to put off completely the "old man" and to put on the "new man." (1473)

Carlo cited Scripture to explain the reason behind suffering. He said that Christ took on the entire weight of evil:

> Make many to be accounted righteous;
> and he shall bear their iniquities.
> Therefore I will divide him a portion with the great,
> and he shall divide the spoil with the strong;
> because he poured out his life to death,
> and was numbered with the transgressors;
> yet he bore the sin of many,
> and made intercession for the transgressors. (Isaiah 53:11–12)

Even though the Prophet Isaiah was writing around seven hundred years before the coming of Jesus, he intuited that the suffering of the just can also redeem the sins of others. With his passion and death on the cross, Christ gave suffering a new meaning and assimilated us into his redemption.

The apostle James invites us to intercede on behalf of others:

> The prayer of a righteous man has great power in its effects. Elijah was a man of like nature with ourselves and he prayed fervently that it might not rain, and for three years and six months it did not rain on the earth. Then he prayed again and the heaven gave rain, and the earth brought forth its fruit.
>
> My brethren, if any one among you wanders from the truth and some one brings him back, let him know that whoever brings back a sinner from the error of his way will save his soul from death and will cover a multitude of sins. (Jas 5:16–20)

When Carlo was younger, Jacinta appeared to him and told him that there are no words on earth that can describe the horror of hell. For this reason, he often meditated on the ultimate realities, including hell and the possibility of ending up there. Every so often, he would say to me: "Mom, but do you realize what it means to go to hell for all of eternity? Try to imagine being in a place forever and ever and ever and ever ..." It was this deep awareness of the risk that pushed him to create his exhibit "Hell, Purgatory, and Heaven."

Carlo would become upset that so many risk losing themselves for all of eternity. He found it a disturbing reality. He made note of the writings of some saints who described this place. He used them to catechize those who did not believe in the existence of hell. Here is one text on hell from the diary of Sister Faustina Kowalska, the saint of Divine Mercy:

> Today, I was led by an angel to the chasm of hell. It is a place of great torture; how awesomely large and extensive it is! The kinds of tortures that I saw; the first torture that constitutes hell is the loss of God; the second is perpetual remorse of conscience; the third is that one's condition will never change; the fourth is the fire that will penetrate the soul without destroying it — a terri-

ble suffering, since it is a purely spiritual fire, lit by God's anger; the fifth torture is continual darkness, and a terrible, suffocating smell, and despite the darkness, the devil and the souls of the damned see each other and all the evil, both of others and of their own; the sixth torture is the constant company of Satan; the seventh torture is horrible despair, hatred of God, vile words, curses and blasphemies. These are the tortures suffered by all the damned together, but that is not the end of their sufferings. There are special tortures destined for particular souls. These are the torments of the senses. Each soul undergoes terrible and indescribable sufferings, related to the manner in which it has sinned. There are caverns and pits of torture where one form of agony differs from another. I would have died at the very sight of these tortures if the omnipotence of God had not supported me. Let the sinner know that he will be tortured throughout all eternity, in those senses which he made use of to sin. I am writing this at the command of God, so that no soul may find an excuse by saying there is no hell, or that nobody has ever been there, and so no one can say what it is like.

We had been given three lithographs by Salvador Dalí depicting hell, heaven, and purgatory, and we discovered that the Fátima vision of hell had converted Dalí, who immediately began work on some religious and ecclesiastical works. These included *The Madonna of Port Lligat* and *The Ecumenical Council*, which was an homage to the Second Vatican Council, as well as some illustrations of *The Divine Comedy* commissioned by the Italian government.

In addition to the Fátima apparitions of the Virgin Mary, Saint Jacinta received various private visits from her while sick and bedridden. The Blessed Mother explained, "The sins which cause most souls to go to hell are the sins of the flesh. Certain fashions will be introduced that will gravely offend my son. People who serve God should not follow fashions. The Church has no fashions; Our Lord is always the same."

Carlo was also devoted to St. John Bosco, who was also brought to visit hell accompanied by his guardian angel, during which he saw there were young people there. Saint John also said that the angel revealed to him that the sins which bring the most souls to hell are those against the Sixth Commandment and immodesty. This is why Carlo cared so deeply about this virtue and acted as an apostle among his classmates to help them respect this commandment.

Vocal prayers, which Carlo considered to be an effective means for uniting oneself with God, were also very important to him. Carlo said that prayer makes us look at everything from the point of view of eternity. The difficulties of this world seem to be insignificant if viewed from this perspective. For Carlo, immersing himself in God through meditation and prayer was like entering into heaven through a secret door and sitting down in his place in eternity for a moment. Carlo had a contemplative spirit. He was always thinking of God, who became the guide of his heart and his actions.

He found the daily reciting of the holy Rosary to be an effective means of meditating on the life of Jesus. Mary lived with her gaze fixed on Christ, treasuring his every word: "But Mary kept all these things, pondering them in her heart" (Lk 2:19). In reciting the Rosary, we experience these mysteries through the heart of Mary, and it becomes easier to set up our life in imitation of that of Jesus and Mary. As Carlo said, "In accepting the message of the angel who announced the birth of the Savior with her 'yes,' Mary gave us the perfect icon on which to model our own lives." In union with Christ and obedient to him, she collaborated in obtaining the grace of salvation for all of humanity in a manner that was unique and unrepeatable. In suffering with him as he died on the cross, "in this singular way, she cooperated … in the work of the Savior" (*Lumen Gentium,* 61). As a compendium of the entire Gospel, the Rosary helps us relive the mysteries of the Incarnation and the redemption for our salvation.

• • •

The Virgin Mary also told the shepherds at Fátima, "Pray the Rosary every day in order to obtain peace for the world and the end of the war." Many saints have recommended this prayer. Sister Lucia said, "Through the power that the Father has given lately to the Rosary, there is no personal, familial, national, or international problem that cannot be solved with the Rosary." St. Pius of Pietrelcina, who loved to say many Rosaries every day, also told his brothers on multiple occasions that which would become his final spiritual request: "Love Our Lady and make her loved. Always recite the Rosary. … Talk about the Rosary, about my Blessed Mother, talk to souls about the great means of salvation: the Eucharist and the Rosary."

The founder of the Shrine of the Virgin of the Rosary of Pompei, Barolo Longo, who Carlo adored and often invoked, once heard an angel tell him: "If you want salvation, propagate the Rosary. This is Mary's promise: those who propagate the Rosary will be saved." The saintly Curé d'Ars used to say, "A single Hail Mary recited well makes hell tremble." And, finally, my son would say, "After the holy Eucharist, the holy Rosary is the most powerful weapon for fighting the devil and the shortest ladder for climbing into heaven."

Carlo also recited it in pieces, while he went to school, or on the bus, or while we took walks. He knew that the Church grants plenary indulgence if the Rosary is prayed by a family, as part of a community, or in church, or with someone else, and for this reason he always tried to meet this condition so that it could be applied to souls in purgatory.

I remember that during the Jubilee Year 2000, on the occasion of the feast of Our Lady of the Rosary in October, we were able to get tickets for an open-air ceremony in St. Peter's Square where all the world's bishops were invited to consecrate the millennium to Our Lady of Fátima and her Immaculate Heart in the presence of St. John Paul II. We had invited Carlo's cousin from Rome, Umberto, to come with us, along with his mother and father. The ceremony made a strong impression on Carlo, and I am certain that he prayed intensely in his heart for many intentions, for all young people, and that the world would move closer to God, reserving the cult of praise and adoration for him which he is owed. Carlo was moved to see all those bishops praying in front of the statue of Our Lady which had arrived directly from Portugal. Over the course of his life, we had performed seven acts of entrustment to Our Lady of Pompei, who is Our Lady of the Rosary, with a powerful blessing from a priest.

There is a little church on Via Sant'Antonio in Milan where a priest celebrates Mass every Sunday and then immediately consecrates the faithful who so desire to Our Lady. As a reminder of this act of entrustment, at the end of the ceremony each person is given a Miraculous Medal with blue ribbon, the color of Mary. Carlo had collected many such medals. I remember that Carlo's young cousins once came to visit us from Rome to spend the Christmas holidays with us. Carlo insisted they also be consecrated to the Virgin Mary in that church. I remember that it was a day to remember, because right after the consecration, as we crossed Piazza del Duomo, some young people came up to us. They were members of the Work of Brother Ettore, a holy priest who dedicated his life to serving the homeless and whose cause for canonization has been initiated. They had a lot of rosaries with them and gave us many of them. Carlo and his cousins saw it as a sign that the Virgin Mary was pleased with them, and through these unexpected gifts she was inviting all of us to recite the Rosary and spread the devotion.

In 2017, my children Francesca and Michele and I went to renew our consecration to the Virgin Mary in this church in Milan. We also received a beautiful sign on this occasion. We had just finished the consecration and we were leaving. While we crossed Piazza del Duomo, without knowing why, I was attracted to some posters outside the Museo del Novecento. I felt like something was pushing me to bring the children to see it. To our great surprise, while we were entering the museum, we practically ran into the postulator of the cause for canonization of the shepherds of Fátima, Sister Angela Coehlo. I had already had the pleasure of meeting her at the 2016 exhibit at the Fátima Sanctuary in honor of the hundredth anniversary of the apparitions, where Carlo's rosary and backpack were displayed beside some objects belonging to Sister Lucia. This nun was part of an order which was founded in 1974, Aliança de Santa Maria, which continues the spiritual work of Fátima by spreading the Rosary and the Virgin Mary's appeals for reparation and consecration to her Immaculate Heart. Sister Angela came to Milan for work, and she had also had the idea of visiting the museum. The fact that we met her so unexpectedly, and in Milan, seemed like a real sign from Providence and confirmation that the Virgin Mary wants people to consecrate themselves to her Immaculate Heart. Carlo used to say that it is very important to help the Virgin Mary accompany people in entrusting themselves to her Immaculate Heart, "a safe port for all the shipwrecks of this world," as Sister Lucia defined it.

The hour of triumph of the Immaculate Heart of Mary will coincide with the coming of the universal reign of the Sacred Heart of Jesus. As St. Maximilian Kolbe stated:

> Modern times are dominated by Satan and will be more so in the future. The Immaculata alone has from God the promise of victory over Satan. However, assumed into heaven, the Mother of God now requires our cooperation. She seeks souls who will consecrate themselves entirely to her, who will become in her hands effective instruments for the defeat of Satan and the spreading of God's kingdom upon earth.

The Church was formed on Pentecost, and Mary was present and continues to accompany it maternally and to intercede for the People of God. Following the Immaculate Heart of Mary means renouncing the judging of others, an action which is born for love of oneself. It means learning from her to deny oneself:

> Judge not, that you be not judged. For with the judgment you pronounce you will be judged, and the measure you give will be the measure you get. Why do you see the speck that is in your brother's eye, but do not notice the log that is in your own eye? Or how can you say to your brother, "Let me take the speck out of your eye," when there is the log in your own eye? You hypocrite, first take the log out of your own eye, and then you will see clearly to take the speck out of your brother's eye. (Matthew 7:1–5)

Carlo used to say, "Every baptized person is a prophet" — that is, prophet in the true, precise, and complete sense of being a witness of tomorrow. A witness with faith that is courageously professed, with a hope experienced with warmly cultivated and expressed charity. The theological virtues which baptism infused are to be cultivated and brought to fruition with the daily exercise of our virtues and the daily fight against our flaws. The Christian is a prophet if he can influence his environment in such a way as to radically transform it. Carlo believed that

> being a prophet means giving the world proof that we are in continual, efficient, effective contact with heaven. Contact which is made evident by means of our smile, our helpfulness, our patience, our understanding, and our intelligence in understanding others. Contact that is prophetic is supernatural. Prophecy is documentation of a life in grace. Prophecy is providing evidence of the Gospel brought to life and vitality. ... Everyday life should be understood in the atmosphere of baptism. This atmosphere is a different air, a different climate, a different land, a different region. If we enter into this order of ideas and ideals, evangelization becomes a new and renewing fact. So much is said about "new evangelization." It is this. Nothing else!

Carlo also spoke on healing, especially that what truly counts is the healing of the soul, of our hearts. My son believed that, yes, the physical healing which occurs in holy places is important, but what truly make these places special is that through them the Lord gives us the possibility of repentance and of starting a new life defined by the Resurrection. Astonishing acts of healing have occurred. Paralyzed people have begun to walk again, blind people have gotten their sight back, the deaf have begun to hear again, and the dumb have started to speak.

But there have also been conversions of doctors and scientists, including two Nobel prize winners. The first was Alexis Carrel, who won a Nobel prize in medicine. After visiting Lourdes in 1903 as an agnostic, as a doctor following a train of sick people, he converted after becoming an eyewitness to the inexplicable healing of a young, terminally ill woman. As Louis Pasteur wrote, "Little science takes you away from God, but more of it takes you to him." The second, Luc Montagnier, who was director of the Pasteur Institute, discovered the HIV virus, and won a

Nobel prize in medicine, wrote, "As far as the miracles of Lourdes that I've studied, I believe it really is something inexplicable. … I don't have an explanation for these miracles, and I recognize that there are healings that are not included within the current limits of science."

"Every one who drinks of this water will thirst again, but whoever drinks of the water that I shall give them will never thirst; the water that I shall give him will become in him a spring of water welling up to eternal life" (Jn 4:13–14). Through these miraculous waters, grace is given to us, if we are there in good faith and sincerely willing to walk a path of conversion.

13

"The Eucharist Is My Highway to Heaven"

The *Admonitions* by St. Francis of Assisi includes the following:

> Behold, each day he humbles himself as when he came from the royal throne into the Virgin's womb; each day he himself comes to us, appearing humbly; each day he comes down from the bosom of the Father upon the altar in the hands of a priest. As he revealed himself to the holy apostles in true flesh, so he reveals himself to us now in sacred bread. And as they saw only his flesh by an insight of their flesh, yet believed that he was God as they contemplated him with their spiritual eyes, let us, as we see bread and wine with our bodily eyes, see and firmly believe that they

are his most holy body and blood living and true. And in this way the Lord is always with his faithful, as he himself says: Behold I am with you until the end of the age (Matthew 28:18-20).

Jesus promises to be with us always. This is the new and definitive alliance with which God bound himself to his people. God the Father revealed through his messenger, "'A virgin shall conceive and bear a son, / and his name shall be called Emmanuel' / (which means, God with us)" (Mt 1:23). Also, the Prophet Isaiah says, "Therefore the Lord himself will give you a sign. Behold, a virgin shall conceive and bear a son, and shall call his name Immanuel" (Is 7:14).

These were Carlo's comments on Jesus' words of promise to "be with us always" until the end of the world:

"With you" means existence as a pair. "With" means life together. And life together means cohabitation, co-partnership, collaboration, making plans together, interaction, organizational harmony, questions and answers, concerted actions, innate ideas, ideals pursued together, values lived together, values defended together, values improved together. "With you": this is the understood tabernacle, the aided tabernacle, the collaborated tabernacle. The two words are brought to life. And they come to life if they are "life" on the inside. In taking cognizance of the tabernacle, reappropriating the tabernacle, managing the tabernacle, maneuvering the tabernacle, the words "with you" are finally brought into effect. The Trinitarian plan for the rational being is clear: elevation to a supernatural state, adoption as a son, inheriting co-eternity.

God said to Moses, "I will be with you" (Ex 3:12), and Jesus Christ repeats this to each and every one of us, baptized in his name, who tries to live in observance of his Gospel. Carlo was so deeply aware of this that he set up his entire existence as a daily encounter with Jesus through the Most Holy Sacrament.

To understand Carlo's spirituality, you have to delve into the Eucharistic mystery. When he took his first Communion at the age of seven, he began to go to Mass and perform Eucharistic adoration before Mass or afterward every day. He said:

> If we truly reflect, we are much, much luckier than those who lived more than 2,000 years ago with Jesus in Palestine. The apostles, the disciples, and the people of those times could meet him, touch him, talk to him, but they were limited by space and time. Many had to travel for miles on foot to meet him, but it was not always possible to approach him because he was always surrounded by crowds. Just think of Zacchaeus, who climbed a tree to see him. All we need to do, however, is go into the nearest Church, and we have "Jerusalem" right outside our front door!

He further wrote:

> People who lived alongside Jesus could not eat his Body and drink his Blood like we can. They could not perform Eucharistic adoration, through which Jesus transfigures us and makes us more like him. It is He who told us, "Be perfect, as your heavenly Father is perfect" (Mt 5:48), and in "hiding himself" in the Eucharist, he gives us all of himself, his Body, his Blood, his Soul, and his Divinity, and he helps us realize our sanctification. Jesus invites us to come to him: "If any one thirst, let him come to me and drink. He who believes in me, as Scripture has said, 'Out of his heart shall flow rivers of living water'" (Jn 7:37–38).

St. Ignatius of Antioch believed the Eucharist was a "medicine of immortality." My son believed the Eucharist was the most supernatural thing that existed on earth, because God our creator is present within it. He said, "If people understood the importance of the Eucharist, there would be such long lines to go take Communion that you would not be able to enter the churches."

It was Msgr. Pasquale Macchi, who had been Pope Paul VI's personal secretary, in anticipation of Carlo's first encounter with the Eucharistic

Jesus, who suggested to us that we celebrate the Sacrament in a place that favored meditation, silence of the soul, and union of the spirit with God. So, on June 16, 1998, on a beautiful day full of sun and joy, when Carlo had just turned seven, we went to the Monastero della Bernaga in Perego for this important event. It is difficult to describe the feelings that my son experienced.

Certainly, union with the Eucharistic Jesus was at the heart of Carlo's day and from that moment onward. Starting on that day, he went to Mass every day. His relationship with the Body of Christ had become "LIFE." During Mass, he conversed with him, he spoke to him, he listened to his words, and he took inspiration and energy from his actions. His creativity and constructive energy flowed outward from his daily Mass attendance.

I remember many things from his first Communion, including the trip in the car from Milan. Before arriving at the convent, while we were walking up the hill, a shepherd with a little white lamb crossed the street. My husband had to stop the car. I remember Carlo's smile, the joy on his face. He adored lambs. He said that that lamb which appeared out of nowhere seemed to him like a sign come down from heaven, like a little gift just for him. He was beaming. Carlo was aware of what he was going to do. The Eucharist became so important to him that he declared, "My plan for my life is to always be united with Jesus." After his death, I found the following words on his computer: "Loving tomorrow is giving the best fruit to today."

And Carlo certainly trusted in the Eucharist to ripen these fruits, through which the doors of heaven are opened for us. The then-mother superior of the convent, Mother Maria Emanuela, to whom Carlo remained attached for the entirety of his earthly existence, gifted us with a beautiful description of that memorable day:

> The memory of that June 16, 1998, which was certainly reawakened following his unexpected flight to heaven, is alive in me, just as it is in the entire convent community. It was the Tuesday after the feast of Corpus Christi when Carlo received his First Holy Communion at the altar of our convent church. It was private, since he had not yet reached the prescribed age for receiving the Sacrament of the Eucharist with his classmates but was already

ready and eager. He was calm and composed during holy Mass, but he started to show signs of something like impatience as the moment for receiving holy Communion approached. With Jesus in his heart, after holding his head in his hands for a short while with a prayerful attitude, he started to move as though he could not sit still. It seemed like something had happened inside him, something of which only he was aware, something so big that he was not able to contain it. ...

The nuns closest to the altar could not keep themselves from watching him, deeply moved, even through the thin blinds on the grate, and realizing that it was as if Carlo was fulfilling a long-awaited desire. For this reason, he remained in all of our hearts. I was struck by his harmonious physical development but even more by the clarity of his gaze, the brightness of his smile, and the peace that you could see on his face with such beautiful features! Before us was a young man who was distinguished but not refined, simple and free in his expressions, and always very polite. I remember that when he addressed his parents, it was ... cordial and [with] respectful filial spontaneity, which I dare say is a bit uncommon today! ... I was also very struck by the fact that on that occasion, and also on later ones, Carlo always asked me before leaving to accompany him in prayer so that he could bring the plans that the Lord had for his life as a student and young man in historic times such as these to fruition.

At the Monastero della Bernaga, Carlo had already demonstrated that he had made this message his own. It was one of the "places of silence" of his land of birth, atop a mountain where each word that you heard seemed to take on particular meaning. A few phrases written by Mother Maria Candida Casero, a twentieth-century hermit nun, made a strong impression on him:

The Holy Spirit is a fire that easily spreads to purified souls, like natural fire does to dry leaves. The Body of the Lord is on the al-tar stone! It is his heart, so beautiful, resting on flames and overflowing with flames: dive into it! Everyday Communion gives you all of this. During the Resurrection, the Soul of Jesus gave life to his Body; in holy Communion, the Body of Jesus gives life to your soul … God made into a Sacrament! Have you ever thought deeply about this? He is alive, real, and the bounds of accidents keep him forever bound as a victim. … Drink from the holy Host purity, life! May your heaven contemplate it in spirit as well. Delight in the Lord, and he will grant you what you ask. Where your treasure is, there your heart will be also. Jesus, your treasure, sits at the right hand of the Father and lives in the holy tabernacle. Enclose your heart within it, and send your thoughts to heaven. Not wishing to know or seek heavenly things. … A day without Communion can be compared to a day without sun, without bread, without smiling, without rest. Pray that this never occurs because of you. … This "over-essential Bread" tastes of every virtue! When you come to receive it, yearn to acquire first one and then another virtue, and obey his instructions. … When you attend holy Mass, you are also the offerer of much sacrifice, and that Most Precious Blood is also yours. Immerse yourself in it, trusting fully, and it will communicate to you the ardor to sacrifice yourself with generosity. May your sacred wonder before your Eucharistic God be ever renewed: the Body of the Lord is there! It is his beautiful heart, overflowing with flames! It is his immense Soul, a sea of light and holiness! Communion every day gives you all of this. … Would it be too much to go crazy with love? This little Host is capable of setting the world on fire: May it set you on fire, too! It can wound more than a sharp sword. Abandon your heart to it! The Eucharist is all of heaven fallen down here in exile! When you go to church, think "I am going to heaven!" The Eucharist is a flame. Always circle this flame lovingly, or little Eucharistic butterfly, you will wind up falling in and be incinerated. You will find everything in this little Host, because everything is in it. It is a lever for raising oneself toward holiness, a spark for setting yourself on fire, a bath for washing your stains, a supplement for your flaws, a door which leads you to heaven. The Eucharistic soul does not only live in the Eucharistic Jesus every day during holy Mass, but rather seeks to maintain its thought and its affection before the Eucharistic throne. It always endeavors to transfuse the vitrtues of the holy Host in all of its acts!

Carlo made these words his own. It was no accident that Carlo took his first Communion in that convent, where you could feel the Eucharistic mysticism so strongly.

I believe that the fact that Carlo's destiny was bound to those holy nuns by Divine Providence and that they have always continued to pray for him even after his departure is a sign from heaven and confirmation of how his spirituality was connected to the Eucharist right from the beginning. These nuns, who spend all day in silence and prayer, follow the stories of the world and of the people who live in it with a unique profoundness and dedication, and Carlo cared deeply about being looked after and helped by their prayers. It is incredible how they accompanied Carlo's journeys even while remaining within the walls of the convent.

Carlo loved them deeply and was fascinated by their union with Jesus. He wanted to experience it with the same intensity. After meeting them, he wrote, "The more Eucharists we receive, the more similar we become to Jesus, and we get a taste of heaven while we are still on earth." Evidently, it was precisely these nuns, who Carlo defined as "living tabernacles," who inspired him.

Carlo often stopped to worship Jesus during the Eucharist. He asked his friends to try to do as he did: "Do as I do," he said, "and you will see what kind of revolution will occur within you." It was from here, from this deep attachment to the Eucharist, that his love for the small, the needy, and the poor was born. I am certain that so many of the homeless people that came to his funeral had met him because of the impulse he had towards them thanks to his daily encounter with Jesus through the Eucharist. It is there that God teaches us to give to others by giving himself to us. As St. Teresa of Calcutta wrote, "If you cannot recognize Christ in the poor, you will not be able to find him in the Eucharist, either. A single, identical, equal faith illuminates both."

I found this beautiful meditation in Carlo's notes which explains how the Holy Trinity has really taken residence among us on our planet for over two thousand years:

> And the Word became flesh ... taking on human nature, associating it to a divine nature in a single divine person ... and came to live among us. But the word "lives" should be understood not in the common sense of taking up residence, of making its home on this earth. This is not what it means. When we use the term "to live" in our language, we instinctively think of something like this: it made its home in a certain place. This term, "to live," is a word that leads us to conclusions which are terrifyingly reductive. The word "to live" [*abitare*] is a Latin verb which comes from the word "to have" [*avere*] ... also has many other meanings when used as an auxiliary verb. It means ... off the top of my head ... to have, but it also means to hold, to visit, to possess, to sanctify, to assimilate, to make inherent, to put into pairs, and many other things. ... So, we have to take this word ... he lived among us ... as a much more general, much more universal, much broader, infinitely broader term, so when I say, "And the Word became flesh and lived among us," what I am saying is on its face very reductive if the sense of the word inspired by the Evangelist John is not translated. John wished to say many things in writing through the Holy Spirit. When Jesus took on human nature and was made man, he came down to this planet not as an alien but as "One" who in living outside of time and space entered with [human] nature into time and space and as if he incorporated it, assimilated it, made it connatural, twinned it. Therefore, Jesus became, as the apostle Paul says, "All in all," and took the true reality and the true substantiality from this planet, this planet earth which is part of creation and therefore of the universe. Before the Incarnation, humanity, prisoners in original and actual sin, marched forward through the centuries inside an abyss that appeared unfathomable and insurmountable. But at a certain point, love prevailed over justice, mercy prevailed

over punishment, and sin was defeated by the Incarnation. ... In you, this planet saw the second person of the most Holy Trinity for a generation, incarnate. And since that moment more than twenty centuries ago, it has never been the same. Yes, astronomically, scientifically, geologically, it might be the same planet, but from the point of view of the Gospel, of the Incarnation, it is no longer the same planet, it is a planet that has been absorbed into eternity, as part of a divine plan, and so for twenty-one centuries we have truly been inserted into this plan. We must think of this so-called inhabitation as an appropriation of the planet by Jesus, that Jesus who still moves within the Eucharist, as he does in faith, among us, and so he walks among us, lives among us, and shares our everyday lives with us, both in the Eucharist and in faith. For this reason, we must see this "inhabitation" as Christ truly residing on this planet earth. We see Jesus among us, we see Jesus with us, we see Jesus truly within us.

And so the Eucharist, which is a "second Incarnation," truly becomes not so much a Sacrament in the ritual sense but rather a Sacrament in the supernatural sense. For this reason, when we take Communion, Jesus pauses among us for fifteen minutes, hidden in the form of bread and wine, substantially present, truly residing, in the sense that I explained previously — that is, he shares this day with us and continues, after the forms of bread and wine have decomposed, with his grace, his residence with us. So, we become his house, his home, and so Jesus, present, alive, and real, is not only a fact of faith, not only a fact of "sacramentality," but a fact of "Life!" In other words, Jesus is with me and I with him, as an extremely personal, individual fact. This direct contact between Jesus and I occurs through the Eucharist and the Faith. When Jesus came to this planet earth, he tried to summarize, or as Paul says, to recapitulate all of eternity, all of humanity in himself. Humanity before him, humanity in him, humanity after him. This is residing. And Jesus, residing in this sense, recapitulated in himself, day by day, hour by hour, the entire human race, in every sense. ... And so we have before us a miracle which leaves us in awe and which leaves us truly surprised. It is the miracle of redemption, it is the miracle of Jesus's life with us, who in recapitulating all of humanity in himself, made himself truly, really Redeemer, Savior, and Sanctifier of each and every one of us.

Carlo believed that "through the Eucharist, we are transformed into love." Just like how after consecration, bread and wine become the Body and Blood of Jesus through the power of the Holy Spirit, we are also "transubstantiated" in Christ. Jesus himself assures us, "I am the bread of life" (Jn 6:35). And he reemphasizes with authority that it was not Moses who gave us the bread of heaven, but rather his Father who gives us the true bread of heaven (see v. 32). Jesus is the true Living Bread come down from heaven which will never perish, unlike that which the people of Israel ate in the desert, the manna, which is a bread that does perish.

I found these beautiful meditations on the Bread of Heaven in Carlo's notes:

> When Jesus says that it was not Moses who gave us the Bread of Heaven, but rather his Father that gives the Bread of Heaven, the true Bread of Heaven, he is introducing the Eucharist. His grand design, his famous plan, his marvelous project, is taking shape, is prefiguring reality. He introduces the Father, who he declares to be the giver of Bread, the real bread. He defines himself as the "Bread of God." We are entering the world of the Eucharist. "He who has come down from heaven": this is an expression that should be rewritten and meditated upon and studied and contemplated without fail. Heaven: eternity. We speak of a descent because we think of heaven as an entity of the above. The word simply means "coming" or "arrival" from eternity to time. From outside space to planet earth. This is a unique intervention: the most Holy Trinity places itself in personal contact with the rational being. There is an encounter which occurs. The Bread of God: Life. And so the Jews asked him, "Sir, give us this bread always." And Jesus answered, "I am the bread of life. Whoever

comes to me will never be hungry, and whoever believes in me will never be thirsty." Here we are. Jesus declares unequivocally and inescapably to be the "Bread of Life." He defines himself as "Bread." And he specifies, "Of life." His plan is taking form in his words. He promises to be "food." If we really think about this, it is astonishing. A historic event. The expression, "I am the bread of life," means that the abnormal and enormous weight is assumed by Christ, supported by divine nature, and made fully celestial by the divine Person so that we no longer hunger or thirst. Christ truly and substantially present in the form or appearance of bread and wine. It is the Bread which turns existence toward the beyond. And he adds, "But I said to you that you have seen me and yet do not believe." He accuses them of a lack of faith. They mutter about his unusual expression "I am the bread come down from heaven." They refer back to their knowledge of his personal details. They know Mary and Joseph. We have a valuable demonstration or proof of the historical significance of Christ. They find this to be so strange, so absurd, that it is unheard of. They clearly heard him say, "I am the bread come down from heaven." What kind of bread is this? What heaven is he talking about? What is this descent? And they discuss, and they reason (or fail to reason), and they make inferences. They are agitated. Almost anguished. Jesus confronts them: "Do not grumble among yourselves. No one can come to me unless the Father who sent me draws him. And I will raise him up on the last day. Truly, truly, I say to you, whoever believes has eternal life." Jesus has brought supernaturalism to Earth. Jesus explains, "If anyone eats of this bread, he will live forever. And the bread that I will give for the life of the world is my flesh." He made his will explicit: he wants to give himself through bread and drink. He is not expounding on a theory. He does not take refuge in the absolute. He does not complicate things with abstruse reasoning. He talks about manna, about the desert, about fathers, about the dead. They cannot argue with this. The Bible is there in the synagogue and everyone can read it and remember. But immediately, like a lightning strike on a clear day, he adds that He is the living bread which ensures eternity. He talks about his flesh for the life of the world. It is his physical, psychological, and spiritual reality. This reality is the bread of life. Bread which must be eaten if you want to live in eternity. Otherwise, eternal death awaits. He threw a boulder into the pool: the great, enormous, amazing declaration — affirmation — promise. He spoke so clearly, he expressed himself with words that were so completely precise and unequivocal, that "the Jews then disputed among themselves, saying: 'How can this man give us his flesh to eat?'" They understood correctly. They come close to accusing him of instigating cannibalism. "Flesh to eat": they have gotten right to the center of the problem/issue. Of course, Jesus' affirmation-declarations are not the most obvious. They are exploding expressions. They are glimpses of heaven. But Jesus says: "Truly, truly, I say to you, unless you eat the flesh of the Son of Man and drink his blood, you have no life in you. Whoever feeds on my flesh and drinks my blood has eternal life, and I will raise him up on the last day. For my flesh is true food, and my blood is true drink. Whoever feeds on my flesh and drinks my blood abides in me, and I in him. As the living Father sent me, and I live because of the Father, so whoever feeds on me, he also will live because of me. This is the bread that came down from heaven, not like the bread the fathers ate, and died. Whoever feeds on this bread will live forever." These six verses are a center of gravity. They are ultra-magnetic. They are six verses from the beyond. They are six verses of eternity. They do not speak in generic or approximate terms. They do not ease into the subject from far away. They do not circle around it. Immediately and very concretely, they ask that we feed on him or suffer non-life. He offers himself to us as food and drink. He wants us to feed on him. His divine-human reality is placed at our complete, total, global disposal. If this is not love, what is? Jesus enacts a very tight and very intimate bond with him. A bond that deals in terms of life. A bond that leads to eternity. Jesus and us. Jesus with us. Jesus for us. Jesus in us. As you can see, an interpersonal relationship is created. The individual man and woman are unequivocally interested in establishing this coexistence. Eating and drinking means consuming our daily food and drink. Consuming means admitting into our organism. Until these things in the form of bread and wine dissolve, the presence of the Body and Blood and Soul and Divinity of Christ is within us. Our living organism is intimately bonded to Jesus Christ, a true God and true Man. Jesus promises eternal life to those who take Communion. And he does not say "will have" but rather "has" eternal life. Life, therefore, and life that is eternal. In other words, co-eternity. With Communion, we have eternal life. Having eternal life means possessing everything that is necessary and indispensable for entering into co-eternity. We are registered in heaven's "registry office." We are citizens of co-eternity in every effect. And he insists, "My flesh is true food, and my blood is true drink." Everything is given. And later, "Whoever feeds on my flesh and drinks my blood abides in me, and I in him." Whoever takes Communion creates a home. A home together. Together under the same roof. "In me," "in him": beyond living together, it is the cohesion of organisms that do not become confused or fused with one another but rather suffused with one another and united to one another. This union is not symbolic, not poetic, not sentimental. What is it, then? Clearly, it is the opposite of being outside or of closeness. It is a reality which touches the roots, which reaches the depths, which emerges in the intimate. Jesus wants to realize and create this union by giving himself through his Body and Blood and Soul and Divinity. And this is how it ends: "As the living Father sent me, and I live because of the Father, so whoever feeds on me, he also will live because of me. This is the bread that came down from heaven, not like the bread the fathers ate, and died. Whoever feeds on this bread will live forever." Jesus, the Revealer of the Trinity, presents us the Trinity as an absolute unity. And he tells us their respective names: Father, Son, Holy Spirit. The Father generates. The Son is generated. The Holy Spirit proceeds from the Father and Son. We have existence. Through Communion, this leads to life. Jesus talks of life, promises life, gives life. That life is the Eucharist. The Eucharist is Christ, a true Man and true God. The Bread of Life is Christ. It is bread come down from heaven. From eternity to time. From heaven to planet earth. Come down: to bring oneself from on high to down low. The on high opens itself in the fullness of all times and communicates with the down low. Communion: the substantial and substantive injection of life into existence. In conclusion, Jesus makes himself substantially present in terms of his Body, Blood, Soul, and Divinity in things in the shape of bread and wine. The Council of Trent spoke of "transubstantiation." After consecration, the surface level traits — color, taste, smell, quantity — of the bread and wine remain. Bread and wine on the surface. Jesus in substance.

Carlo copied a few quotes by saints which explain the mystery of transubstantiation. As the great Doctor of the Church St. John Chrysostom wrote:

Let us be blended into that flesh. This is effected by the food which he hath freely given us, desiring to show the love which he hath for us. On this account he hath mixed up himself with us; he hath kneaded up his body with ours, that we might be a certain one thing, like a body joined to a head. ... He hath given to those who desire him not only to see him, but even to touch, and eat him, and fix their teeth in his flesh, and to embrace him, and satisfy all their love. Let us then return from that table like lions breathing fire, having become terrible to the devil. ... Parents often entrust their offspring to others to feed; "but I," saith he, "do not so, I feed you with mine own flesh."... For your sake I shared in flesh and blood, and in turn I give out to you the flesh and the blood by which I became your kinsman. (*Homilies on the Gospel According to St. John*, 46, 3).

He also really liked St. Thomas Aquinas, and used him to meditate on the true presence of Jesus in the Most Holy Sacrament:

> We see its truth when he says, "For my flesh truly is food." Some might think that what he was saying about his flesh and blood was just an enigma and a parable. So Our Lord rejects this, and says, my flesh truly is food. As if to say: Do not think that I am speaking metaphorically, for my flesh is truly contained in this food of the faithful, and my blood is truly contained in this sacrament of the altar: "This is my body ... this is my blood of the new covenant," as we read in Matthew (26:26). ... "He who eats my flesh and drinks my blood abides in me, and I in him." Now, Our Lord proves that this spiritual food has such power, that is, to give eternal life. And he reasons this way: Whoever eats my flesh and drinks my blood is united to me, but whoever is united to me has eternal life: therefore, whoever eats my flesh and drinks my blood has eternal life. ... And there is another way by which those who eat do not abide in Christ nor Christ in them. This is the way of those who approach [the sacrament] with an insincere heart: for this sacrament has no effect in one who is insincere. There is insincerity when the interior state does not agree with what is outwardly signified. In the Sacrament of the Eucharist, what is outwardly signified is that Christ is united to the one who receives it, and such a one to Christ. Thus one who does not desire this union in his heart, or does not try to remove every obstacle to it, is insincere. Consequently, Christ does not abide in him nor he in Christ. (*Commentary on the Gospel of Saint John*, Book I, Chapter VI)

Carlo used to say that through the Most Holy Sacrament present in the tabernacle, the healing love that only God can effect is irradiated and we join ourselves to the triumphant Church, that which is in paradise and which in that moment is prostrate in prayer before the Lamb of God to ask for graces and blessings for the whole Church. In the tabernacle, Jesus is present in the attitude of worship of the Father to which he wishes to associate all of mankind. Jesus wants to teach us how we, too, should worship the Father. Before the Eucharist, we too must have this attitude of reverence.

• • •

In ancient times, the Greek word *proskýnesis* and its Latin equivalent *adoratio* were used to refer to acts of veneration, worship, submission, and respect toward divinities. Christian submission is nothing other than a kind of love and trust in the God that first loved us and that makes himself our travel companion each day in the Most Holy Sacrament. Carlo would say that submission means "being at the complete, total, global disposition of God." He had read St. John Paul II's encyclical *Ecclesia de Eucharistia*, which urges all believers to place themselves "at the school of Mary, a woman of the *Eucharistia*." In fact, no one can better introduce us than Mary on how to worship her son, [present] in each Eucharist for our salvation: "The body given up for us and made present under sacramental signs was the same body which she had conceived in her womb!" (56). This is the close connection between Mary and the Eucharist. Mary's womb was Earth's first "tabernacle." Like John who welcomed Mary into his home, we must also welcome her to let her help us become "living tabernacles": "When Jesus saw his mother, and the disciple whom he loved standing near, he said to his mother, 'Woman, behold, your son!' Then he said to the disciple, 'Behold, your mother!' And from that hour the disciple took her to his own home" (Jn 19:26–27).

Carlo said:

> This woman, who never would have thought that she was immaculate, this woman, who always thought of herself as the servant of the Messiah, this woman who never would have dreamed in that moment, this noblewoman of the people of David, this woman who was chosen and desired by the Trinity, knew how to cry out, "Here am I, the servant of the Lord; let it be with me according to your word." Servant, she says. In the corresponding Greek, "slave." That is, at the complete, total, global disposal of

God. Slave: entirely prostrate to God's orders. Slave: without any ifs, ands, or buts. Slave: in entirety, body and soul. Slave: in every aspect. Slave: obeying orders without question. Slave: does not object, does not dispute, does not intervene, does not place conditions, but rather kneels, raises her hands, turns her gaze, and exclaims, "Yes!"

Even though there are no explicit references in the Gospels, how could we not think that it is precisely the spiritual participation of the Blessed Virgin with the disciples at the Eucharistic banquet that revitalized her heart to this complete willingness to do the will of God and the community that was being created? The gestures of worship, which are those of bowing our heads, kneeling, and prostrating ourselves express reverence, affection, submission, obliteration, and the desire of union, to be of service, and never, naturally, groveling. True worship does not mean moving away or creating distance but is rather an identification of love. St. Thomas Aquinas explains that in authentic worship the external humiliation of the body manifests in and excites the internal devotion of the soul and the yearning to submit oneself to God and to serve him. In imitation of the angels, we must also have the same spiritual attitude toward God of praise and thanksgiving.

• • •

So as not to be overcome by spiritual tepidity and aridity during prayer, Carlo would say the position of the body assumed while we pray was very important, that when we attend Mass, our body must also demonstrate that which we believe. To worship, it is important to orient our heart toward God with our body, to worship the Lord with all our heart, with all our soul, and with all our strength: "Hear, O Israel: The LORD our God is one LORD; and you shall love the LORD your God with all your heart, and with all your soul, and with all your might. And these words which I command you this day shall be upon your heart" (Dt 6:4–6).

Worshiping means offering the best that we have to God. It is trusting in Jesus, and with Jesus in the Father and in the Holy Spirit. My son believed that during Eucharistic adoration two abysses met: the abyss of our poor, sinful humanity, and that of Divine Mercy. The Prophet Malachi assures us that we will be healed by the sun of the righteousness of God: "The sun of righteousness shall rise, with healing in its wings" (Malachi 4:2). This sun of righteousness is Jesus in the consecrated Host, and the healing which he brings regards all of humanity, suffering and wounded, in purgatory and on earth. The entire mystery of the Church is there. Rays of love. God always wants to associate man with the mystery of the work of sanctification and the spreading of his grace, and Eucharistic adoration is one of the ways in which he performs this redemption.

Carlo was greatly devoted to tabernacles. He said that they should be visited on each pilgrimage that we made. He wrote, "If Jesus stays with us always, everywhere that there is a consecrated Host, what need do we have to make a pilgrimage to Jerusalem in order to visit the places where Jesus lived more than 2,000 years ago? So, we should also visit tabernacles with the same devotion!"

Carlo lamented the fact that they were often deserted. On this topic, this was his message:

The tabernacle is a synonym for a cradle of grace. The most Holy Trinity operates in the tabernacle. I see the tabernacle as dynamic. The Eucharistic reality is the proof and confirmation and verification of this destination of holiness. Holiness which is achieved through faith in the Eucharist, with the heroic practice of the seven virtues: the three theological virtues (faith, hope, and charity) and the four cardinal or moral virtues (prudence, justice, fortitude, and temperance). The model is God. The instruments are reason and grace. Grace is given or regiven by the sacraments. The tabernacle is close to that which is holy. It is intimate with it. Spending time with that which is holy makes it holy, as well. So, visiting the tabernacle means making oneself a candidate for holiness. And there might be a nonanswer, nonfaith, hypocrisy, selfish expression, a risky nonsolution, a dangerous one-way journey. We present ourselves for who we are with humility and simplicity. Humility does not alter the terms.

Simplicity does not complicate relationships. With this presentation, the interview begins. An interview which can only be characterized by familiarity and intimacy. This visit must be qualified by worship. Worshiping. We recognize that we are before the One God. The distance is infinite, even though the tabernacle is a few meters away. Worship: paying homage with a deference reserved only for God. Using words of dialogue with an Absolute Interlocutor. Reflecting … that you are before the Eucharist. The visit passes through the respectful feelings of worship interwoven with faith in the One God, hope for One God, and love for the One God. We also confess ourselves, climbing up to the top to the commandments of Sinai and continuing along the commandments of the Church and walking down the paths of the duties of one's state of life. And it then becomes opportune to recite the Lord's Prayer, Hail Mary, Glory Be, the guardian angel Prayer. … The visit comes to a close. We submit the day's plans to the Lord, professing that everything will be done for the glory of God. The farewell can be externalized with the use of a few short prayers such as, "Oh Jesus, make me love you even more," "Lord, take me as I am and make me as you wish." "I will try to offend you less." "Lord, I abandon myself to you." And similar prayers.

• • •

Carlo believed that the episode of Moses praying on Mount Sinai before the burning bush was an anticipation of Eucharistic adoration. If Moses prayed in the presence of God, the people of Israel were victorious over the Amalekites, but when he stopped praying to him, they lost. It is in worshiping God, the manifestation of which is found in the burning bush on Mount Sinai, that Moses receives the mandate of the Lord to free the people of Israel from the slavery and oppression of Egypt. The burning bush in which the Lord manifests himself to Moses is a symbol of the Eucharist, of Eucharistic worship, which frees us from the slavery of sin.

The worship of the Magi and the shepherds of the Baby Jesus placed in a manger is another prefiguration of Eucharistic adoration. Carlo was amazed when he discovered that in choosing to be born in that little town called Bethlehem, Jesus already implicitly manifested his destiny: to become our bread and wine. The word Bethlehem means "house of bread" in Hebrew and "house of meat" in Arabic (*Bayt Lahm*). Jesus himself will later say about himself, "I am the living bread which came down from heaven; if any one eats of this bread, he will live for ever; and the bread which I shall give for the life of the world is my flesh" (Jn 6:51).

In worshiping God, who is present in the consecrated Host, we find the whole universe present, and we can intercede to obtain graces for the whole world and to obtain many vocations. Carlo believed that before the Eucharist we become holy, and we become already transfigured on this earth.

I found these beautiful words on the importance of tabernacles in his notes:

> We must enter the mindset of the tabernacle. This is an entirely special mindset. Baptism is spiritual regeneration. Confirmation is spiritual growth. The Eucharist is spiritual food. The Sacrament of the Eucharist, although it is made of multiple materials, is a single entity in its form and perfection. In an absolute sense, the Eucharist is a single sacrament. The Eucharist is the sacrament of unity. Even though there are two elements, bread and wine, from which the entire Sacrament of the Eucharist is made, we profess on the basis of the Church's teachings that it is a single sacrament. Baptism is necessary for beginning spiritual life. The Eucharist is necessary for bringing supernatural life to bear. The Sacrament of the Eucharist has three meanings: the first involves the past, since it commemorates the Passion of the Lord. For this reason, it is known as a Sacrifice. The second involves the unity of the Church. For this reason, it is known as Communion or Eucharistic Assembly. The third involves the future: it foreshadows eternal beatitude, and for this reason, it is known as the viaticum. There are three elements in the sacrament of the Eucharist: *Sacramentum tantum*, or bread and wine. *Res et sacramentum*, the true Body of Christ. And *Res tantum*, or the

effect of this sacrament. The Paschal Lamb is the main figure of the Eucharist. Christ instituted this sacrament in the form of bread and wine. The result of the Gospel. In the Eucharist, we consume bread and wine, common aliments for rational beings. In this sacrament, the bread, as the sacrament of the Body, and the wine, as the sacrament of the Blood, are consumed separately. This sacrament is in memorial of the Lord's Passion, when the Blood and Body were separated. The Body of Christ for the salvation of the body. The Blood of Christ for the salvation of the soul. And do not think to take the "with you" in vain! We must demonstrate, document, and bear witness to the fact that the Eucharist exists. It is enough to turn the corner, to open the door, to enter any given church. ... There are people kneeling. There is a ceremony going on. Something is there. Someone is there. We must enquire. We must ask. It is documentary evidence, it is testimonial evidence, it is near palpable evidence of the influence of the Eucharist. So, it has the sacrosanct right of citizenship. We must speak about it. We must recognize the reality. We must! We are speaking of five continents: Europe, Asia, Africa, America, and Oceania. It undergoes and sustains each and every story on the planet. We do not think about it, we do not notice it, we do not prepare, but when there is an earthquake, an eruption, a flood, or anything like this, the tabernacle is devastated just like everything else. When a catastrophic event is announced, we do not pay any attention to the involvement and overturning of the tabernacles. It is a presence that shares, which takes part ... a presence that is presence. In the tabernacle and from the tabernacle it is the divine, substantial, substantiating, substantive presence which acts. It absolutely cannot not be taken into account. It has been there for over twenty centuries. It is near. Inside the tabernacle, there is Life. There is Being. There is Eternity. There is the Infinite. It is a world apart. It is a new planet. It is a new start. It needs to be included in geography books, not just history books. The tabernacle must become everyone's home, everyone's residence, a place where people can meet, the point of reference, the parameter, the unit of measurement. Adoration: We must make it deeper. We must make it more personalized. We must give thanks for this gift. Giving thanks means recognizing the benefit. It is feeling and knowing that we are recipients of grace. Giving thanks, saying thanks, appreciating God's gifts. The tabernacle is one of the greatest of God's gifts. The tabernacle is the place of thanksgiving. Here, Jesus gives thanks. He gives thanks to the Father. He gives thanks to the Holy Spirit. He gives thanks for the Church. He gives thanks for each and every one of us. He gives thanks for me, for you, for him, for her, for them. Emanations of thanksgiving leave the tabernacle. But also propitiation. The Passion continues. Forgiveness must be earned. In our name, the tabernacle raises its hands to heaven.

My son believed that Jesus' presence in the tabernacle was like a super powerful magnet. As soon as you get close, it fatally attracts all the souls that sincerely look for it and makes them fall in love with Jesus. Those who are ready to tune into "his voice," even if this means effort, perseverance, commitment, and sacrifice, will sooner or later be able to. And the more we continue along this path, the more we will be able to perceive the beat of Jesus' heart, which throbs incessantly with love for us. Carlo believed:

> The history of tabernacles is the history of salvation, which for over two millennia has been bloodlessly renewed every minute and every second throughout the globe. They accompanied it. They followed it. They marked it. Each tabernacle has its own chronicle, its own story, its own history. And not the simplest ones. Each time that a tabernacle is installed, it means that a church or chapel has already been built. For over twenty centuries, year after year, there has been an admirable proliferation of tabernacles. If we could only make a lit-up map, at least continent by continent, we would see millions of little lights turn on. The Eucharist must enter this world and mingle with everyone who lives in this world. The world must be freed, it must be purified, it must be humanized with the Eucharist. This is not a

strange and incomprehensible discussion. It involves rehuman-izing, re-civilizing, reintegrating. The living, vital presence of the Eucharist is decidedly helpful in this regard. We must try to spread the idea of religion. Religion leads to worship. We run the serious risk of having our originality, our exclusivity absorbed by a cultural blockage. We must "eucharisticize" all of this. This does not appear to be something that could only happen in a utopia. Yes, it is a giant effort, but not impossible. If the Eucharist is able to enter into this world, to make progress, to spread broadly, to invest itself in this world, then it is done. Victory! Fresh air! A button, a gesture, a tap of a finger and we are in contact with the world of small and large industry. Telephones, radios, TVs, computers, and internets are in homes twenty-four hours a day. If we are "eucharisticized," we take flight. An "interethnic," inter-continental, cosmic flight. And everything passes before us. If we are able to "eucharisticize" it, then it is done. And if we are able? Then an impetuous current will form and everything will be sucked in, collected, consolidated, conformed. Since the Eu-charist exists substantially and vitally, we must spread it through this current. It is a current which is called multimedia. It is an enormous flow of information. An enormous influx. It is an ocean of news, ideas, words, advice, suggestions, proposals, in-sinuations, attempts, interferences, and much more. And we are in it up to our necks. We risk being pulled under. It is a vortex which swallows up everything. It is the opportunity — I do not want to say the last opportunity — to put the Eucharist into the vortex. Almost violently. Almost presumptively. Talk about it, discuss it. With the way it is confined to the tabernacles, it risks "life imprisonment." Closed up, locked, behind armor … the Omnipotent. … Inside, in secret, the Omniscient. There, Being. There, the Essential. There, the Only. There, the One. There, the Three. There, heaven. There, twenty-four hours a day. Without a break. Without release. Without rest. Without anything. The In-finite in the finiteness of a box. The Infinite in the finiteness of a container. The Infinite in the finiteness of an inside.

According to Carlo, the more that we feel we are flawed, the more we must approach the Eucharist as a viaticum for personal salvation. He himself did not feel that he was in any way better than anyone else. Quite the contrary. He considered himself to be a boy like many others, who, however, unlike others, had discovered that the secret for a happy life lay in abandoning everything to Jesus, in meeting him in the Eucharist, and in placing God at the center of our lives.

He was convinced that through encounters with the Most Holy Sacrament, each person could bring their entire selves — that is, all that we are — without fear of judgment. In the Eucharist, Jesus gives himself to us as "pure love." Carlo had discovered this "love" and decided never to let it go. He had learned in Assisi and in the La Verna Sanctuary to perform Eucharistic adoration. We visited these places so many times — especially the La Verna Sanctuary, where Saint Francis received the gift of the stigmata. Here, we could truly feel that this was a place of grace, where the presence of God was strongly felt. It is there that my son and I went on spiritual retreats.

One year, during summer vacation, Carlo and I stayed there for a month. It was a time of spiritual growth. In this exact place, Carlo received the grace of feeling the Passion of Christ on the inside. He had this powerful experience which made a deep impression on him and helped him better understand the sacrifice of Mass. I remember that it took him a long time to collect himself, and I saw that he was very moved. After this powerful experience, he started to recite the prayer of the Stations of the Cross. It was then that he began to build wooden crosses with the branches that we found on our walks in the Verna woods. He liked to spread them throughout the paths in the woods as a gift for the person who would later find them. On some, he wrote a few words, including those spoken by Pope John Paul II during the homily at the Mass for the inauguration of his pontificate, October 22, 1978: "Do not be afraid. Open wide the doors for Christ."

Carlo used to say, "Before the sun, we become tan, but before the Eucharistic Jesus, we become holy." For him, standing before the Eucharist was like standing in front of a radiant sun. To explain what happens in your soul when you worship God in the Most Holy Sacrament, he used the following metaphor:

> When a thin ray of light shines in a semi-dark room, you can see the dust in the air with your naked eye. In fact, it is the specks of dusts found along the beam of light themselves which spread the light in every direction, just like how you can see the moon in the night sky. The same thing happens to our soul. During Eucharistic adoration, we are struck by the light that radiates from the Eucharist. In this way, we are able to see all the "dust" that pollutes our soul and keeps us from progressing along the path to holiness that we cannot normally see with our naked eye.

Adoration satisfies that deep desire to remain in "silence," to "listen to the voice of God," which so many people, often without realizing, hear. In worshiping God, who humiliates himself for love of us, remaining with us in the form of bread and wine, we also learn to love. And because love always tends to humble itself, we learn from Jesus how to imitate him and grow in humility. Through worship, Jesus helps us decenter ourselves from ourselves in order to open us up to divine will. Just as the Earth revolves around the sun, the entire universe with all its infinite galaxies, stars, and planets revolves around the Eucharist!

St. Thérèse of Lisieux wrote:

> Think, then, that Jesus is there in the tabernacle expressly for you — for you alone; he burns with the desire to come into your heart. … The nature of love is to humble oneself. In order that love be fully satisfied, it is necessary that it lower itself, and that it lower itself to nothingness and transform this nothingness into fire. … Spiritual advice: Consider your allotted hour of adoration as an hour of paradise; go there as one goes to heaven, to the divine banquet, and this hour will be desired, greeted with happiness. Sweetly keep alive the desire for it in your heart. Tell yourself: in four hours, in two hours, in one hour, I will go to our Lord's audience of grace and love; he invited me, he awaits me, he desires me.

A perpetual chapel of Eucharistic adoration will be like a "nuclear power plant" which spreads the Light of Christ throughout the whole world, abundantly pouring divine mercy and blessing on us all. In the Bible, two paths are described: a "narrow" one, which leads to salvation and eternal happiness and a "wide" one, which leads to perdition and eternal unhappiness. Let me be clear: We are free to refuse his help and his "rules," but this will inexorably lead us to fall into an abyss from which we can no longer emerge. Jesus did not come to abolish the commandments but rather to bring them to fruition by giving us the key for interpreting them: love. Deuteronomy even speaks of a curse: Nothing good can come without God. Eucharistic adoration gives souls a preview of the Beatific Vision to which all those who have been redeemed are destined through the will of God. In the presence of the Most Holy Sacrament, souls who have hearts that are so predisposed will be taught about heavenly things because Jesus, who is really present in this marvelous sacrament, makes himself their teacher, as he was for his disciples during his three years of public ministry. In the Eucharist, we find the good Samaritan and the heavenly doctor who binds the wounds of broken hearts and gives them strength and vigor, transforming the souls which are sinners and wounded by the ancient sin into authentic witnesses, ready to give their lives for their Lord and Savior, and for their brothers. To live through love, souls must feed off love and the spiritual nutrition that we receive by feeding on the bread of eternal life and standing beside the One who, as a prisoner of love, decided to stay with us forever until the end of the world. The Eucharist is the visible and tangible sign of God, who in the person of the Son, wants people, for all of time, to be able to live in his constant presence until God is there to wipe every tear from their eyes, as the prophetic book of Revelation states.

• • •

Carlo believed that the consecration was a very important part of Mass: "During consecration, we have to ask for grace from God the Father through the merits of his only Son, Jesus Christ, his five holy wounds, his most Precious Blood, and the tears and sadness of the Virgin Mary, who as his mother, can intercede on our behalf more than anyone else." After consecration, he always said the following prayer: "For the Sacred Heart of Jesus and the Immaculate Heart of Mary, I offer you all my requests and ask you to grant them to me." As soon as Carlo received the Eucharistic Jesus, he said, "Jesus, come in! Make yourself at home!" He often repeated, "If we approach the Eucharist every day, we will go straight to heaven!" When we take Communion, we must have the same feelings that the disciples had in Emmaus when they recognized Jesus: hearts burning with love (see Lk 24:13–35).

My son also believed that "being true disciples of Jesus" means loving God above all things and therefore, also, our neighbor as ourselves. In an extreme act of love, God gave us his only-begotten Son, who in dying on the cross readmitted us to divine life by instituting the sacraments and especially the Eucharist, the sacrament that best expresses this immense love that God has for his creatures. In this sacrament, he sacrifices himself every day on the altar for our salvation. Every minute and every second in the world, when a Mass is celebrated, this sacrifice which occurred over two thousand years ago on the cross is ritualized bloodlessly. Just think what an extraordinary thing is occurring!

Saint John, the beloved disciple, writes, "Let us love one another; for love is of God, and he who loves is born of God and knows God. He who does not love does not know God; for God is love" (1 Jn 4:7–8). And where can we find the help we need to grow in our capacity to love, if not by feeding on the Eucharist, which contains the same God of which John speaks who is none other than "love"? That same God who died on the cross for the human race! Jesus is love, and the more we feed on the Eucharist, which truly contains his Body, the more we will feed our capacity to love. He himself will help us, joining into our DNA and transforming us. The Eucharist will configure us in a unique way toward God. We can only become holy like God wishes us to be by loving him above all things and our neighbors as ourselves. By feeding on the Eucharist, which is none other than the sacrament of the love with which God loves us, we will bind ourselves more and more to the heart of Christ.

• • •

To show how all of Scripture speaks of Christ, Carlo loved to recount episodes in the Bible that clearly depict the figures of Jesus, the sacraments, and especially the marvelous gift of the Eucharist. The Church affirms that this is the entire story of the People of Israel, who prepare for and await the coming of Jesus Christ, who is God and who was made man and who chose to dwell among us and to offer himself in sacrifice to save us. To cite just a few of these prefigurations, let us recall, for example, the Passover (see Ex 12:1–11), the early stages of the liberation of the People of Israel from slavery in Egypt and entry into the Promised Land. At this Passover dinner, the people were to offer a lamb "without blemish" in sacrifice. To be spared by the Angel of Death, they painted the door frames of the houses where the family would spend their Paschal dinner with the blood collected from the lamb. They also ate unleavened bread and wine, which are clear prefigurations of the Eucharistic table, in which Christ is sacrificed for our salvation. During the Exodus, other Eucharistic images are presented — for example, manna (a Hebrew word which means "What is it?", *Man-hu*) is a food which came down from heaven resembling bread. Thanks to this food, the people of Israel had nourishment in the desert and did not die of hunger (see Ex 16:11–15). Another prefigurement is the baked bread (see 1 Kgs 19:4–8) which the angel brings to the Prophet Elijah, hungry and disheartened, which allows him to continue his arduous journey to Mount Horeb. And let us not forget the suffering servant, who was described by the Prophet Isaiah, about seven hundred years before the coming of Jesus, in the following manner: "Like a lamb that is led to slaughter, / and like a sheep that before its shearers is silent, / so he opened not his mouth" (Is 53:7). There are also numerous examples in the New Testament, such as the multiplication of the bread and fish (see Jn 6:11–13), the wedding in Cana (Jn 2:1–12), and the resurrection of Lazarus (Jn 11:1–44), to cite a few.

There are Eucharistic miracles which help confirm that the heart of Jesus burning with love is found in the consecrated Host. In the miracle of Lanciano (A.D. 750), for example, the consecrated Host was transformed into flesh, which numerous scientific analyses have confirmed to be a piece of myocardium, the muscle which forms part of the heart wall and which is responsible for spreading the impulse to contract to the various parts of the heart. The fact that the flesh of the heart is myocardium is of theological significance. In fact, without this muscle, the heart would not beat. This gives our organism life, just like the Eucharist does for the Church. According to the *Catechism of the Catholic Church*, "The Eucharist is 'the source and summit of the Christian life.' 'The other sacraments, and indeed all ecclesiastical ministries and works of the apostolate, are bound up with the Eucharist and are oriented toward it. For in the blessed Eucharist is contained the whole spiritual good of the Church, namely Christ himself, our Pasch'" (1324).

Before Carlo died, I told him to ask Jesus to perform other Eucharistic miracles like the one in Lanciano, where it was clear that he was truly present in the consecrated Host. I think that my son's intercession was heard, because only ten days after his death, on October 21, 2006, a Eucharistic miracle occurred in Tixtla, Mexico, and soon after, two more in Sokolka, Poland, in 2008 and in Legnicka, Poland, in 2013. All of these miracles, which have been studied by eminent scientists and confirmed by the ecclesiastical authorities, are similar to the Eucharistic miracle of Lanciano. In each of these, the consecrated Host was transformed into flesh, which was shown to be heart tissue — myocardium — after careful scientific examination.

Jesus performs these miracles to help us rekindle our faith, which often wavers. While he was still on earth, John tells us in chapter 6 of his Gospel, Jesus promised the gift of the Eucharist. To prepare his disciples for the fact that he would make himself present in consecrated bread and wine, he performed two miracles to clearly demonstrate that he had the power to suspend the laws of nature. He multiplied the bread and fish and crossed Lake Tiberias by walking on water. In this way, Jesus showed that he had the power to transform bread and wine into his Body and his Blood. And through Eucharistic miracles, Jesus continues to do the same. He teaches us about his true presence in the Eucharist by suspending the laws of nature — something only he can do.

Carlo went to the Sanctuary of Merciful Love in Collevalenza, Italy, on multiple occasions. He told me he had received special interior graces there. Servant of God Maria Esperanza had apparitions of Jesus and the Virgin Mary. Through a vision she had of Jesus crucified with the Eucharist behind him, we have confirmation that in instituting the Sacrament of the Eucharist, God performed the greatest act of love that he could for us. The Sacrifice of the Cross and the Eucharist coincide.

In the Eucharist, Carlo caught a glimpse of the Sacred Heart, hidden to the senses, but which can be perceived by faith. For this reason, he wanted his entire family to consecrate themselves to the Sacred Heart of Jesus, which was performed by a Jesuit priest in the Centro San Fedele in Milan. Mindful of Jesus' words to St. Margaret Mary Alacoque, the visionary of the Sacred Heart, Carlo usually dedicated the Communion of the first Friday of the month for the reparation of sins and the offenses committed against Christ. He copied down the revelation that the saint received between June 13 and 20, 1675, on the octave of the feast of Corpus Christi:

> Behold this Heart which has so loved men, that It has spared nothing, even to exhausting and consuming Itself to prove to them Its love. In return, I receive from the greater number nothing but ingratitude, contempt, irreverence, sacrilege, and coldness in this Sacrament of My love. But what I feel still more is that there are hearts consecrated to Me who use Me thus. Therefore, I ask of thee that the First Friday after the Octave of the Blessed Sacrament shall be kept as a special Feast in honor of My Heart, to make reparation for all the indignities offered to It, and as a Communion day in order to atone for the unworthy treatment It has received when exposed upon the altars. I also promise that My Heart shall shed in abundance the influence of Its divine love on all those who shall thus honor It or cause It to be so honored.

Jesus' great promise of final perseverance, revealed to Saint Margaret Mary, made to anyone who takes Communion on the first Friday of the month, made a strong impression on him. Carlo shared this practice with everyone he knew and tried to get them involved in reparation. He felt this invitation to pray and offer sacrifices for sinners and for those who were far from divine grace deeply. During the Passion, Christ's heart was pierced with a lance in order to make certain that he was dead. For this reason, the wound in the Sacred Heart of Jesus, who had by then expired, must remain a vivid image through the centuries of the immense gift that God himself gave humanity: the offering of his only-begotten Son for the redemption of the world.

Christ loved all of us so intensely that he offered himself as the victim of a cruel immolation on Calvary: "And walk in love, as Christ loved us and gave himself up for us, a fragrant offering and sacrifice to God" (Eph 5:2).